DIVIDED SCOTLAND?

Divided Scotland?

The Nature, Causes and Consequences of
Economic Disparities within Scotland

Edited by

DAVID NEWLANDS
University of Aberdeen, UK

MIKE DANSON
University of Paisley, UK

JOHN McCARTHY
University of Dundee, UK

ASHGATE

Published by
Ashgate Publishing Limited
Gower House
Croft Road
Aldershot
Hants GU11 3HR
England

Ashgate Publishing Company
Suite 420
101 Cherry Street
Burlington, VT 05401-4405
USA

Ashgate website: http://www.ashgate.com

British Library Cataloguing in Publication Data
Divided Scotland? : the nature, causes and consequences of
    economic disparities within Scotland. - (Urban and regional
    planning and development)
    1. Scotland - Economic conditions - 1973- - Regional
    disparities
    I. Newlands, David A., 1953- II. Danson, Mike III. McCarthy,
    John
    330.9'411085

Library of Congress Cataloging-in-Publication Data
Divided Scotland? : the nature, causes and consequences of economic disparities within Scotland / [edited by] by David Newlands, Mike Danson, and John McCarthy.
    p. cm. -- (Urban and regional planning and development series)
    Includes bibliographical references and index.
    ISBN 0-7546-1527-8
    1. Scotland--Economic conditions--1973---Regional disparities. 2. Scotland--Economic policy. 3. Income--Scotland--Regional disparities. I. Newlands, David A., 1953- II. Danson, Mike. III. McCarthy, John, 1961- IV.
Series: Urban and regional planning and development.

    HC257.S4D58 2004
    330.9411--dc22

                                                                2004014001

ISBN 0 7546 1527 8

Printed and bound in Great Britain by Antony Rowe Ltd, Chippenham, Wiltshire

Contents

List of Figures and Tables

List of Figures

List of Tables

List of Contributors

Nick Bailey, Senior Lecturer, Department of Urban Studies, University of Glasgow

Stuart Black, Chief Executive, Inverness and Nairn Executive

Mike Danson, Professor, Department of Economics and Enterprise, University of Paisley

John Fairley, Professor, Department of Environmental Planning, University of Strathclyde

Tom Hart, Chair, Scottish Transport Studies Group

Barbara Illsley, Lecturer, Geddes Institute, Department of Town and Regional Planning, University of Dundee

M. Greg Lloyd, Professor, Geddes Institute, Department of Town and Regional Planning, University of Dundee

John McCarthy, Senior Lecturer, Geddes Institute, Department of Town and Regional Planning, University of Dundee

Ronald W. McQuaid, Professor, Employment Research Institute, Napier University

David Newlands, Senior Lecturer, Department of Economics, University of Aberdeen

Peter Roberts, Professor of Regional Planning, Department of Civic Design, University of Liverpool

Douglas Scott, MA (Hons), MPhil, MBA, MRTPI

Ivan Turok, Professor, Department of Urban Studies, University of Glasgow

Chapter 1

Introduction

David Newlands, Mike Danson and John McCarthy

1.1   Divided Scotland?

In recent years, there has been much debate about the relative economic performance of the Scottish economy. While this has not changed altogether – indeed, the comparisons of Scotland and Ireland become ever more common – there has been some shift in focus. A growing concern with economic disparities between areas of Scotland is discernible.

This is partly because, by many measures, such disparities are considerable. For example, in 1995, the gross value added (GVA) per capita, which is a measure of average income, in the richest Local Area in Scotland, Edinburgh, was 2.3 times that in the poorest Local Area, the Western Isles (National Statistics Office, 2003). Such figures have to be treated with caution. The figures for areas of in-commuting, like Edinburgh, are inflated because commuters boost the income attributable to such areas but not the population base used to calculate average income. In addition, allowance has to be made for differences in the cost of living. Nevertheless, these figures are indicative of very substantial disparities in income and standard of living across Scotland, and are confirmed by other evidence. Average earnings in Aberdeen in 2002 were 46 per cent higher than in the two local authorities, Moray and Scottish Borders, where pay rates were lowest (Scottish Executive, 2003). There are also dramatic differences in job opportunities across Scotland as manifested by rates of economic activity, employment and unemployment. More detail is presented in Chapter 2.

Not only are economic disparities within Scotland large but they are increasing. By 2001, the ratio of GVA per capita in the richest Local Area (still Edinburgh) to the poorest (now East & West Dunbartonshire and Helensburgh & Lomond) had increased from 2.3 to 2.6, in just six years. While the Edinburgh economy is expanding rapidly, perhaps symbolised most vividly by booming house prices, many other areas of Scotland continue to experience severe economic problems of narrow employment opportunities, low pay, a poor skills base, and inadequate infrastructure.

The size and significance of the economic divisions within Scotland which it inherited have been recognised by the Scottish Executive, although somewhat ironically the location of the Scottish Parliament itself in Edinburgh has further fuelled the economic growth of the city.

In its *Framework for Economic Development in Scotland*, the Scottish Executive argued that 'economic development should raise the quality of life of the Scottish people through increasing economic opportunities for all, on a socially and environmentally sustainable basis' (Scottish Executive, 2000, Executive Report, p.1). To this end, four main objectives are set out: the furtherance of economic growth, addressing regional disparities within Scotland, promoting social justice, and the more effective management of Scotland's environmental resources.

The *Framework* is a coherent and detailed statement of an economic strategy for Scotland but the prospects of it achieving the difficult balancing act of raising the economic growth rate in Scotland, while simultaneously meeting social, regional and environmental objectives, are poor. While the probability of conflicts between the four outcomes is recognised, there is no serious consideration of the implications of such conflicts because nothing is said about the weights attached to each outcome. Thus, for example, there is no indication of what increase in interregional disparities – if any – the Executive would consider an acceptable trade-off for an increase in the trend rate of economic growth in Scotland.

This is a realistic example because, in practice, efficiency, productivity and growth objectives are prioritised over the *Framework*'s equity objectives. The specific measures by which the former are to be addressed are spelled out in much more detail than the corresponding initiatives to address the latter. This partly reflects political priorities but partly the fact that even more of the channels by which the equity issues can be tackled lie outwith the powers and responsibilities of the Executive than is true of the economic growth objective, with the UK government or with the market decisions of businesses and individuals.

On the other hand, the translation of the *Framework per cents* objectives into more specific initiatives has begun. The development agencies, Scottish Enterprise and Highlands and Islands Enterprise, are the vehicles for many of these initiatives. *A Smart, Successful Scotland* (Scottish Executive, 2001) resets the directions and priorities of the agencies in light of the policy ambitions of the *Framework*. The Scottish Executive is seeking to improve the performance of the Scottish economy and address economic disparities within Scotland by measures which seek to improve the transport infrastructure, labour skills, the scale and quality of urban regeneration, and the effectiveness of the economic development and planning frameworks. All these issues, and more, are discussed in this book.

1.2   Structure of the Book

The next chapter, by David Newlands, sets out the changing regional economic structure of Scotland over the last fifty years and then plots some of the different – and not always consistent – ways in which economic disparities within the contemporary Scottish economy manifest themselves.

Chapters 3-6 consider detailed case studies of four different areas of Scotland. Chapter 3, by Ron McQuaid, analyses the economic impact of the Scottish

Parliament on Edinburgh and considers the opportunities to use the current buoyancy of the local economy to tackle problems of social exclusion in Edinburgh. In Chapter 4, Ivan Turok and Nick Bailey explore the paradoxes of the Glasgow economy. There has been a significant change in Glasgow per cents economic performance over the last decade, some of the signs of which are particularly visible in the city centre, but many poorer parts of the city remain depressed and suffer from a host of socio-economic problems. Chapter 5, by Stuart Black, analyses the recent economic record of the Highlands and Islands. While there have been improvements, with the development of new industries, particularly in information technology, income levels are still below the national average and there remain problems of decline in some of the more remote parts of the region. In Chapter 6, Douglas Scott, discusses the South of Scotland and argues that it shares many of the same problems as the Highlands and Islands but has not received the same recognition or policy support.

Chapters 7-11 discuss a number of cross cutting issues which affect all areas of Scotland but often very differently. Chapter 7, by Mike Danson, examines the framework of economic development and argues that the institutional landscape in Scotland is ossifying, with limited institutional and corporate learning and innovation, in contrast with former times. In Chapter 8, John Fairley discusses the provision of vocational education and training (VET). VET in Scotland is fragmented, often separated from other parts of the educational system, based on voluntarism, and is still being driven by UK priorities although it is a devolved policy area. Chapter 9, by Tom Hart, addresses the whole range of transport issues. While there is scope for using transport policies to reduce overheating around Edinburgh and encourage a shift in the balance of economic activity towards north, west and south, the main opportunities for action to reduce disparities in access to transport facilities is within Scotland per cents regions and travel-to-work-areas. Chapter 10, by Peter Roberts, considers the recent record of urban regeneration in Scotland and discusses some of the future challenges if urban regeneration policy is to continue to be as innovative as it has been in the past. In Chapter 11, Greg Lloyd and Barbara Illsley examine the progress made in introducing community planning and discuss the ways in which community planning could improve the social, environmental and economic management of different areas of Scotland.

Finally, Chapter 12, by Mike Danson and John McCarthy, summarises the principal themes of the book and seeks to draw out the major policy implications, for the Scottish Parliament, for development agencies and local authorities, and for the communities of different parts of Scotland.

Many of the contributors to this book are active in the Scottish Branch of the Regional Studies Association (RSA). The RSA is an international learned society interested in regional development, policy and research. The Scottish Branch includes academic researchers from most of Scotland per cents universities and policy makers from the Scottish Parliament, development agencies and local government. Most of the chapters of the book were first presented as papers at a conference held by the RSA Scottish Branch in Inverness.

References

National Statistics Office (2003) *NUTS3 GVA Tables*.
Scottish Executive (2000) *The Way Forward: Framework for Economic Development in Scotland*, Scottish Executive, Edinburgh.
Scottish Executive (2001) *A Smart, Successful Scotland: Ambitions for the Enterprise Networks*, Scottish Executive, Edinburgh.
Scottish Executive (2003) *Scottish Economic Statistics*, Scottish Executive, Edinburgh.

Chapter 2

The Changing Nature of Economic
Disparities within Scotland

David Newlands

2.1 Introduction

Scotland has a distinctive regional structure, largely rural areas in the Highlands
and the Borders and a highly urbanised and developed central belt in between. At
the beginning of the twentieth century, its shipbuilding and engineering complex
made Clydeside the dominant region of Scotland in economic terms. By the end of
the century, the discovery of North Sea oil and the increased importance of
services, particularly the financial sector, had led to an eastern shift in the centre of
gravity of the Scottish economy.

This chapter has two main objectives. First, it seeks to explain the pattern of
economic disparities at the turn of the millennium by examining the processes of
regional economic development in Scotland in the half century after 1945. Second,
as a backdrop to the subsequent chapters of the book, it describes and analyses
some of the more important of the current socio-economic indicators for the
different areas of Scotland.

2.2 The Postwar Development of Scotland's Regional Economies

In the middle of the twentieth century, the industrial distribution of Scotland still
showed the imprint of the pattern which developed in the Victorian period
(Lenman, 1977). The major part of industry and population was in the central belt
of the Lowlands and of this the greatest concentration was in the Clyde Valley
centred on Glasgow. The industrial specialisation in shipbuilding and marine
engineering remained prominent. Shipbuilding was much the biggest
manufacturing industry in Scotland.

The Ayrshire plain was effectively an extension of the central belt, sharing the
industrial development of the Glasgow area although agriculture and coal mining
were also important. The Borders were largely agricultural although there was
some manufacturing. Woollen cloth was particularly important in the south east. In
the south west, manufacturing was more various, including chemicals, food
processing, textiles and engineering. Aberdeen and the coastal areas of the north

east had a variety of manufacturing industry, particularly engineering, but were also very dependent on agriculture and fishing. The Highlands and Islands depended mainly on agriculture, forestry, fishing and tourism. The chief manufacturing industry in the Highlands and Islands was woollen textiles.

While textile industries remained important to a number of Scottish regions after the war, they had all ceased to be expanding sectors. Industrial adjustment was particularly traumatic in Dundee with the decline of jute but the gap was filled in due course by the expansion of new light engineering industries producing cash registers, watches and sound equipment. A number of the incoming firms were American, attracted by cheap female labour, among them Timex which established a large factory to manufacture clocks and watches. In this regard, Dundee was typical of much of Scotland. Between 1950 and 1975, over a quarter of the 230,000 jobs created in firms opening in Scotland were in foreign owned businesses.

Changes to Scotland's industrial structure accelerated from the 1950s onwards (Johnston et al, 1971). For example, Grangemouth grew rapidly in the 1950s and 1960s on the back of a number of large petrochemical plants which are still important local employers. Many of the new industrial developments of this period were due in part to the development of government regional policy. In 1958, a new steel strip mill was allocated to Ravenscraig in Lanarkshire and a cold strip mill to Gartcosh. The location of a British Motor Corporation factory at Bathgate in 1961, producing trucks and tractors, and a Rootes plant at Linwood in 1963, producing Hillman Imp cars, were other government responses to pressure to provide new jobs in the west of Scotland.

In the Highlands, the pulp mill at Corpach outside Fort William was established in 1962. Then, in 1965, the government created the Highlands and Islands Development Board (HIDB). Partly as a result of the establishment of the HIDB, by the end of the 1960s, the Highlands was securing 10 per cent of government expenditure in Scotland despite having only 5 per cent of the population. The HIDB helped persuade the government to locate a fast breeder nuclear reactor at Dounreay in Caithness and a large aluminium smelter at Invergordon on the Moray Firth.

Among older industries, shipbuilding underwent a period of turmoil in the late 1960s and early 1970s. Employment in shipbuilding on the Clyde was 98,000 in 1945. Thirty years later it was one quarter of that figure. This painful process of contraction was not confined to the Clyde. In 1969, the Burntisland Shipping Company on the Forth went bankrupt leaving Robb Caledon of Dundee and Leith and Hall Russell of Aberdeen as the only significant shipbuilders on the east coast.

Income and employment levels reflected the regional distribution of industry and the relative health or otherwise of different industries. The lowest rates of unemployment in the 1950s were in the Borders, Edinburgh and the Lothians. The highest rate was in the Highlands and Islands. Unemployment rates were also above the Scottish average in Glasgow and the adjacent counties of Lanarkshire, Renfrewshire and Dunbartonshire. The familiar response was that many emigrated. In the 1950s, over three quarters of the natural increase in population left Scotland, mainly to jobs in England (Lee, 1995).

There were also important population shifts within Scotland in response to changes in industrial structure. The concentration of Scotland's population in the central belt, which had been a marked feature of the early twentieth century, continued after the war. By the 1950s, the Clydeside conurbation accounted for about one third of the population of Scotland and the central industrial belt about three quarters. While, in 1801, nearly half the Scottish population lived in the northern and Highland counties, by the 1950s fewer than 20 per cent did. The long process of urbanisation was slowing by the mid twentieth century but three of the four Scottish cities – Edinburgh, Aberdeen and Dundee – were still growing. However, Glasgow's population decline had already begun.

The new towns such as East Kilbride, Glenrothes and Cumbernauld expanded very rapidly, their growth bound up with the introduction of overspill policies, particularly from Glasgow. In parallel, Glasgow sought to deal with housing problems in the city by creating a number of peripheral working class estates such as Drumchapel, Easterhouse and Castlemilk. However, lacking social amenities and local employment opportunities, they soon became as bad as the inner city areas they were supposed to replace.

The role of housing in the postwar economic development of Scotland and its constituent regions received much attention. In some areas, there was an absolute shortage of housing and in other areas an unsatisfactory quality of housing. The effect was to limit the geographical mobility of labour and the overall flexibility of the Scottish economy. There were familiar criticisms of the housing system, particularly council housing. Low rents and complex points systems for the allocation of local authority housing meant that in many areas the existing stock of housing was not used effectively and waiting lists remained long despite heavy postwar building programmes. Housing scarcities were exacerbated by rent controls in the private rented sector. These problems were encountered throughout the UK but were particularly severe in Scotland because the number of owner occupied houses and new houses built for sale was distinctly smaller than in England.

Ravenscraig, Gartcosh, Bathgate, Linwood, Corpach, Dounreay and Invergordon were all the result of political responses to high levels of unemployment in different parts of Scotland. However, even at the time, there was an awareness of the possible drawbacks of giving such prominence to the immediate provision of employment: that effectively resources were devoted to the propping up of dying industries and that potential growth areas were denied support. 'The build-up of industrial complexes and centres which offer prospects of becoming zones of growth cannot be the only aim but it should be one of the principal aims of policy' (Toothill, 1961, p.154).

There was serious contemporary debate about the role of inward investment in improving the performance of the Scottish economy and in tackling regional disparities in unemployment within Scotland but again some recognition of the risks of over dependence on inward investment, particularly of subsidiaries which had limited strategic and operational independence from their foreign owned parent companies.

There was a flurry of government plans relating to parts of Scotland beginning with the *Central Scotland Plan* in 1963. The *Grangemouth-Falkirk Plan* appeared in 1968 and *Tayside: Potential for Development* in 1970. In 1966, the government published *Plan for Expansion*, a White Paper detailing plans for the future development of the Scottish economy. This argued that old declining industries should be slimmed down and modernised and that resources and employment should be shifted into new growing industries such as cars and electronics. Declining regional economies such as the north east and the Borders would require specific assistance to achieve such changes. In the end, the whole of Scotland, except the Edinburgh-Leith area, was proposed as a development area.

Despite this denial of development area status to Edinburgh, the concentration of industry and population in the central belt meant that it remained the principal political and planning focus within Scotland although there was also an effective Highland lobby, especially after the creation of the HIDB.

By the end of the twentieth century, the Scottish economy had become ever more closely integrated into the UK economy. GDP per head in Scotland has hovered about 92-96 per cent of the UK average (Storie and Horne, 1999). The only major gap in terms of income is between Scotland and the South East of England. Compared to the other regions of England, and indeed compared to many other countries in Western Europe, Scotland is a middle income region. Unemployment in Scotland was higher than the UK as a whole for most of the twentieth century, distinctly higher than the southern regions of England and comparable with the northern regions. In recent years, however, the gap between Scotland and the UK average has closed somewhat and, while unemployment is still higher than in the South, it is significantly lower than in the North.

The last twenty five years have seen a massive restructuring of the Scottish economy. The traditional metal and metal using industries of steel, shipbuilding, transport equipment and mechanical engineering have all experienced sharp decline. Another notable trend of recent decades is the increase in external ownership of Scottish industry, partly as a consequence of merger and takeover activity, partly as a result of the attraction of foreign direct investment from North America and East Asia. While most small and medium sized firms are still Scottish owned, only 33 per cent of Scottish businesses in the employment size band 250-499 in 1998 had Scottish headquarters. For the largest businesses of all, with employment of 500 or more, the figure was a mere 19 per cent (Campbell and MacDonald, 1999).

While agriculture, forestry and fishing is now a very small part of the Scottish economy, and there are areas with almost no representation in these sectors, the primary industries remain important in some parts of Scotland. The local authority areas with most jobs in agriculture, forestry and fishing are Aberdeen, Dumfries and Galloway, Shetland and Orkney (each around 11 per cent of employment).

Manufacturing also has distinct regional patterns of location. By the end of the twentieth century, the three largest manufacturing sectors in Scotland were food and drink (3.5 per cent of total Scottish output), metalworking, mechanical engineering and transport equipment (4.7 per cent) and electrical and instrument engineering (6.0 per cent). Food and drink employed 58,000 people in 2000, of whom about a quarter were employed in the whisky industry. However, whisky accounted for about one fifth of all manufacturing exports. The largest whisky company was Distillers, operating a large number of distilleries and bottling plants throughout Scotland. Elsewhere in the drinks industry, Scottish and Newcastle and Tennent Caledonian are major brewing concerns, concentrated in Edinburgh and Glasgow respectively. The bulk of the remainder of the food and drink sector is accounted for by meat and fish processing and the manufacture of bread, biscuits and confectionery. This sector is particularly important to the regional economies of Orkney, Shetland, Grampian and Strathclyde.

Metalworking, mechanical engineering and transport equipment was the sector which drove the whole Scottish economy a hundred years. Although now a rump of what it was, it still employed 73,000 people in 2000. There are some companies in this sector all round Scotland but, apart from Fife and the Highlands (mainly the oil platform construction yards), it remains concentrated on Clydeside, with the surviving shipbuilding and repair yards and engineering firms such as Anderson Strathclyde (mining equipment) and Weirs (pumps and valves).

Electrical and instrument engineering employed 61,000 people in 2000. This sector is concentrated in central Scotland with Silicon Glen stretching from Fife through Edinburgh and West Lothian to Inverclyde, west of Glasgow. Production covers electronic data processing equipment, including computers, electronic components and, latterly, mobile phones. There are some indigenous companies, notably Ferranti (now part of the BAE group) but a striking feature of the electronics industry has always been the number of inward investors including IBM, Honeywell, NCR, Digital Equipment, Motorola, National Semiconductors, NEC and Mitsubishi. This has raised concerns about Silicon Glen being a branch plant economy and certainly comparison with other concentrations of electronics in the UK, such as Silicon Fen in the Cambridge area, suggests that the Scottish cluster is weaker. Employment within Scotland is skewed towards partly skilled employment such as assembly work while other clusters have higher concentrations in management and R&D (Fraser of Allander Institute, 2001).

By the end of the twentieth century, most Scots worked in the service sector. In terms of their contribution to Scottish output in 1995, the main service sectors were hotels and restaurants (3.0 per cent), financial services (4.1 per cent), transport and communications (7.6 per cent), wholesale and retail trade (10.4 per cent), property and business services (15.3 per cent) and public services (21.2 per cent).

An important distinction can be drawn between dependent or local services and autonomous or exporting services. The scale and range of dependent or local services depend upon the amount of local spending or in some cases, such as education and health care, the size of the local population. Autonomous or exporting services are ones which serve a national or international market. The boundary between dependent and autonomous services is not easily drawn since, in practice, many services have both local and national or international markets. Nevertheless, the distinction is of great significance, not least for the pattern of economic activity in different areas. Dependent or local services are, almost by definition, found everywhere in Scotland and to that extent the increased importance of the service sector has been a force for the greater uniformity of the regional economies of Scotland. In contrast, autonomous or exporting services can be as, or more, geographically concentrated than coalmining, shipbuilding and mechanical engineering were in Scotland a hundred years ago. The continued existence of regional economic disparities within Scotland is largely attributable to the appearance of new specialisations in these types of service industries.

New clusters of service industries were emerging as the twentieth century ended, such as one in biomedical sciences in Dundee, but over the preceding thirty years the two significant clusters which accounted for much of Scotland's economic growth, as well as the eastward shift in the balance of the economy, were financial and business services and oil related services.

The financial and business services sector provides employment for about 150,000 people, more than twice that employed in metalworking and mechanical engineering, although its importance is not reflected in the availability of data (Perman, 2001). The sector covers an enormous range including banking, finance, insurance, property, accountancy, commercial law, advertising, consultancy and IT.

Financial services in particular account for some of the most profitable, innovative and fastest growing companies in Scotland. Ten of the largest 20 companies located in Scotland are in financial services. They account for 62 per cent of the turnover, 70 per cent of the profits and 33 per cent of the employment of the top 20 firms. Scotland is the sixth largest fund management centre in Europe (by institutional equity holdings) while in the banking sector alone Scotland again ranks sixth in Europe (Dunlop, 2001).

Edinburgh is Scotland's financial centre, helping explain why by the end of the twentieth century it had become the most dynamic regional economy in Scotland. Edinburgh is the headquarters of the Royal Bank of Scotland, the Bank of Scotland, merchant banks, insurance companies, investment managers and numerous other financial institutions. However, Glasgow is also an important base for a range of financial services. Just over half, 51 per cent, of all financial services employment is located in Edinburgh and 16 per cent in Glasgow although, for data reasons, these figures probably understate the dominance of the two cities. A few other areas also have a significant concentration in parts of the financial services sector, generally because of the presence of one or two companies with large offices there. These include Fife (in Building Societies), Tayside (in insurance and fund management) and Grampian (again in fund management) (Dunlop, 2001).

Aberdeen is Edinburgh's closest rival in terms of a prosperous regional economy. Aberdeen is the main onshore base for the North Sea oil industry although there are smaller bases on Shetland and Orkney. Aberdeen's economy has been transformed since the first commercially viable discoveries of oil were made in 1969. Prior to that, the Aberdeen economy was relatively depressed with low wages and large scale emigration of people from Aberdeen in search of better employment prospects elsewhere. The arrival of the oil industry radically changed Aberdeen's economic circumstances with significant growth of employment and a reversal of the trend of population movements.

The oil industry now dominates the Aberdeen economy (Newlands, 2000). The jobs created by oil are relatively well paid. As a result, average earnings in Aberdeen for men have risen markedly compared to the rest of the country, and are distinctly higher than the national average. The same is not true, however, for women, only a comparatively small number of whom are employed in the oil industry. The oil industry is the biggest single individual employer in Aberdeen with some 50,000 people working for the oil companies and numerous oil supply firms. Relatively small numbers are now employed in Aberdeen's traditional industries, only a few thousand in fishing, only some 15,000 in total in manufacturing. Most of the oil businesses in Aberdeen are foreign companies. The Wood Group is one of the few examples of a local business exploiting the opportunities offered by oil.

Shifts in the relative fortunes of different industries within Scotland have had important implications for the distribution of population, income and employment. Strathclyde region accounted for 49 per cent of the total Scottish population in 1971. By 2001, the corresponding local authority areas made up only 44 per cent of the Scottish total. The former Lothian, Grampian, Tayside, Fife and Central regions come next in population size, in that order. All these regions have experienced an increase in their share of the Scottish population. For Grampian, the increase was substantial, a rise of nearly 20 per cent between 1971 and 2001. Overlaying the general shift in population distribution from west to east, Glasgow and Dundee have experienced major declines due in part to people moving out of the cities to surrounding areas. The increased extent of commuting, particularly in the central belt, has been partly a response to increasing disparities in house prices between different parts of Scotland with prices rising particularly sharply in Edinburgh from the 1980s onwards. Even with commuting, differentials in house prices risk becoming as much an impediment to the movement of labour around the country as were council housing allocation procedures forty or fifty years ago.

The principal vehicles of regional and industrial policy within Scotland over the last quarter of a century have been the development agency networks. To the Highlands and Islands Development Board (HIDB), created in 1965, was added the Scottish Development Agency (SDA) in 1975, with responsibilities for the economic development of lowland Scotland. In 1991, the HIDB and the SDA were reconstituted as Highlands and Islands Enterprise (HIE) and Scottish Enterprise (SE) when they took over the training functions previously exercised in Scotland by the Training Agency. At the same time, there was a further decentralisation of economic development and training responsibilities to Local Enterprise Companies (LECs) throughout Scotland.

There were a variety of other policy initiatives in the late twentieth century. A number of areas of Scotland benefited from European Union regional aid, notably the Highlands and Islands which was an Objective One region. The government created four Enterprise Zones in Scotland in the 1980s and 1990s. The Tayside Enterprise Zone covered a number of sites, in Dundee and Arbroath, but the other three were all intended to attract business to areas which had experienced the closure of a single major employer: the Singer sewing machine factory at Clydebank, the aluminium smelter at Invergordon and the steelworks at Ravenscraig. The latter two were of course symbols of the failure of earlier regional policy measures.

2.3   Economic Disparities within Scotland at the Beginning of the Twenty First Century

First of all, it is important to stress that, for various reasons such as small sample sizes, detailed information about the different areas of Scotland is severely limited. On the other hand, the quality of data is improving, through the appearance of new surveys, such as the Scottish Household Survey, and Scottish 'boosts' to existing UK surveys, such as the Annual Business Inquiry (Scottish Executive, 2003).

Table 2.1 shows gross value added (GVA) per capita in 1995 and 2001 in the Local Areas of Scotland and in four larger regions. There is a fairly consistent ranking. Among the four larger regions, GVA per capita is highest in North Eastern Scotland, followed by Eastern Scotland and then South Western Scotland and finally the Highlands and Islands.

Table 2.1   Gross value added (GVA) per head, current prices, 1995 and 2001, local areas of Scotland

Local Area	GVA per head, 1995, £	GVA per head, 2001, £	Increase 1995-2001, %
SCOTLAND	10861	13660	26
North Eastern Scotland	15031	19300	28
Aberdeen City, Aberdeenshire and North East Moray	15031	19300	28
Eastern Scotland	11304	13886	23
Angus and Dundee City	10447	12289	18
Clackmannanshire and Fife	8429	10061	19
East Lothian and Midlothian	7511	8931	19
Scottish Borders	9146	9298	2
Edinburgh City	16464	22168	35
Falkirk	10857	12114	12
Perth & Kinross and Stirling	10320	12085	17
West Lothian	12739	15154	19
South Western Scotland	10006	12831	28
East & West Dunbartonshire and Helensburgh & Lomond	7103	8498	20
Dumfries & Galloway	9213	10293	12
East Ayrshire and North Ayrshire Mainland	8651	9934	15
Glasgow City	13233	19110	44
Inverclyde, East Renfrewshire and Renfrewshire	10785	11974	11
North Lanarkshire	7883	10010	27
South Ayrshire	10056	12783	27
South Lanarkshire	8678	11729	35

Table 2.1   *continued*

Local Area	GVA per head, 1995, £	GVA per head, 2001, £	Increase 1995-2001, %
Highlands and Islands	8262	9954	20
Caithness & Sutherland and Ross & Cromarty	6941	9090	31
Inverness & Nairn and Moray, Badenoch & Strathspey	8650	10440	21
Lochaber, Skye & Lochalsh and Argyll and the Islands	8317	9428	13
Eilean Siar (Western Isles)	7153	9969	39
Orkney Islands	9921	10321	4
Shetland Islands	11305	13034	15

Source: National Statistics Office (2003) *NUTS3 GVA Tables*.

The three highest income Local Areas in both 1995 and 2001 are Edinburgh followed by Aberdeen, Aberdeenshire and North East Moray (the North Eastern Scotland region) and then Glasgow. The three lowest income Local Areas in 1995, in ascending order, are: Caithness & Sutherland and Ross & Cromarty; East & West Dunbartonshire and Helensburgh & Lomond; and the Western Isles. The three lowest in 2001, in ascending order, are: East & West Dunbartonshire and Helensburgh & Lomond; East Lothian and Midlothian; and Caithness & Sutherland and Ross & Cromarty.

However, as already noted in Chapter 1, these figures cannot be taken at face value. The figures for both Edinburgh and Glasgow are overestimates of the income of city residents since, with extensive commuting into both cities, GVA is inflated by the activity of commuters while the population base, used to calculate GVA per capita, is not. GVA per capita gives a very misleading impression of the Glasgow economy in particular, an impression which is corrected by examination of other data considered shortly, and again in Chapter 4.

The counterpart to the inflation of the GVA per capita figures for Local Areas which have extensive in-commuting is the deflation of the figures for areas with out-commuting. Out-commuting deflates GVA but not the population base. This factor explains at least part of the poor showing of East & West Dunbartonshire and Helensburgh & Lomond and of East Lothian and Midlothian.

A major contributory factor to differences in GVA per head is variation in earnings. Table 2.2 shows average earnings in 2002 for 24 local authority areas. Data constraints, especially small sample sizes, mean that figures for the other eight local authorities are unavailable.

In 2002, weekly full time earnings were highest in Aberdeen, 18 per cent above the Scottish average and 46 per cent higher than in the two local authority areas with the lowest pay, the Scottish Borders and Moray. Edinburgh ranks second highest after Aberdeen but Glasgow only sixth, with earnings below the Scottish average. Other local authority areas (in addition to the Scottish Borders and Moray) with low pay, below 90 per cent of the Scottish average, are Angus, Inverclyde, North Ayrshire, Perthshire and Kinross, and West Dunbartonshire.

Table 2.2   Average gross weekly earnings, full time employees on adult rates, local authority areas, 2002

Local authority area	Earnings, £	Scotland = 100
Aberdeen City	504.5	118.1
Aberdeenshire	414.1	97.0
Angus	380.6	89.1
Argyll and Bute	390.3	91.4
Dumfries and Galloway	386.7	90.6
Dundee City	411.4	96.3
East Lothian	399.6	93.6
Edinburgh City	480.6	112.6
Falkirk	391.7	91.7
Fife	390.1	91.4
Glasgow City	421.4	98.7
Highland	411.8	96.4
Inverclyde	354.7	83.1
Midlothian	397.5	93.1
Moray	346.1	81.1
North Ayrshire	372.8	87.3
North Lanarkshire	413.2	96.8
Perthshire and Kinross	369.4	86.5
Renfrewshire	447.7	104.8
Scottish Borders	346.2	81.1
South Ayrshire	421.1	98.6
South Lanarkshire	434.2	101.7
West Dunbartonshire	376.5	88.2
West Lothian	430.1	100.7
SCOTLAND	427.0	100.0

Source: Scottish Executive (2003) *Scottish Economic Statistics*.

Turning to employment opportunities in different areas, Table 2.3 shows economic activity, employment and unemployment rates. The economic activity rate measures people in employment or seeking employment as a proportion of the relevant population (16-59/64). The employment rate is those in employment as a proportion of the same population. The economic activity and employment figures in Table 2.3 are for 2001. There are incomplete data for unemployment rates across Scotland employing the ILO definition of unemployment (essentially those who state they want a job). Instead, Table 2.3 shows the figures for those claiming unemployment related benefits in 2002.

Each of these three indicators picks up on slightly different labour market characteristics and the rankings of local authority areas by each measure vary a bit. However, there are some consistent patterns. Eight local authority areas have economic activity rates below 80 per cent, employment rates below 70 per cent and claimant count unemployment rates above 4.5 per cent. They are Dundee, two areas in the central belt (Clackmannanshire and Falkirk), Glasgow, and four areas in the west of Scotland (East Ayrshire, North Ayrshire, Inverclyde and North Lanarkshire).

Very similar patterns emerge from the work of Bramley et al (2000) who employ data on the take up of social security benefits, specifically Income Support (IS) and Housing Benefit (HB), to describe the geography of poverty in Scotland (in 1996). The average for the whole of Scotland was 32 per cent of households (for IS alone) or 33 per cent (for IS and HB together). The lowest poverty figures were for Aberdeen (16 per cent for IS and 17 per cent for IS/HB) and then relatively affluent commuter areas, such as Aberdeenshire and East Renfrewshire, and two of the island groups, Shetland and the Western Isles. By far the highest figures were for Glasgow (52 per cent for both measures). Other high poverty areas were Dundee, North Lanarkshire, South Ayrshire and West Dunbartonshire (all in the range 36-40 per cent). The figures for Edinburgh were 27 per cent (IS) and 32 per cent (IS/HB), close to the Scottish average.

Table 2.3   Rates of economic activity, employment and unemployment, local authority areas

Local authority area	Economic activity rate, %, 2001	Employment rate, %, 2001	Claimant count, %, 2002
Aberdeen City	81.2	76.2	2.1
Aberdeenshire	84.3	81.6	1.7
Angus	85.9	81.6	3.6
Argyll and Bute	81.8	76.6	3.6
Clackmannanshire	66.4	64.9	4.7
Dumfries and Galloway	78.9	74.7	3.5
Dundee City	75.9	68.8	6.0
East Ayrshire	75.1	69.1	5.6
East Dunbartonshire	80.6	76.5	2.4
East Lothian	78.5	76.1	2.1
East Renfrewshire	82.8	75.9	2.6
Edinburgh City	80.6	77.5	3.2
Eilean Siar (Western Isles)	84.7	78.5	4.3

Table 2.3   *continued*

Local authority area	Economic activity rate, %, 2001	Employment rate, %, 2001	Claimant count, %, 2002
Falkirk	76.5	69.3	4.3
Fife	79.2	72.3	5.3
Glasgow City	68.2	60.6	6.0
Highland	83.4	78.8	3.8
Inverclyde	74.6	67.5	4.6
Midlothian	86.9	84.5	2.2
Moray	83.3	79.3	2.6
North Ayrshire	75.1	67.8	6.6
North Lanarkshire	74.6	68.0	4.7
Orkney Islands	78.6	75.9	2.2
Perthshire and Kinross	85.3	81.2	2.5
Renfrewshire	81.1	75.8	4.2
Scottish Borders	82.9	81.6	2.6
Shetland Islands	87.1	84.8	1.9
South Ayrshire	79.3	71.4	4.7
South Lanarkshire	79.9	75.0	3.9
Stirling	78.3	72.8	3.8
West Dunbartonshire	77.6	70.3	6.1
West Lothian	83.9	78.7	4.2
SCOTLAND	78.5	73.2	4.1

Source: Scottish Executive (2003) *Scottish Economic Statistics*.

2.4   Conclusions

To some extent, the continued existence of very distinctive regional economies is surprising since Scotland is a relatively small place. Even fifty or a hundred years ago, the Scottish economy was fairly well economically integrated and the extent of that integration has increased over time with improved transport and communication networks and greater migration and commuting. It has been suggested that, while regional economic differences pose a number of problems, regional diversity also brings strength to the economy as a whole (Peat and Boyle, 1999), the argument being that diversity provides protection against adverse events within one or a small number of industries. This is perhaps true but only if the period of dominance of prosperous, growing sectors is used to good effect, to open up opportunities for their successors. It would be hard to argue that this process has been well managed in Scotland. In 1945, the Clydeside shipbuilding and engineering complex was still the dominant sector of the Scottish economy. In the early twenty first century, the financial services sector based in Edinburgh is the driving force. However, it has taken the sixty years in between and more to achieve the transition from one to the other.

References

Bramley, G., Lancaster, S. and Gordon, D. (2000) 'Benefit take-up and the geography of poverty in Scotland', *Regional Studies*, 34(6), pp.507-520.

Campbell, A. and MacDonald, D. (1999) 'Small and medium sized enterprises in Scotland', *Scottish Economic Bulletin*, 58, pp.33-41.

Dunlop, S. (2001) 'Financial services and the Scottish economy', *Quarterly Economic Commentary*, 26(1), Fraser of Allander Institute, Strathclyde University, pp.31-38.

Fraser of Allander Institute (2001) 'The Scottish electronics sector', *Quarterly Economic Commentary*, 26(2), Fraser of Allander Institute, Strathclyde University, pp.22-23.

Johnston, T., Buxton, N. and Mair, D. (1971) *Structure and Growth of the Scottish Economy*, Collins, Glasgow.

Lee, C.H. (1995) *Scotland and the United Kingdom: The Economy and the Union in the Twentieth Century*, Manchester University Press, Manchester.

Lenman, B. (1977) *An Economic History of Modern Scotland 1660-1976*, Batsford, London.

Lythe, S.G.E. and Butt, J. (1975) *An Economic History of Scotland 1100-1939*, Blackie, Glasgow and London.

National Statistics Office (2003) *NUTS3 GVA Tables*.

Newlands, D. (2000) 'The oil economy' in Fraser, W.F. and Lee, C.H. (eds) *Aberdeen: A New History*, Tuckwell Press, East Linton, pp.126-152.

Peat, J. and Boyle, S. (1999) *An Illustrated Guide to the Scottish Economy*, Duckworth, London.

Perman, R. (2001) 'Living in the past: why is Scotland's financial services sector ignored?', *Scottish Economic Report*, June, pp.91-95.

Scottish Executive (2003) *Scottish Economic Statistics*, Scottish Executive, Edinburgh.

Scottish Office (1988) *Scotland: An Economic Profile*, HMSO, Edinburgh.

Storie, G. and Horne, J. (1999) 'Economic review', *Scottish Economic Bulletin*, 58, pp.5-22.

Toothill, J.N. (1961) *Inquiry into the Scottish Economy 1960-1961*, Report of a Committee Appointed by the Scottish Council (Development and Industry) under the Chairmanship of J.N. Toothill, Scottish Council (Development and Industry), Edinburgh.

Chapter 3

Edinburgh and its Hinterland

Ronald W. McQuaid

3.1   Introduction

The early part of the twenty first century saw a growth in Edinburgh's economy,
due partly to its industrial structure linked to financial services and tourism, but
also due to a limited extent to the direct and indirect impacts of the new Scottish
Parliament. This chapter considers some of the impacts upon the local economy of
locating the Parliament in Edinburgh. These impacts include: those directly
associated with the Parliament (construction of the new Parliament building; the
Parliament's operation; other government departments and Non Departmental
Public Bodies; associated private and non governmental organisations), as well as
wider positive and negative impacts on organisations not directly associated with
the Parliament and the wider multiplier and displacement effects.

The next section briefly sets the analysis within the context of the current
geographical distribution of government and Non-Departmental Public Bodies
employment, as the location of the Parliament can directly influence many of these.
Section 3.3 then discusses the possible direct and indirect impacts of the
Parliament upon Edinburgh. Section 3.4 considers some of opportunities to use the
employment benefits of the Parliament and, more significantly, the buoyancy of
the local economy to tackle the problems of social exclusion and particularly that
of long term unemployment among the most disadvantaged of the city. This is
followed by some conclusions.

3.2   The Distribution of Civil Service and Non Departmental Public Body
Employment

Edinburgh has historically benefited disproportionately in terms of the number and
quality of jobs in government departments and Non Departmental Public Bodies
(NDPBs or 'Quangos'). These continue to have a positive impact upon the
Edinburgh economy, although new polices of the Executive of the Parliament are
seeking to distribute some of these jobs and associated benefits to other parts of the
country.

3.2.1 The Geographical Distribution of Civil Service Employment

It is useful to start by considering the geographical distribution of government related employment in Scotland. In Scotland as a whole in 2001 there were 46,228 permanent full time equivalent posts (FTEs) in government departments. With approximately 9 per cent of the Scottish population, the city of Edinburgh has nearly a quarter (24 per cent) of all civil service jobs. The wider Lothian region (which approximates to the Edinburgh travel-to-work-area) contains around 15 per cent of the Scottish population and 26 per cent of civil service jobs. While many civil servants are part of UK wide departments, a significant number were transferred to the control of the Scottish Parliament. There has thus been a debate on whether the Parliament should seek to change the location of these jobs and disperse some existing or new posts to other parts of the country.

Most of the other civil service posts (around 70 per cent of the total in Scotland) are part of UK, not Scottish Executive, departments. Their activities usually relate to services directly to the Scottish population (e.g. social security services), although some deal with other parts of the UK (e.g. parts of the Inland Revenue). Of particular importance are Social Security and the Inland Revenue (especially the East Kilbride and Cumbernauld and Edinburgh offices), Education and Employment spread across job centres in urban areas and the Ministry of Defence employing both non industrial and industrial staff at both military bases and support services such as Contracts and Central Purchasing and some Payroll. Hence the distribution of civil servants to a large extent reflect UK rather than Scottish Parliament policies.

The Scottish Executive, dealing with specifically Scottish policies, employed 4170 FTEs (excluding those working in Agencies). The Scottish Executive jobs were concentrated in Edinburgh with 3175 jobs (76 per cent of Scottish Executive employment excluding Agencies). However, the Agency jobs were more widely distributed (for example, Economic and Industry Affairs in Glasgow, some Fisheries Research Laboratories in Aberdeen and Pitlochry, the Liaison Office in Dover House in London and some regional HMI Schools offices), although more than half of the staff of the Scottish Executive and its agencies (such as NDPBs discussed below) are located away from Edinburgh (Scottish Executive, 1999a).

A further 4344 FTE posts were in the Scottish Prison Service largely concentrated in the main prisons throughout the country. The remaining civil servants were located throughout Scotland, although largely headquartered in Edinburgh. These included Fisheries Research Services (316), Historic Scotland (748), Scottish Agricultural Scientific Agency (141), Scottish Courts Service (850), Scottish Fisheries Protection Agency (272), Scottish Office Pensions Agency (185), Student Awards Agency Scotland (135), Crown Office and Procurator Fiscal Service (1235), General Register Office (Scotland) (242), National Archive for Scotland (134), Scotland Office (71), and Registers of Scotland (1061). The number of civil servants has been increasing in the early 2000s, partly as increased expenditure in the rest of the UK feeds through to Scottish expenditure through the Barnett formula.

Data from the Cabinet Office (Cabinet Office, 2003) in Table 3.1 show the distribution of all civil service posts by Unitary Authority. Overall, the data show that civil service employment is widely, but unevenly, dispersed with smaller urban and rural areas generally under represented.

Table 3.1   Civil service staff in post in Scotland by unitary authority, FTEs, October 2001

Unitary Authority	FTEs	Civil servants per 10,000 population
Border	256.4	24
Clackmannan	489.3	102
Falkirk	2064.3	142
Stirling	820.1	95
Dumfries and Galloway	591.2	40
Fife	1814.6	52
Aberdeen City and Aberdeenshire	2177.8	50
Moray	894.4	103
Highland	951.3	46
East Lothian	294.9	33
Edinburgh City	11229	250
Midlothian	180.3	22
West Lothian	744.9	47
Argyll & Bute	155.5	17
East Dunbarton	77.0	7
North Lanarkshire	1649	51
North Ayrshire	842.9	62
West Dunbartonshire	3283.5	352
Glasgow City	9345.6	162
South Lanarkshire	3289.6	109
Inverclyde	751.0	89
East Ayrshire	156.1	13
South Ayrshire	757.7	68
Renfrewshire and East Renfrewshire	734.2	28

Table 3.1   continued

Unitary Authority	FTEs	Civil servant per 10,000 population
Angus	321.5	30
Dundee City	955.7	66
Perth & Kinross	1161.4	86
Orkney	38.8	20
Shetland	98.7	45
Western Isles (Eilean Siar)	96.1	36
(Not allocated geographically)	5.0	0
TOTAL (rounded)	46228	91

Note: population based upon GRO (Scotland) figures for 2001; figures rounded.

Source: Based on Cabinet Office, personal correspondence, 2003.

The City of Edinburgh is greatly over represented in terms of civil service jobs with 11229 FTE posts, notably 3175 in the Scottish Office but a further 8054 in over 45 Departments or units including 1502 in the Inland Revenue, 867 in Registers Scotland and 748 in Historic Scotland. Glasgow has the second highest number of FTEs with 9346, including 2068 in the Benefits Agency and 610 in the Employment Service. However, on the basis of jobs per 10,000 population, Edinburgh has close to double the concentration of civil service jobs in Glasgow with 250 and 162 FTE posts respectively. Both are well above the national average of 91. Indeed Edinburgh has more civil servants per capita than anywhere else in Scotland other than West Dunbartonshire (due to naval bases). Other areas with high rates of civil servants (but well below Edinburgh's rates) include Moray (also linked to the Ministry of Defence), South and North Lanarkshire (particularly linked to the Inland Revenue centres at East Kilbride and Cumbernauld), Falkirk (a major Child Support Agency office) and Clackmannan (with a Young Offenders Institute).

Around Edinburgh, the rest of Lothian has relatively few civil service jobs with 47 (per 10,000 people) in West Lothian, 33 in East Lothian and 22 in Midlothian. The per capita rate for the Lothians as a whole was still a high 160. In neighbouring Fife (52 per 10,000 population) most civil service jobs are located in Dunfermline immediately across the Firth of Forth from Edinburgh and there appears to be a distance decay effect from Edinburgh in that region.

3.2.2   The Distribution of Employment in Non Departmental Public Bodies

Employment in Non Departmental Public Bodies (or Quangos) is biased towards Edinburgh, although they serve the whole of Scotland (McQuaid, 1999a). In 1996, a third (2641) of the national total of 8102 full time equivalent NDPB posts were located in Edinburgh. Despite its much larger population, only 1489 (18 per cent of the Scottish total) were in Glasgow (and relatively few others in Greater Glasgow). Aberdeen had 764 posts (9 per cent), Dundee 500 (6 per cent), Stirling 255 (3 per cent) and Inverness had 333 (4 per cent).

In terms of per capita measures Edinburgh had notably more jobs than the other cities with 63 posts per 10,000 population compared to 22 for Glasgow, 37 for Aberdeen, 30 for Dundee, 32 for Stirling, 54 for Inverness and 16 for Scotland (the population based used for Inverness was the old District population rather than Highland Council as the Council area is extremely large and contains NDPB jobs not included in the Inverness statistics). Updated figures for 2002 in Hassan and Warburton (2002) show that there has been limited change, although the number of Quango jobs was 8866 in total. An exception is Inverness which gained considerable numbers of jobs, so the figures per 10,000 population were 68 for Edinburgh, 24 for Glasgow, 32 for Aberdeen, 34 for Dundee, 46 for Stirling, 89 for Inverness and 17 for Scotland. The high share of jobs in Inverness reflects its role as an administrative centre for the Highlands. These figures do, however, ignore the effect of commuting into the cities. Also most NDPB headquarters were in Edinburgh probably representing better than average jobs and larger multiplier effects (in terms of wages, supply of services etc).

There were also 6616 employees of the three Water Authorities although these are spread around the country as many are linked to 'production' with only 714 employees (11 per cent of the national total) of the East of Scotland Water Authority located in Edinburgh, 1267 in Glasgow, 403 in Aberdeen, 370 in Dundee, 226 in Stirling and 253 in Inverness. If Water Authority jobs are included, then the numbers of NDPB jobs per 10,000 population in 1996 were 80 (Edinburgh), 42 (Glasgow), 57 (Aberdeen), 52 (Dundee), 61 (Stirling), 94 (Inverness) and 29 (Scotland). By 2002 these figures had changed to 82 (Edinburgh), 40 (Glasgow), 44 (Aberdeen), 59 (Dundee), 70 (Stirling), 130 (Inverness) and 26 (Scotland). So again Edinburgh has an over representation of such publicly funded jobs, although all the cities are over represented.

In addition to the number of jobs in different locations there may be distinctions between types of jobs or expenditure and between the impacts of the expenditure and jobs upon the local economy. The higher level jobs are concentrated in Edinburgh and it is expected that these would have greater positive multiplier effects on the local economy (due to the salary levels and as greater discretionary budgets, such as the use of advertising agencies, may be associated with such posts). Expenditure patterns and policies are important. For instance, Scottish Enterprise National in Glasgow may have greater discretionary expenditure associated with each staff member than many other organisations, leading to a greater local multiplier effect and possibly local expenditure (if there is a distance decay in expenditure patterns).

There are other differential multiplier effects of the distribution of functions and related jobs. For instance, the Royal Botanical Gardens and the National Library, Galleries and Museums provide important tourism attractions for Edinburgh, funded by the Scottish Executive, while Glasgow's Kelvingrove Art Gallery is not funded directly through them. There may also be a substitution effect whereby the local government can provide a lower level of facilities and services in these areas, as there is no need to provide as high a standard of, for instance, library services when the National Library is available locally. Hence local government expenditure on such services can be relatively lower than other cities (and Edinburgh has a low per capita expenditure on Museums). This difference in local expenditure on such services is exacerbated in the case of other major regional cities where such services support a wider hinterland (such as Dundee serving Tayside and North Fife or Glasgow's Mitchell Library which provide specialist services and books for much of the west of Scotland). It is unclear whether government support to local governments fully takes these different spending needs into account.

There are also other major government funded bodies, such as the National Health Service, but these tend to follow population distribution although they are concentrated in major urban rather than rural areas. To provide a complete picture public posts (such as Universities, Further Education Colleges, the NHS, UK wide publicly funded agencies, and local government posts funded partly by central government) should be included. Also many posts are directly or indirectly funded through government initiatives such as voluntary or private sector training agencies for the unemployed and social inclusion initiatives, which are likely to favour the less prosperous areas of greatest need, and so Edinburgh may possibly be 'under represented' although in terms of outsourced government employment and government contract expenditure (e.g. computer services or defence contracts) it may be 'over represented'.

In summary, when the location of Scottish departments which serve the new Parliament is considered there is a current bias of government and NDPB employment in favour of Edinburgh. However, when all civil service jobs, including those in UK Departments, are considered this geographical bias is considerably reduced. In the case of NDPBs, there is a strong concentration in Edinburgh. Hence the staff distribution and wider impact of expenditure needs to be considered more fully.

3.2.3 *Scottish Executive Policy on the Location of Civil Service and NDPB Jobs*

The then First Minister, Donald Dewar, set out the policy on the location of those civil service posts falling under the remit of the Scottish Parliament. He stated that 'the Scottish Executive is committed to ensuring that government in Scotland is efficient and decentralised, as part of a wider vision of more accessible, open and responsive government' (Scottish Executive, 1999a). Two objectives were set out as governing the location and relocation decisions of civil servant posts in Scotland. First, the location of the Departments and agencies of the Scottish Executive and the bodies it funds should promote efficiency and effectiveness.

Second, and subject to the first objective, the people of Scotland expect that the work of the Scottish Executive and related bodies should be close to the communities they serve.

Most of the headquarter functions of Scottish Executive Departments are located in Edinburgh (although the Enterprise and Lifelong Learning Department has historically been and remains in Glasgow). The Executive clearly expected higher level posts to remain in Edinburgh since headquarters functions 'typically involve frequent meetings with Ministers and the Scottish Parliament it was expected that this was to remain the case' (Scottish Executive, 1999a), although given the relatively short distances (at least in the Central Belt which covers the bulk of the country's population) this need not prevent NDPBs locating elsewhere. It was stated that executive functions can, however, be discharged effectively in other locations. The policy was set out that:

> when the Scottish Executive establishes a new unit or agency, or where an existing unit is merged or otherwise reorganised, there should be a presumption against location in Edinburgh. We have also decided that where a significant property break point is reached – for example, the termination of an existing lease – relocation options outside Edinburgh will be considered. In each case, Ministers will look at alternative locations. Costs will be taken into account in deciding on location, along with operational effectiveness and the position of staff concerned (Scottish Executive, 1999a).

Each case will be considered individually and the potential new locations to be considered cover all parts of Scotland. The issue of costs was elaborated in a further written answer as 'estimated whole-life costs will be considered in relation to each location or relocation opportunity, as will operational effectiveness and the position of any staff concerned' (Scottish Executive, 1999b). These costs will be influenced by inertia, the existing organisational structures and practices (such as the form of links between senior and operational staff) which may be altered by the Executive in order to encourage dispersal, and the location of existing staff (although as these are disproportionately based in Edinburgh this may act as a break on relocations, particularly to more distant parts of the country). It appears that costs are primarily operational or financial costs and it is unclear if, or how, wider social costs and benefits of dispersal (especially to the potential recipient communities) are taken into account by the Executive. A further issue may be the availability of suitable labour. As the Edinburgh labour market is much more buoyant than most of the rest of Scotland, it is likely to be more difficult to recruit suitable labour at equivalent salaries as in many other parts of the country.

This dispersal policy applies to the Departments of the Scottish Executive, to its executive agencies, to the Departments of the non Ministerial office holders and to the Crown Office, and to all Non Departmental Public Bodies funded by the Scottish Executive. The Scottish Executive has stated that it will keep the organisational scope of the policy under review.

In the first few years of the Parliament there was limited relocation of civil service posts, which is unsurprising given the timescale. Lifelong learning staff have been relocated to Glasgow and the Food Standards Agency has been set up in Aberdeen, the Public Guardian's Office in Falkirk, the National Office of the Scottish Commission for the Regulation of Care and the Offices of the Scottish Social Services Council in Dundee, the Scottish Public Pensions Agency in Galashiels and Scottish Water in Dunfermline. From 2004 the plans are for the headquarters of Scottish Natural Heritage to be set up in Inverness (although there has been strong opposition from trades unions and staff), the Office of the Scottish Charity Regulator in Dundee, the Scottish Executive Inquiry Reporters' Unit in Falkirk, the headquarters of Forestry Enterprise Scotland in Inverness, the headquarters of Her Majesty's Inspectorate of Education in Livingston, the Risk Management Authority in Paisley, and the Accountant in Bankruptcy in Ayrshire. There is also planned to be a significant movement of jobs in the Common Services Agency of the National Health Service in Scotland from Edinburgh initially to Aberdeen and to Glasgow and some VisitScotland headquarters posts will be identified for dispersal from Edinburgh (Scottish Parliament, 2004a). Further decisions are expected during 2004 and 2005 on reviews of NHS Health Scotland, NHS Education Scotland, the Mental Health Tribunal Service, the Scottish Building Standards Agency, the Scottish Arts Council, Sportscotland, NHS Quality Improvement Scotland, the Registers of Scotland, and the Mental Welfare Commission.

How rigorously the Parliament pursues dispersal will need to be judged over a longer period when both quantity and quality of dispersed posts can be considered. For example, the executive arm of the Food Standards Agency, comprising some 40-45 staff, was located in Aberdeen. There was a clear competition between Dundee and Aberdeen for this Agency. The reasons for choosing the latter were the links to scientific and research interests and the relocation costs (Scottish Executive, 1999c). Particular considerations in the decision were stated as being: the general efficiency and effectiveness of the operation; the need for the Agency to be 'arm's length' from Ministers and thus outside of the Central Belt of Scotland; the need for good communications links with the public, Ministers, the Agency headquarters in London and the media. In the case of the relocation of the Scottish Executive's Inquiry Reporters' Unit to Falkirk, the Communities Minister argued 'Falkirk is well served by public transport and was the best option in terms of value for money' (Scottish Executive, 2003). This partly reflected lower rents compared to Edinburgh.

Tavish Scott, Deputy Minister for Finance and Public Services stated in a Written Answer (Scottish Parliament, 2004a) that the reasons for dispersal included efficiency and effectiveness of service provision, level of investment needed (especially as Edinburgh is one of the most buoyant labour markets and hence finds it difficult to attract and retain staff) and social reasons:

We have made good progress with the relocation policy. The Executive is committed to ensuring that government in Scotland is efficient and decentralised as part of the wider vision of more accessible, open and responsive government.

Relocation policy is part of this vision. It can also help us to address particular problems in certain parts of the country. Relocation can provide more cost effective solutions for service delivery by allowing organisations to operate away from some of the pressures of the Edinburgh market. It can assist areas with particular social and economic needs. The impact of a relocation such as the Accountant in Bankruptcy on communities in Ayrshire can be significant. Our small units policy also addresses this issue though with the focus on smaller and more remote communities. The final main objective of relocation policy relates to our vision of a decentralised Scotland. We do not wish to see devolution mean a concentration of all things in Edinburgh or indeed in the central belt ... However, headquarters functions of the Scottish Executive departments are currently based in Edinburgh and Glasgow because of the frequent meetings with ministers and the Scottish Parliament (Scottish Parliament, 2004a).

New bodies are also subject to the dispersal policy with the location of the proposed National Transport Agency and the Royal Fine Arts Commission for Scotland (Architecture and Design Scotland) to be determined in accordance with the relocation policy with the presumption against an Edinburgh location. A location review is to be carried out on a case-by-case basis in which options outwith Edinburgh must be considered. Similar policies appear to be being developed in the rest of the UK following the Lyons Review of the potential relocation of central government departments and agencies (HM Treasury, 2003; see also Marshall et al, 1997).

It seems likely that there will continue to be strong political pressure to ensure that other centres such as Dundee are chosen as the location for other agencies or departments, although unless the location criteria and information are made transparent there is likely to be suspicion that political criteria are paramount. If the social benefits to the recipient location are not explicitly considered then rural areas are unlikely to receive much of the benefits of dispersal due to their difficulties and costs particularly of physical communication.

With a currently buoyant labour market in Edinburgh the loss of relatively small numbers of new or existing civil service or agency posts is unlikely to have a significant impact upon the local economy. Even should the local economy deteriorate the city has a greatly disproportionate share of such jobs, particularly at the higher levels.

3.3   Impacts of the Parliament on the Local Economy

The location of the new Parliament has a number of direct and indirect impacts upon Edinburgh and other local economies. These include the jobs and expenditure directly associated with the Parliament and linked industries, and wider impacts in terms of the development of the economy and property prices as well as multiplier and displacement effects (these are discussed more fully in McQuaid, 1999a).

3.3.1 Direct Impacts of the Parliament

The Scotland Act 1998, s.21, created the Scottish Parliament Corporate Body (SPCB) to provide (or ensure the provision of) property, staff and services required for the Parliament's purposes. The government's White Paper *Scotland's Parliament* (Scottish Office, 1997) estimated that the additional running costs of the Parliament would be £20-30m, including staff and operating costs. This included the salaries and allowances of the 129 Members of the Scottish Parliament (MSPs). Even after taking inflation into account these estimates were extremely optimistic, as the SPCB revenue expenditure for the year ended 31 March 2003 was £47.9m (SPCB, 2003). This comprised: parliamentary staff salaries of £13.5m and MSP salaries of £9.1m, members' costs of £7.5m, which enable MSPs to secure staff and accommodation to assist them in the discharge of their parliamentary duties, and £17.8m to meet the administration and property running costs of the Parliament. So the direct employment, and subsequent multiplier effects, of the Parliament are notably larger than first expected. There will be greater displacement of expenditure elsewhere in Scotland than initially expected, as the transfers from the UK Treasury to Scotland as a whole are not expected to increase to take account of the costs of running the Parliament.

Amidst much political controversy, estimates of full final capital costs of the new Parliament building at Holyrood, and associated infrastructure including roads, have risen dramatically over time from £50m to £109m in June 1999 to £195m in March 2000 and over £396.5m in late 2003, including fees and VAT, and is likely to be well over £430m finally (SPCB, 2003; Scottish Parliament, 2004b). As evidence to the Holyrood (Fraser) Inquiry has indicated, this is due to factors such as changing specifications, poor project control and the choice of design. The initial direct employment impact of the construction of the Parliament was estimated at around 417 worker years of construction jobs (see McQuaid, 1999a, for a discussion). This figure now looks a considerable underestimate. Most of this is due to the over tenfold increase in construction and related costs. Not all of these jobs can be considered to be productive as the Inquiry evidence suggested that, due to poor project management, many workers spent long periods waiting for earlier phases to be completed before they could continue working (Holyrood Inquiry, 2004). So ironically this could be included in job generation but is inefficient and undesirable.

There are also displacement effects on capital and other expenditure elsewhere in Edinburgh and Scotland that are not insignificant. One point is that the construction industry in Edinburgh has been particularly 'overheated'. There has been large scale private and public developments during the construction of the Parliament including the replacement of the major hospitals with the new Edinburgh Royal Infirmary Private Finance Initiative funded hospital in the south east of the city and major works at Leith and the western edge of the city near the Gyle (including the new Royal Bank of Scotland campus headquarters), as well as considerable housing development. Evidence suggests that many construction firms were suffering labour shortages and wage rates for skilled workers rose considerably. One report indicates that the hospital project had a shortage of some 20 per cent of construction workers. So it is unfortunate that the impact of construction of the Parliament exacerbated the 'overheating' of the sector.

3.3.2   *Wider Impacts of the Parliament*

The impacts of the Parliament discussed above will have multiplier (indirect and induced effects) and displacement effects. For instance the multiplier effects of salaries to MSPs and new employees, firms providing services directly to the Parliament, as well as firms lobbying or seeking to influence the Parliament, consulates, industries associated with the effects of the Parliament such as the media and hotels, and local government. The full effects of these are difficult to estimate, as can be seen from the wide divergences in estimates cited below. Since an impact of around 2400 jobs would represent around 0.7 per cent of the Edinburgh travel-to-work area workforce (nearly 1 per cent of the City Council area workforce), the figures are small but reasonably significant. Of course, those getting such jobs may often commute and the availability of such jobs may increase in-migration, although lower skilled workers are less likely to commute as far as high skilled workers and so may not gain as many benefits from jobs in Edinburgh (McQuaid et al., 2001).

Research on the full range of likely local impacts of the new Parliament was undertaken for various agencies. Edinburgh City Council (1997) estimated that there would be approximately 5500 new jobs in Edinburgh of which 600 would be associated with the Parliament, 4500 with new and relocating businesses and organisations, 200 with business tourism and 200 with construction and refurbishment (Table 3.2). These figures were based upon an assumed 10 per cent growth in employment in Business Services, a 25 per cent growth in industry/employer/professional organisation employment, and 25 per cent growth in media employment, as a result of the Parliament. Glasgow City Council (1997) and their consultants (Pieda, 1997) estimated that the impacts would be around half of those of Edinburgh City Council with 2700 direct and indirect jobs and 417 construction job years (or 41.7 permanent job equivalents assuming 10 years is equivalent to a permanent job), of which 2500 and 367 respectively would be in Edinburgh.

A later study for The Scottish Office, City Council of Edinburgh and Lothian and Edinburgh Enterprise (Pieda, 1999) increased the total employment linked to the new Parliament to 2405, made up of 1751 direct jobs plus 654 indirect or induced jobs. Within this figure there were major changes in the likely sources of the employment gains from the other two reports and a larger average multiplier was used. Clearly such estimates of future events need to be treated with some caution, as it must be remembered that these are working reports and were not intended as in-depth definitive studies.

The latter study was carried out after some of the decisions on the Parliament had been finalised and there had been time to interview a wider sample of firms. In the Parliament itself (Members of the Scottish Parliament (MSPs), researchers, Civil Servants and Parliamentary staff) there were estimated to be 698 jobs plus an

Table 3.2   **Approximate employment effects of the Scottish Parliament on Edinburgh**

	1997 Edinburgh City Council estimates	*1997 Glasgow City Council/Pieda estimates*	*1999 Pieda estimates*
Employment associated with the Parliament, including MSPs	729*	704	1036*
New and relocating businesses and organisations	4500*	c.1531*	865*
Related tourism	200	96	412*
Construction and refurbishment	200	40	92*
Jobs elsewhere in Scotland	N/A	205	
TOTAL (rounded)**	5629	2834	2405

Note: each estimate uses different assumptions and figures are approximate; * Figures include 129 MSPs' jobs and multiplier effects; ** Rounded totals quoted in the reports referred to.

Source: Based on Edinburgh Council (1997), Glasgow Council (1997) and Pieda (1997), and Pieda (1999).

additional 338 associated indirect or induced jobs (total 1036). In early 2004 the actual figures were 129 MSPs, 349 people employed by them, and 472 staff in post at the Parliament (excluding staff employed by contractors) – a total of 950. Estimates of construction jobs rose (as the costs of the Parliament building had begun to rise and a capital expenditure estimate of £59 million was used) to 71 FTE direct jobs (710 person years) and 21 indirect or induced jobs (total 92) although at a cost of £400 million these figures are more likely to be over 600 FTE jobs. The construction employment may increase due to the further increase in cost estimates (see above). Assuming an average output per employee of the construction industry there would be around 2294 person years (or, say, 229 FTE jobs). However, the techniques and speed of production, use of imported materials may alter this figure. In addition there would be indirect employment, although as many workers are brought in from other parts of Scotland and the UK (partly due to the 'overheated' local construction industry) these may be more widely spread beyond Edinburgh than in the past.

Further impacts are upon services used by those working in, or with, or visiting the Parliament, especially restaurants, hotels, speciality shops etc. Around 2000 extra hotel rooms are expected to be developed in the next few years, some of which are linked to the extra business and tourism travel linked to the Parliament and the associated organisations around it. Edinburgh estimates varied from 96 to

412 jobs in business and related tourism. The different estimates for the impact of improvements to transport (e.g. air travel) may also result from greater travel to the city, although the scale of this effect may be relatively small, at least in the short run. Indeed Edinburgh airport has surpassed Glasgow airport in both domestic and international scheduled air passengers and is likely to have the highest total passenger numbers of any airport in Scotland (Scottish Transport Review, 2003; Department for Transport, 2003). There have been transport improvements (e.g. to the airport and rail services to Edinburgh), although these could act as a force helping to centralise more economic activity in the capital.

Tourism job numbers are quite high in the Pieda (1999) report (317 direct plus 95 indirect), although it is claimed that in the early years of the Parliament there will be a 'window' of interest and after that numbers may decrease. The various jobs in media, lobbyist organisations, overseas representatives and various other private sector firms are estimated at 665 plus 200 indirect and induced jobs (total 865). This was estimated after interviewing a sample of relevant firms. It is considerably lower than estimates in the earlier studies but in the medium term is likely to be a more realistic.

The studies of the impacts of Scottish Parliament did not estimate new specific multipliers but used generally accepted estimates. Using a multiplier figure of 1.32 Pieda (1997) estimated the income multiplier effects to be 861 FTEs, plus 96 FTEs in tourism and 40 FTEs in construction. Edinburgh Council (1997) used an income multiplier of 1.2 and supplier multiplier of 1.1. These figures appear to be for the multiplier effects within Edinburgh, although it is important to distinguish these from the wider multiplier effects on the rest of Scotland and beyond. Pieda (1999) used a higher average multiplier of around 1.8. Detailed study would be required to estimate more precise figures. However, the geographical distribution of these multiplier effects within Scotland is less certain, although it is expected that the effects would be concentrated in Edinburgh. The purchasing policies of the Parliament and others (e.g. the construction firms) will affect the geographic distribution of the multipliers.

The three studies vary quite considerably from each other in terms of the employment attributed to different factors. The variation between the reports reflects different estimates and assumptions (e.g. concerning construction compared to refurbishment) and in particular different estimates of growth in businesses attracted by the Parliament. The methodology used by each differed, with Edinburgh assuming a certain percentage growth in broad related industries (see above), while Glasgow considered each specific industry and the likely impact upon it and the 1999 study used a survey of firms. The multipliers used in each study were fairly similar, although the likely displacement effects elsewhere in Scotland (e.g. of industry/ employer/professional organisations) is not explicitly considered. The timescale for the impacts is important and it is unclear from the reports when the estimated employment figures would be reached. Many of the wider impacts upon property markets, congestion and changing perceptions of Edinburgh on employment and industrial location have been considered elsewhere (McQuaid, 1999a) and are not repeated here.

3.4 Inclusion and the Long-term Unemployed

The city's claimant count unemployment rate stood at 2.3 per cent in 2002 (these averages use the working age population denominator as now favoured by the Office for National Statistics, NOMIS), well below the Scottish and United Kingdom averages of 3.3 per cent and 2.6 per cent respectively and at near its lowest for three decades. Taking account of 'hidden unemployment' a rough estimate of the 'real' unemployment (as opposed to the claimant count rate) suggests a rate of up to 22 per cent (based upon UK figures, see Beatty et al, 2002), which is low historically and compared to most other parts of Scotland, other than Aberdeen and Shetland. In addition Edinburgh's economy has a high share, or location quotient, of fast growing industries such as Financial Services (although this may be an overdependence in the case of a contraction in the industry).

However, a key issue is the exclusion of certain groups of the population from the benefits of the economic prosperity, in particular the position of the long term unemployed. The local Council has sought to develop policies in response to such localised long term unemployment, and the wider social problems that both reflect and contribute to the exclusion of individuals and groups from the active labour market (Edinburgh Council, 1999; Lindsay and Sturgeon, 2003).

This has involved a partnership and community based approach to the development of employment and regeneration initiatives and detailed analysis of the characteristics of the long term unemployed, particularly in the five areas of unemployment concentration largely on the city's periphery: North Edinburgh, including the Pilton, Muirhouse and Granton areas; South Edinburgh, including the Prestonfield, Kaimes, Inch and Gilmerton areas; Leith, including the Fort, Lorne and Harbour areas; Wester Hailes, including the North Hailes and South Hailes areas; and Craigmillar, including the Niddrie area. Here unemployment remains a significant problem with 20-25 per cent of unemployed claimants having been out of work for at least a year.

Different localities are undoubtedly distinguished by different flows of employed and unemployed people in and out of the labour market and work (or 'labour market flow regimes'), reflecting both the underlying economic and industrial conditions and the characteristics of the local economy (Martin and Sunley, 1999). These conditions and characteristics are in turn influenced by both labour supply and local employer demand factors (Adams et al, 2000). Accordingly, the skills levels within the local labour force, the types of opportunities that are available, and the role of employers in setting rates of pay and conditions all significantly impact upon the ability of residents in high unemployment localities to find appropriate work.

In the case of Edinburgh the buoyant economy has resulted in the late 1990s and early 2000s in levels of labour demand that are particularly high, providing the opportunity to influence employers towards recruiting the long term unemployed. This arguably offers a greater opportunity to tackle this issue than at any time in at least the last 30 years, as it reduces one of the main weaknesses of supply side policies, such as the New Deal, of an inadequate local labour demand side.

Conventional models of 'mismatch unemployment' usually highlight supply side factors such as skill shortages, wage demands in specific markets, interregional spatial mismatch and the search channels used by job seekers (Layard et al, 1991). Significant barriers to work for the long term unemployed include lack of education, qualifications and relevant recent work experience, together with other traditional supply side factors such as creche facilities, employer prejudice against the long term unemployed and older job seekers, gender roles, and personal adaptability to the workplace. However, a number of analysts have stressed the importance of forms of spatial mismatch specifically linked to geographical immobility within local labour markets (Holzer, 1991). Individuals from excluded or peripheral areas tend, it is argued, not to take up employment opportunities outwith their immediate localities, further limiting their job prospects (Webster, 1999).

Indeed, the reluctance of unemployed people to travel in order to pursue work has been identified as a factor limiting the success of their job search (McQuaid and Lindsay, 2002). While this may be a problem in many areas, Edinburgh is a relatively small city and evidence from a recent survey of 115 long term unemployed people suggested that most respondents were willing to travel beyond their immediate area of residence for employment. Less than 5 per cent of respondents indicated a strong desire to work only within their immediate locality. Some 44.5 per cent of the sample expressed a willingness to travel anywhere in Edinburgh and 51 per cent would travel anywhere in the wider Lothian area (Edinburgh travel-to-work-area) or beyond (McQuaid et al, 2001). Almost 81 per cent expressed a willingness to travel for thirty minutes or more to work. Indeed, there was little evidence to be found that labour market insularity – in the sense of a psychological aversion to travel beyond one's own locality – was a significant barrier for long term unemployed people in that area.

So policies may take a broader perspective including skills, experience, psychological and other supply side barriers together with working with employers (as the City Council has done on major construction and other projects) in order to improve employment among the most disadvantaged groups. Policies and support are likely to need to be increasingly focused upon the specific requirements of individuals (rather than standardised 'volume' initiatives). Such intensive support may be more expensive per person, but more likely to succeed and so be more cost effective, while the overall level of resources required may fall due to the declining numbers of unemployed. This will require effective partnership working between the relevant agencies and bodies (McQuaid, 1999b and 2000). The quality of support will be crucial and efforts will need to be made to properly monitor and improve the quality and effectiveness of support.

In addition, as the overall economy is so buoyant the numbers of unemployed in the various disadvantaged areas is decreasing, so consideration may need to be given to whether some job search services and training schemes should be increasingly provided at the city rather than neighbourhood level, in order to reap economies of scale, improve services and avoid duplication. However, some local services are likely to be necessary in order to identify and work with local people requiring assistance. In terms of national support for local economic development in Edinburgh, there will be pressure to shift resources to areas of Scotland with greater need. So initiatives in Edinburgh will need to show that they are particularly effective and also that they are significantly increasing the size of the Scottish economy rather than primarily redistributing resources within the economy.

3.5 Conclusions

This chapter has considered the wide range of impacts of the Scottish Parliament upon the local economy in Edinburgh. The positive impacts, particularly direct and indirect employment and expenditure should be relatively significant to the local area. There will also be some of the negative issues of congestion, labour market pressure, rising house prices, and displacement of employment elsewhere. The current geographical distribution of civil service and Non Departmental Public Body employment considerably favours Edinburgh. Although the number of civil servants serving the Parliament is relatively small, it is higher than originally expected. The Parliament and Executive have set policies to aid the decentralisation of civil service and Non Departmental Public Body jobs, although the long term results of this policy remain to be seen and higher level jobs are less likely to be decentralised despite communication improvements.

A key issue for Edinburgh is how to reduce the exclusion of certain groups of the population from the benefits of the economic prosperity, in particular the long term unemployed. Little evidence has been found of travel being a barrier to work for this group, although other factors such as training, experience and personal factors are. Future policies and support may need to increasingly focus upon the specific requirements of individuals with high quality rather than standardised 'volume' initiatives. The buoyant economy means that there is a major opportunity to tackle the problems of the more disadvantaged in an intensive manner, although unless these initiatives are very effective there will be calls to divert more of these resources to the many other areas in Scotland where need is greater.

References

Adams, J., Greig, M. and McQuaid, R.W. (2000) 'Mismatch unemployment and local labour market efficiency: the role of employer and vacancy characteristics', *Environment and Planning A*, 32, pp.1841-1856.

Beatty, C., Fothergill, S., Gore, T. and Green, A. (1997) *The Real Level of Unemployment 2002*, Sheffield, Centre for Regional and Social Research, Sheffield Hallam University.

Cabinet Office (2003) *Cabinet Office Statistics website*. Home Civil Service Staff Branch, London. www.civil-service.gov.uk/statistics.

Department for Transport (2003) *Air Traffic Demand in Central Scotland*, DfT Report by Arup, London, DfT.

Edinburgh Council, The City of (1997) *Implications for Edinburgh of a Scottish Parliament*, report to the Economic Development Committee, 9 June.

Edinburgh Council, The City of (1999) *Access to Employment*, Edinburgh.

Glasgow Council, The City of (1997) *Potential Impact of a Scottish Parliament on Glasgow's Economy*, report to the Policy Formulation and Monitoring Subcommittee.

Hassan, G. and Warburton, C. (2002) *Anatomy of the New Scotland*, Edinburgh, Mainstream Publishing.

HM Treasury (2003) *Independent Review on Public Sector Relocation (Lyons Review)*. www.hm-treasury.gov.uk/lyonsreview.

Holyrood Inquiry (2004) *Holyrood Inquiry Transcript*, 23 March 2004, evidence of Paul Curran. www.holyroodinquiry.org/transcripts_documents/23-03-2004am/transcript23-03-2004-am.htm

Holzer, H.J. (1991) 'The spatial mismatch hypothesis: what has the evidence shown?' *Urban Studies*, 28, pp.105-122.

Layard, R., Nickell, S. and Jackman, R. (1991) *Unemployment, Macroeconomic Performance and the Labour Market*, Oxford, Oxford University Press.

Lindsay, C. and Sturgeon, G. (2003) 'Local responses to long-term unemployment: delivering access to employment in Edinburgh', *Local Economy*, 18(2), pp.159-173.

Marshall, J.N., Hopkins, W.J. and Richardson, R. (1997) 'The Civil Service and the regions: geographical perspectives on Civil Service restructuring', *Regional Studies*, 31 (6), pp.607-13.

Martin, R. and Sunley, P. (1999) 'Unemployment flow regimes and regional unemployment disparities', *Environment and Planning A*, 31, pp.523-550.

McQuaid, R.W. (1999a) 'The local economic impact of the Scottish Parliament' in McCarthy, J. and Newlands, D. (eds) *Governing Scotland, Problems and Prospects: The Economic Impact of the Scottish Parliament*, Aldershot, Ashgate, pp.149-166.

McQuaid, R.W. (1999b) 'The role of partnerships in urban economic regeneration', *International Journal of Public-Private Partnerships*, 2, pp.3-28.

McQuaid, R.W. (2000) 'The theory of partnerships – why have partnerships' in Osborne, S.P. (ed.) *Managing Public-private Partnerships for Public Services: An International Perspective*, Routledge, London, pp.9-35.

McQuaid, R.W., Greig, M. and Adams, A. (2001) 'Unemployed job seeker attitudes towards potential travel-to-work times', *Growth and Change*, 32(4), pp.356-69.

McQuaid, R.W. and Lindsay, C. (2002) '"The employability gap": long-term unemployment and barriers to work in buoyant labour markets', *Environment and Planning C*, 20(4), pp.613-628.

Pieda (1997) *The Potential Impact of a Scottish Parliament on the Glasgow Economy*, Edinburgh, Pieda.

Pieda (1999) *Scottish Parliament Economic Impact and Regeneration Impacts*, Report for The Scottish Office, City Council of Edinburgh, and Lothian and Edinburgh Enterprise, Edinburgh, Pieda.

Scottish Executive (1999a) *Parliamentary Written Answer S1W-01558*, 15 September.

Scottish Executive (1999b) *Parliamentary Written Answer S1W-2086*, 3 November.

Scottish Executive (1999c) *Scottish Executive Press Release SE0801/1999*, 5 October.

Scottish Executive (2003) *Scottish Executive Press Release SEC289/2003*, 18 July.

Scottish Office (1997) *Scotland's Parliament*, Cmnd 3658, Edinburgh, HMSO.

Scottish Parliamentary Corporate Body (2003) *Annual Report for 2003*, Edinburgh, SPCB.

Scottish Parliament (2004a) *Parliamentary Written Answer* S2W-5401 by Tavish Scott, 13 January 2004, Edinburgh, Scottish Parliament.

Scottish Parliament (2004b) Scottish Parliament Financial Summary January 2004. www.scottish.parliament.uk/sp/spcb/holyrood-letters/financial-jan2004.pdf.

Scottish Transport Review (2003) 'Air passengers', *Scottish Transport Review*, Issue 23.

Webster, D. (1999) 'Targeted local jobs: the missing element in Labour's social inclusion policy', *New Economy*, 6, pp.193-198.

Chapter 4

Glasgow's Recent Trajectory: Partial Recovery and its Consequences

Ivan Turok and Nick Bailey

4.1 Introduction

Popular images of Glasgow are surprisingly disparate. For more than a decade the city has been portrayed as an inspiring story of urban transformation and civic pride recognised worldwide. During the 1980s and early 1990s this was often attributed to the initiative of local public organisations. They launched new community based housing schemes, supported the rehabilitation of old warehouses and tenements, promoted cultural events and festivals, invested in major tourist and visitor attractions, encouraged local design and awareness of the city's architectural heritage, and developed a host of innovative employment and training projects (Donnison and Middleton, 1987; Keating, 1988; Urry, 1990; McCrone, 1991; Booth and Boyle, 1993). These initiatives were often accompanied by a dose of civic boosterism that placed Glasgow at the forefront of entrepreneurial cities in Britain (Paddison, 1993; McCarthy and Pollock, 1997; Glasgow Development Agency, 1999).

Sentiments have developed in more subtle ways since then, with increasing private investment in smart hotels, fashionable bars and restaurants, new shopping arcades, designer clothes stores, modern cinemas, nightclubs, fitness centres and stylish loft apartments, mostly in and around the revamped city centre. They have coincided with changes in lifestyle for sections of the population with increased eating out, spending on clothing and entertainment, weekend breaks and city centre living. Glasgow has acquired a trendy, exciting and even glamorous image in certain circles as a place to shop, visit, live and socialise. Public investment has complemented the city's attractiveness as a regional service centre with new museums, art galleries, concert hall, iconic science centre, conference and exhibition facility, and extensive environmental improvements. This cocktail of amenities has conveyed considerable vitality to observers and been widely cited as proof of Glasgow's resurgence, particularly as a place of consumption (e.g. Arlidge, 1996; Scottish Enterprise Glasgow, 2000; Howard, 2001).

A wave of prominent inward investments in financial services, software and call centres have coincided with these changes. They have generated optimism about the city's ability to compete as a national, even European business location, as well as an important retail, leisure and tourist destination (Glasgow City Council, 2001a). They have enhanced the city's reputation for having successfully 'reinvented' itself and transformed the conditions for prosperity through a new economic base in knowledge intensive services and cultural or creative industries (Economist, 1998; Leadbeater and Oakley, 1999; Scottish Business Insider, 2001). Local agencies are reputed to have improved Glasgow's competitive position through their responsive approach towards external opportunities, pragmatic collaboration and active pursuit of new ideas in economic regeneration (Landry, 2000; Maver, 2000; OECD, 2002).

Yet, an altogether more sobering image of Glasgow persists alongside all this. Pervasive themes include continuing industrial closures, persistent unemployment, violent crime and ongoing depopulation through out-migration and high mortality. These problems are linked rather casually in the media with bad housing, environmental dereliction, concentrated poverty, educational under-achievement and religious sectarianism. For example, Glasgow was recently dubbed the 'sick city of Europe' following several comparative studies of health conditions (Shaw et al, 1999; Office for Public Health in Scotland, 2001). Accompanying them are some newer concerns relating to personal and community stress, high debt, family break-up, drug addiction, low political participation, racial tension, neighbourhood abandonment, increasing residential segregation and a declining tax base (Glasgow City Council 1998; Bailey et al, 1999; Fitzpatrick, 2000; Webster, 2000a).

Commentators vary widely in their assessment of Glasgow's fundamental condition and how these economic and social attributes relate to each other. Consequently their views of what needs to be done differ greatly too. It is hard to get beyond partial judgements that seem to serve particular interests to obtain a more comprehensive and coherent picture. It is also important to go beyond single, separate measures of progress in order to explore the causal connections between different aspects of the city's recent development and to construct a more synthetic account and explanation.

One influential perspective holds that the city has turned around completely and that progress is being achieved across a broad front. For example, a recent report concluded: 'Over the past few years Glasgow has changed, both as a place to live and a place to work ... the economy's performance over the last three years is the best there has been for a generation' (Business Strategies, 2001, p.22). The broad policy priority that tends to follow from this analysis involves upgrading the local economy by developing distinctive 'quality' assets, encouraging innovative technologies and raising productivity. This is the thrust of the Scottish Executive's economic strategy *Smart, Successful Scotland* which seeks to increase investment in high level skills, better telecommunications infrastructure for high value tradable services, and commercialisation of university research to develop new knowledge based industries (Scottish Executive, 2001). Higher productivity is expected to raise incomes and generate additional local spending. Remaining concerns, such as the low business survival rates and poor educational attainment, tend to be seen as residual issues to be addressed by targeted initiatives.

An alternative view is that Glasgow's socio-economic challenges are more profound. Recent improvements are deficient in scale and depth to remove the city's pervasive problems. For example, another independent audit published at the same time as that quoted above concluded: 'While there are one or two positive indicators for Glasgow, the area still has a considerable way to go to reach UK levels of competitiveness' (SLIMS, 2001, p.5). There are divergent views on the nature of this challenge. For some, Glasgow's problem is essentially a shortage of employment opportunities, especially for people with manual backgrounds and few formal qualifications, reflecting the city's extensive deindustrialisation (Webster, 2000a). For others, limited aspirations, desire or ability to work among the unemployed is the main brake on progress. The city's low employment rate has been attributed to a lack of 'employability' of its residents, not a shortage of jobs (Scottish Executive, 2001 and 2002). Cultural attributes are sometimes said to lie at the heart of the city's predicament, reflecting a lack of enterprise or high welfare dependency among the local population (quoted in Lever, 1997; Danson and Mooney, 1998; Peat and Boyle, 1999). Parts of the city are periodically portrayed as areas of hopelessness and despair occupied by an 'underclass' (e.g. Murray, 1996). Similarly, sections of the media sometimes represent Glasgow as lacking economic viability, socially unbalanced, deficient in the quality of civic leadership and a drain on national resources (e.g. Sunday Times, 1996; Scotland on Sunday, 2002). There is a long history of negative external perceptions – within government as well as the media – dating back to the portrait of Red Clydeside as a militant working class city unattractive to inward investment, alongside images of overcrowded slums, violent razor gangs and heavy drinking (Pacione, 1995; Robertson, 1998; Levitt, 1999).

The purpose of this chapter is to explore the underlying evidence. Which of these depictions of the city is more accurate and how might one analyse the situation more objectively? Has Glasgow really established the basis for lasting growth and all-round transformation, or are its socio-economic problems showing little sign of diminishing because of inappropriate or inadequate attention?

The assessment is complicated by the intricacies of social and economic change in a sizeable city and deficiencies in national data sources for local areas. The notion of a city turning around may seem straightforward at first sight, but it is not so in practice. Consequently, we focus on two fundamental and interrelated themes: the labour market (reflecting concerns about jobs, unemployment, incomes and poverty) and demographic trends (including concerns about population decline, migration and mortality). Both are central to economic prosperity and the quality of life. The causes and consequences of change and the appropriate policy responses are matters of considerable debate. We consider the prevailing views about these issues and provide a framework that permits a more detailed and systematic assessment of recent developments.

The geographical definition of the city is important in all this. Glasgow is essentially a large conurbation consisting of a core built-up area with extensive commuter suburbs (such as Bearsden, Bishopbriggs and Newton Mearns). It is also surrounded by old industrial towns (such as Clydebank, Coatbridge and Paisley) and former New Towns (East Kilbride and Cumbernauld) that depend on it for certain services and amenities. The whole metropolitan area ('Greater Glasgow') is much larger than the administrative boundary of Glasgow City Council. In order to explore conurbation trends in more detail, we distinguish where the statistics permit between the core city (equated for pragmatic reasons with the City Council boundary) and the outer area (equated with the adjoining six local authorities) (Figure 4.1). In 2000 the core city had a population of 609,000, while Greater Glasgow had a population of 1,717,000.[1]

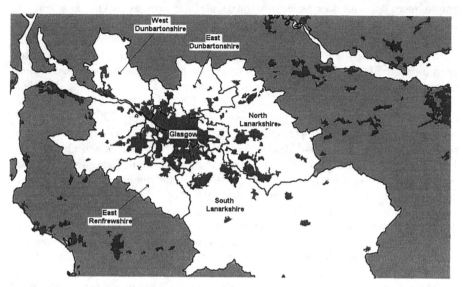

Figure 4.1   Map of Greater Glasgow showing current local authorities

4.2   Overall Economic Performance

The most widely used single measure of economic performance for a nation or region is its gross domestic product (GDP) or output. GDP measures the capacity of the economy to create wealth and income by adding value to basic resources or imports. It includes estimates of the value of public and private services. GDP per capita also corresponds broadly with the average living standards of the population (income per head), although it is a highly aggregate measure and conveys nothing about the distribution of income. The Office for National Statistics has recently produced sub-regional data on GDP for local authorities (ONS, 2001). This enables comparisons to be made between Glasgow's aggregate prosperity and that of other cities and regions, and allows its changing performance over time to be assessed. The data is described by the ONS as provisional at present and has to be treated with caution as a result. It is also only sensible to present GDP per capita statistics for reasonably self contained areas (such as a whole conurbation or functional city-

---

[1] Full details of the statistical sources are given in the technical appendix. The population figure quoted here excludes Inverclyde. If that authority is included, Greater Glasgow had a population of 1,801,000 in 2000.

region) because a large amount of net in-commuting can greatly overstate the prosperity of smaller territories, such as city council administrative areas or even places like Greater London (although this error continues to be made e.g. HM Treasury, 2001a). Greater Glasgow in this context includes Inverclyde.

After making the necessary adjustments for inflation and commuting imbalances, it emerges that Greater Glasgow's GDP per capita was 5 per cent below the British average over the period 1993-98 and 3.5 per cent below the Scottish average (Bailey et al, 2002). This does not suggest a particularly prosperous local economy – on the contrary, it is less prosperous than the average. It is also a full 18 per cent below Greater Edinburgh's GDP per head. Nevertheless, it is not as low as one might have anticipated considering the city's long history of industrial decline. Part of the reason for this is that Glasgow's population also declined, thereby reducing the indicator's denominator. The city's whole economy contracted, at least until recently when other sectors have expanded. Interestingly, Glasgow's GDP per capita was between 10-30 per cent above that of the northern English conurbations over the same recent period (Bailey et al, 2002). In short, Greater Glasgow's recent aggregate prosperity appears to be higher than that of many former industrial cities, but slightly lower than that of the rest of the country. From this evidence it does not conform to the most negative media stereotype of an unviable basket case, although there is clearly room for improvement.

In fact, reporting an average for Greater Glasgow's prosperity over the period 1993-98 obscures what appears to be a notable change during this time. Its level of income per head increased by 3 per cent faster than the British average over the period 1993-98 and nearly 7 per cent faster than the Scottish average. This appears to have reflected strong growth in economic output rather than a sharp fall in the population. Starting from a low base could also have been a factor. No other British conurbation experienced the same rate of increase over this period. It provides some evidence for a turn around or at least an improvement in Glasgow's economic performance during the 1990s. It should be borne in mind that these statistics relate to the whole of the metropolitan area and not simply the core city. The significance of this is explained below.

To provide further insights into Greater Glasgow's economic performance, GDP per capita can be subdivided into a measure of economic productivity (output per employed resident) and a measure of labour utilisation (the employment rate – defined here as the proportion of the resident population in employment). This provides a more specific indication of some of the comparative strengths and weaknesses of Glasgow's economy. The results show that Greater Glasgow's productivity was 5 per cent above the British average over the period 1993-98 and 4 per cent above the Scottish average (Bailey et al, 2002). Glasgow's productivity was considerably higher than that of the northern English conurbations.

The full explanation for this requires further research, but from initial inspection of the industrial composition of these cities, one of the immediate reasons for Greater Glasgow's high and rising average productivity during the 1990s appears to be the disproportionate presence of two relatively high value industries. The first is electronics (mainly involving the production of computers and semiconductors), whose output expanded very rapidly during the 1990s

(Scottish Executive, 2003). The main plants concerned were located in Renfrewshire and Lanarkshire (including East Kilbride, Cumbernauld and separate greenfield locations such as Erskine), rather than in Glasgow City. The second is financial and business services, which grew particularly quickly in Glasgow City during the 1990s and employs a disproportionate number of professional and managerial workers (Bailey and French, 2004; Turok and Bailey, 2004). Although the most recent performance and future prospects for financial services are broadly positive, electronics has experienced a dramatic downturn since 2000 (Scottish Executive, 2003). There have been substantial plant contractions and closures, attributable partly to a global recession in electronics, but also to a significant shift in production towards lower cost locations in Asia and Eastern Europe. The narrow and in some respects vulnerable base to Greater Glasgow's high productivity performance cannot therefore be a source of comfort or complacency.[2] This is reinforced by the fact that the productivity of Glasgow's other manufacturing and service sectors has been no better than the Scottish average, according to the Scottish Production and Services Databases (SLIMS, 2001). In addition, research, development and innovation are generally low, especially in the private sector (Docherty et al, 2001; OECD, 2002).

The employment rate provides some indication of the extent to which the income generated by the city's economy is spread among the population. Greater Glasgow's employment rate was only 91 per cent of the British average over the period 1993-98 and 93 per cent of the Scottish average. It was also lower than most of the northern English conurbations, and it did not improve much over this period (see below). The explanation for this very unfavourable situation is likely to include Glasgow's industrial decline and experience of labour shedding and business relocation, which left a legacy of high unemployment and low economic participation. It may also be a feature of the dramatic shift in the city's economic structure over the last two decades from predominantly manual to non manual occupations, which the resident population of the core city has struggled to adjust to (see below). The combination of relatively high productivity and a low employment rate could also reflect a relatively high level of external ownership and the transfer of surplus income elsewhere – one of the limitations of a branch economy. This has been a feature of the electronics industry, dominated by foreign multinationals using capital intensive techniques to generate high levels of value added with a relatively low labour component and high profit repatriation abroad (Turok, 1993).

Glasgow's combination of relatively high average productivity and a low employment rate is unusual when compared with other cities and regions in Britain (HM Treasury, 2001a; Bailey et al, 2002). Their productivity and employment rates are typically more similar. The contrast between the two variables in Glasgow suggests a more segmented economy, possibly reflecting a more severe history of de-industrialisation and the emergence of a narrower economic base.

---

[2] During 2003 Glasgow lost several high value fund management operations to London as a result of consolidation, including Abbey National and Gartmore.

4.3   Long run Trends in Employment

Glasgow's low employment rate reflects above all the difficulties the conurbation has faced adjusting to industrial decline. Greater Glasgow lost more than two thirds (68 per cent) of its manufacturing jobs between 1971 and 2001, down from approximately 291,000 to 94,000 full time equivalent positions. In the early 1970s manufacturing provided two fifths of all employment in the city directly. It was also a major market for many other local firms engaged in supplying materials and services, and there were substantial knock-on effects from workers' spending. Manufacturing job losses were not compensated for by an equivalent growth in services, which increased by 39 per cent or approximately 145,000 full time equivalent jobs over the same period. Service employment also did not replace the kinds of jobs lost in manufacturing, i.e. full time, well paid jobs mostly filled by men (Turok and Edge, 1999).

The employment performance of the conurbation has been poor across the city core and the outer ring, although the core has done rather worse historically. Glasgow City lost approximately 86,000 manufacturing jobs (74 per cent of its total) between 1971 and 2001, while the rest of the conurbation lost 112,000 (64 per cent). Glasgow City gained approximately 49,000 service jobs (21 per cent) between 1971 and 2001, while the rest of the conurbation gained 97,000 (69 per cent). As a result, there was a net shift or decentralisation of employment from the city core to the surrounding area. Glasgow City accounted for 52 per cent of the region's total employment in 1971 and this had fallen slightly to 50 per cent by 2001.

The rate of decentralisation was greatest in the 1950s and 1960s, when employment was declining in the core but growing in the outer ring (Lever and Mather, 1986). Figure 4.2 shows the year-on-year changes in total employment for the core and outer ring compared with Scotland as a whole between 1971 and 2001. It shows that Greater Glasgow has performed consistently worse than Scotland over the last three decades – either declining at a faster rate or growing at a slower rate. There has never been a period when the combined performance of the city core and outer area has been better than Scotland, until the last few years. There have been short spells when the city core *or* outer area performed slightly better than Scotland (such as in the mid 1980s and late 1980s), but they were always outweighed by the worse performance of the rest of the conurbation. Considering these sectoral and spatial trends together, the central message is that decentralisation was the dominant economic feature of the 1950s and 1960s, whereas de-industrialisation became dominant during the 1970s, 1980s and early 1990s.

The situation has been more positive for the conurbation since the mid 1990s. The conurbation as a whole has performed better than Scotland for the last five years. This implies that Glasgow has experienced a turnaround. Incidentally, Figure 4.2 also shows that Glasgow City's weakest relative performance was during the late 1980s and early 1990s. This was several years after the *Glasgow's Miles Better* campaign and it coincided with many media and academic commentators writing enthusiastically about the city's putative transformation. For instance, Steinle stated at the time that: 'Glasgow (City), which was an economic wasteland fifteen years ago, has turned into a minor San Francisco' (1992, p.316).

The Scottish Office also stated at the time that: 'It is generally agreed that Glasgow is undergoing a transformation' (1988, p.8). In reality, Glasgow City was performing considerably worse than the rest of Scotland. Between 1981 and 1991 it was also one of the three worst performing cities in Britain in employment terms, along with Liverpool and Manchester (Turok and Edge, 1999). Impressionistic assessments of city trajectories can clearly be far off the mark.

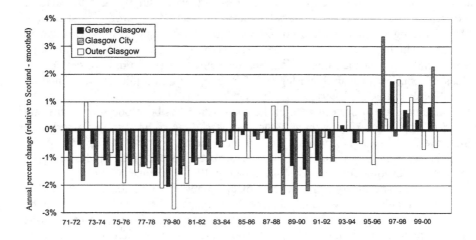

Source: Census of Employment/Annual Employment Survey/Annual Business Inquiry - via NOMIS.

Figure 4.2   Employment change in Glasgow (FTEs)

4.4   Recent Employment Shifts

It is important to consider the most recent period of improvement in more detail, in order to assess the scale and nature of the opportunities created and the extent to which they have benefited people in the core and outer conurbation. Between 1991-93 and 1999-2001 total employment (FTEs) in the city core increased by 38,000 (14 per cent), compared with 34,000 (a 12 per cent increase) in the outer area.[3] This is a major improvement for the city core compared with earlier periods and a significant reversal of the long term trend towards decentralisation. It took the total level of employment in the conurbation back to the level of 1981. The turn around has provided much needed succour and reassurance to the local authority and other city agencies about the underlying economic potential of Glasgow. It comes after a long period of continuous decline during which the government and

---

[3] Averages for successive years are used to reduce variations due to sampling errors in the employment data.

its agencies have tended to neglect the economic needs of the core in favour of development outwith the city, through programmes such as the New Towns, Enterprise Zones and high amenity business parks and industrial sites in peripheral greenfield locations (Pacione, 1995; Robertson, 1998; Levitt, 1999; Webster, 2000b).

The composition of employment change is important because of its influence on the suitability of the jobs for the people most likely to be unemployed, i.e. those with predominantly manual skills and few formal qualifications. Although total employment is back to the level of the early 1980s, the character of the jobs available has changed greatly. The sectors that are by far the most important for less qualified, blue collar job opportunities are manufacturing, transport, distribution and construction (Turok and Edge, 1999). They accounted for just over half (52 per cent) of total employment in Greater Glasgow in 1993. However, there was no growth in these sectors combined in the city core between 1991-93 and 1999-2001, compared with an increase of 17,000 FTEs (10 per cent) in the outer area. This differential expansion is important because travel-to-work data shows that there is little commuting of manual workers from the city core to the outer area (Webster, 1999). Consequently, most of the new jobs in the manual oriented sectors would not have been accessible to Glasgow City residents.

Manufacturing is most important for skilled and semi-skilled manual jobs, but it declined in both areas, and by more than twice as much in the city core as in the outer area. Construction declined a little in the city core but grew elsewhere. Transport and communications expanded a little in both areas, but faster in the outer area. The distribution, hotel and catering sector is most important for unskilled manual jobs. It expanded by about a fifth in the city core and a quarter in the outer conurbation. This uneven pattern of growth in distribution, hotels, etc. runs counter to what one might have expected considering the city centre's reputation as a growing regional service centre during the 1990s and the difficulties known to be facing surrounding town centres such as Paisley, Motherwell and Coatbridge. It cautions against exaggerated claims about the city centre's retail, leisure and tourism functions compared with the surrounding area.

While the city core performed worse than the outer area in the kinds of jobs needed by most non employed residents, it performed much better in the kinds of jobs more likely to be filled by commuters from the surrounding suburbs and towns. The bulk of jobs in business and financial services and in public services are white collar. Employment in business and financial services increased by 24,000 FTEs (45 per cent) in the city core between 1991-93 and 1999-2001, compared with only 5,000 FTEs (17 per cent) in the outer area. Jobs in public services increased by 14 per cent and 12 per cent respectively.

The net result was that the employment profile of Glasgow City shifted in a way that was less favourable to the kinds of people most prone to unemployment than did the economy of the outer conurbation. Figure 4.3 compares the scale of change in the manual oriented sectors of manufacturing, transport, distribution and construction jobs (FTEs) in the city core and outer ring with the change in primarily white collar sectors of business and financial services, public services and other services. The contrast between the pattern of change in the two areas is striking and the reasons for it warrant further research, particularly if this is becoming the prevailing trend. There may be scope for policies to redress the imbalance and promote more manual jobs within the conurbation core, bearing in mind the substantial under-utilised resources of land, labour and infrastructure and the scope for strategic industrial sites to be established. Contrary to the impression sometimes conveyed in the media, Scotland has attracted a sizeable number of manufacturing jobs (29,500) through inward investment since the mid 1990s, less than 3 per cent of which have come to Glasgow City (Scottish Parliament Written Answer, 12 July 2000).

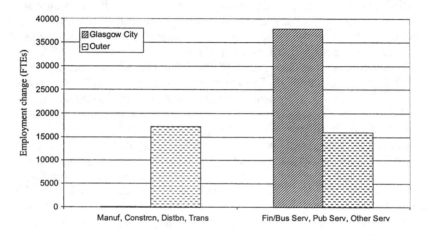

Source: ABI and predecessors, via NOMIS.

Figure 4.3   Employment change, 1991-1993 to 1999-2001

Further confirmation of Glasgow's occupational shift is available from the New Earnings Survey (NES). This provides a more direct estimate of the difference in performance between manual and non manual jobs, based on a 1 per cent sample of PAYE records. The NES suggests that between 1996 and 2000, manual full time jobs in Glasgow city core declined by 12,000 (22 per cent), compared with a decline of 16 per cent in Britain as a whole. In contrast, full time *non manual* jobs increased by 7 per cent in the city core. This is consistent with the recent pattern of Glasgow's sectoral change described above. The NES also shows that by the year 2000 only a quarter (25.7 per cent) of the full time jobs left in the city core were manual. This is substantially less than the proportion of manual jobs in Britain as a whole (32.4 per cent). Decades of industrial decline have left Glasgow City with a disproportionately small amount of manual employment – a striking reversal in what was one of Britain's pre-eminent industrial cities not so long ago. As we shall see, this has had serious implications for the welfare of working class communities and created a more polarised society.

4.5   The Consequences for Unemployment and Economic Inactivity

The effects of these shifts in the scale and character of labour demand on the local workforce are crucial. From the 1991 Census it is known that the decline and restructuring of employment during the previous decade had important consequences for the labour force. These can be usefully unpacked using the framework of 'labour market accounts' (Bailey et al, 1999; Turok and Edge, 1999). First, job loss encouraged substantial out-migration from the city in response to better opportunities elsewhere. Second, it reduced the economic activity rate by almost 10 per cent of the workforce. These were people who apparently stopped actively seeking work by retiring prematurely and/or registering on so-called 'inactive benefits' because of the poor job prospects. Third, there was only a small increase in net out-commuting, indicating the difficulties residents of the core city face in accessing jobs in satellite employment centres. Fourth, there was a modest increase in people on government training schemes. These effects meant that recorded unemployment in Glasgow City actually fell slightly between 1981 and 1991, despite the big loss of jobs. Compared with other cities in Britain, there was a much bigger fall in economic participation and greater out-migration, although some of the latter was movement to the surrounding suburbs and towns for housing rather than economic reasons.

It will not be possible to quantify trends during the 1990s in the same way until the full results of the 2001 Census are published. Instead, the picture needs to be assembled from separate sources, which makes things slightly more complicated. One of the key questions concerns the extent to which local unemployment and inactivity have fallen during this period of employment turn around and growth. Was the rise in economic inactivity during the 1980s a one way process of permanent detachment from the labour market, or was it reversible in more favourable contemporary economic conditions? Alternatively, have local residents who lost their jobs in the 1980s lost out to better qualified people commuting in from elsewhere, or to other sources of labour supply, such as women returning to work after childcare or students engaging in part time work?

Figure 4.4 shows the trend in unemployment drawn from the Labour Force Survey (LFS) (the government's preferred measure) over the last eight years. The LFS is drawn from a small sample of the population, and therefore subject to sampling errors. Use of a four quarter moving average helps to smooth these and remove seasonal fluctuations (see technical appendix for further details). Figure 4.4 shows that the rate of unemployment in Glasgow City has been consistently above that in the outer ring and Scotland as a whole. In fact Glasgow has had one of the highest unemployment rates of any area in Scotland. Over the period 1994 to 2002 there appears to have been a reduction of about four percentage points in the rate of unemployment, which broadly matches the decline elsewhere. This is a definite improvement in absolute terms and compared with earlier trends, although it is not clear whether Glasgow's position has improved relative to Scotland from this data.

During the 1990s the rate of economic inactivity (non participation in the labour market) in Glasgow City stopped rising. Indeed the inactivity rate fell slightly from 33 per cent of the working age population in 1994 to about 30 per cent in 2002. Sizeable data fluctuations from quarter to quarter make it difficult to be confident about the scale of this decline. Meanwhile, the inactivity rate for Scotland as a whole also fell slightly from 22 per cent to 21 per cent over the same period. Consequently, there is tentative evidence that Glasgow's position has improved relative to Scotland, although from a much worse initial situation. The modest reduction in the city's inactivity rate is also something of a contrast with the relatively strong local employment growth over this period. It suggests there may be barriers on the demand and/or supply side to people's re-engagement in the labour market, as discussed below. Growth in Glasgow's population of students in higher education may also be a factor.

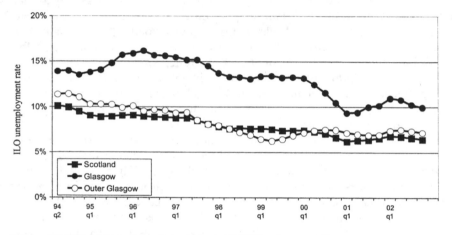

Source: QLFS LADB (re-based) for UA via NOMIS - 4 qrtr moving average.

Figure 4.4   Unemployment rates for Glasgow, core and outer ring

The immediate reason for the reduction in LFS unemployment in Glasgow City between 1994 and 2002 was the rise in the employment rate (the proportion of the working age population with a job), as shown in Figure 4.5. During the mid 1990s the City's employment rate was extremely low (55-57 per cent) compared with the rate for Scotland as a whole (70-71 per cent). By 2002 it appears to have risen to 60-63 per cent compared with the rate for Scotland of 73-74 per cent.[4] This implies that Glasgow City experienced an absolute improvement and slight narrowing of the gap with Scotland. This is an important change from the 1980s and certainly a step in the right direction. Nevertheless, the local employment rate is still very low by national standards and the jobs deficit is over 40,000. This is the number of additional residents who still need to get jobs in order to match the Scottish

---

[4] Once again, fluctuations due to sampling errors make precise statements difficult.

employment rate. It requires an increase of one fifth on the current level of employed residents.

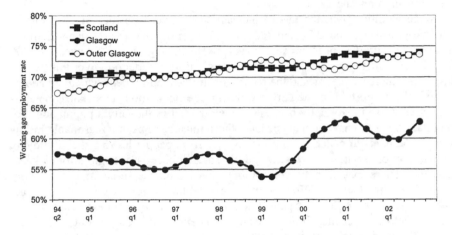

Source: QLFS LADB (re-based) for UA via NOMIS - 4 qrtr moving average.

Figure 4.5   Employment rates for Glasgow, core and outer ring

4.6   Long-term Sickness and Disability

A large section of Glasgow's population has failed to benefit from the employment turn around, particularly those claiming incapacity or invalidity benefits. Glasgow City has a remarkably high proportion of its resident population on these sickness related benefits. Almost one in five (19.4 per cent or 71,200) of the population of working age in the city is on sickness or disability benefits (the latest date for available information is February 2003). This is more than four times as many people as on the Jobseeker's Allowance – the registered unemployment benefit. It is also by far the largest absolute number and the fifth highest percentage of all the 406 local authority districts in Britain (where the figure is 8.7 per cent overall). It is exceeded only by four small former mining districts in South Wales and North East England. Glasgow City's percentage is nearly double the proportion for the rest of Scotland (10.3 per cent) and much higher than the figure for the local authority areas covering the outer ring of Greater Glasgow (12 per cent). In several wards of the City at least one in three people of working age are on sickness benefits.

The number of people claiming these benefits in Glasgow rose roughly fourfold during the 1980s and early 1990s as workers were made redundant, accessible job opportunities declined and people got discouraged from trying to find work. The effective value of sickness benefit payments was also slightly higher than unemployment benefits for certain groups (such as people with savings, pensions or partners in work) because these benefits are not means tested. Welfare advisors and government agencies tended to encourage people to register for sickness rather than unemployment benefits if they had a legitimate ailment because they would be slightly better off and their prospects of getting a job were slim in the prevailing economic circumstances.

Since the mid 1990s the rate of increase has slowed considerably and for the last five years (between 1998 and 2003) the number of Glasgow residents claiming sickness benefits has been broadly constant, fluctuating slightly between 71,200 and 72,200. Most important, it has shown no significant reduction over this period, despite the increase in jobs and the recent rise in the employment rate noted above. Indeed, the proportion of the City's working age population on sickness benefits has actually risen marginally because of a slight fall in the City's population. For the total number to have remained static, there must have been a reasonable inflow of new claimants to match the outflow arising from people leaving the city, dying prematurely or reaching retirement age (when they become ineligible for sickness benefits). There may also be some turnover with people re-entering the labour force. Unfortunately no information is available on the scale, age or other characteristics of the flows of people coming on to and off sickness benefits. This is an urgent issue needing further research. It is known that only about 42 per cent of people leaving the unemployment register in Glasgow go into employment (SLIMS, 2001), but not what proportion goes onto sickness benefits, nor anything about flows in the opposite direction.

The persistent level of sickness claimants indicates a clear limit in the extent to which improved economic opportunities have filtered through to one on the poorest groups in the population, perhaps reflecting their limited capability, skills, confidence and/or motivation to access jobs. Helping more people within this group who want to work and simply to become more active is an outstanding policy challenge.

There is a growing debate nationally about the extent to which people on sickness benefits are ill and unable to work, or more accurately regarded as hidden unemployed who would be in work in a more fully employed economy (Alcock et al, 2003). The number of sickness claimants in Britain rose sharply during the 1980s and 1990s from just over 0.5 million to just over 2.0 million. The fact this occurred when the general standard of health of the population was improving suggests that the main explanation for this growth must have been job loss and rising worklessness. This is supported by the fact that the areas with the biggest increases in economic inactivity and sickness (such as Liverpool, Glasgow and Manchester) were those with the biggest reductions in employment (Turok and Edge, 1999). However, the experience of prolonged or recurrent spells without work and on low income is bound also to have caused psychological and physical damage to some people, therefore their health is likely to have deteriorated over time and their capacity to work must have been affected (Shaw et al, 1999). In the 2001 Census, 26 per cent of Glasgow's population indicated that they had a long term illness or disability limiting their daily activities or work, compared with 19 per cent in 1991 (Registrar General for Scotland, 2003).

Disentangling the two phenomena of disguised unemployment and ill health is complicated because of their interaction. A recent survey of 800 men on incapacity benefit found that half said they would like a full time job, although fewer than one in ten were still looking for a job. Only a quarter said they could not do any work at all, although nearly all said their health limited the kind of work they could do (Alcock et al, 2003). This accords with the findings of a local study in the west of Scotland (McCormick, 2000). Nationally, just under half of people of working age with a disability (3.2m people) already work, and another 1.4m people with disabilities who are without a job say they would like to work (HM Treasury, 2001b). From this kind of evidence of blurred boundaries between hidden unemployment and ill health, it has been estimated that for as many as half of the people on sickness benefits, the principal obstacle may be the lack of appropriate employment opportunities rather than their inability or unwillingness to work (Alcock et al, 2003).

Using these and other survey based and statistical benchmarks, it has also been estimated that the real rate of unemployment in Britain was 9.5 per cent in 2002, compared with the claimant count rate of 3.5 per cent (Beatty et al, 2002). The real rate of unemployment in Glasgow was estimated at 22.7 per cent compared with the claimant rate of 6.9 per cent. The real rate was the fifth highest of all local authorities in the country. To get many of the people on inactive benefits back to work is likely to require an expansion of suitable jobs in the city as well as specific support to help address barriers such as limited information about jobs, training opportunities or in-work benefits, lack of recent work experience, loss of confidence, depression or dependence on alcohol or drugs. A useful start could be made with more active and imaginative use of the 'therapeutic earnings' allowance in Incapacity Benefit to ease the transition into work, as well as more flexibility in the benefits system to enable people to try out employment without putting all their benefits at risk (McCormick, 2000; Arnott, 2001). There is also an established network of highly regarded local employment and training organisations across the poorest areas of the city that is well placed to deliver user friendly, personalised support to this hitherto neglected group (Turok, 2000; OECD, 2002).

4.7 Population Trends

Demographic trends are another key indicator of city performance. A falling population diminishes the use of buildings, infrastructure and public services, the stock of local skills and knowledge, and the availability of public funds in the form of local taxes and government transfers to reverse a general trajectory of decline, since these are largely population driven. The population of a city may decline through net outward movement (out-migration exceeding in-migration) and/or natural change (deaths exceeding births). Out-migration from a core city authority may reflect declining economic opportunities or peoples' preferences to live in surrounding areas on the basis of housing and neighbourhood conditions. Population change also has an immediate effect back on employment because it influences local expenditure on shops, consumer services, leisure facilities and of course a wide range of public services. Consequently, there tends to be a close relationship between the changes in employment and population across cities and regions (Webster, 2000b).

Greater Glasgow's population has been declining since the 1960s, along with all of Britain's northern industrial conurbations. The rate of decline was by far the steepest during the 1970s and 1980s, when the conurbation lost a sixth of its population through net out-migration, at an average rate of 15,000 people a year (Bailey et al, 1999). This corresponded to the period of most severe job loss, affecting the conurbation core and outer area. Most people who left the region moved to the South of England, rather than to other parts of Scotland (Webster, 2000b). During the 1980s Greater Glasgow's population declined faster than any other conurbation in Britain and three times faster than the average rate of decline for those outside London (Champion, 1999). During the 1990s, the average rate of overall decline slowed considerably to 3600 a year (Bailey et al, 1999). This was a significant slowdown bearing in mind the momentum of decline. It coincided with the reversal in Glasgow's economic fortunes and growing obstacles to people moving to the South of England, including rising house prices.

Overlaid on the process of net migration from the conurbation has been a process of suburbanisation within it. Decentralisation of population from the city core to the outer area has been a feature of Glasgow since the 1930s, but it was most pronounced during the 1960s and 1970s. It was influenced by a combination of housing factors (such as the availability of low rise private houses with gardens), neighbourhood factors (such as the perception of better schools and environmental quality), employment reasons (decentralisation of jobs) and public policy (sponsored migration to 'overspill' areas). Many families who could afford to do so chose to move to owner occupied neighbourhoods within surrounding districts, such as Bishopbriggs, Bearsden and Eastwood, partly because Glasgow Council discouraged private housing development within its area until the mid 1980s. Government policy also had a crucial effect in determining priority areas for social housing development and for land release and infrastructure investment for private residential development. Government policy between the 1950s and 1980s was to promote the 'decongestion' of Glasgow's population and industry by clearing old, overcrowded residential and industrial areas, and supporting the growth of new housing and jobs in outlying areas, particularly the New Towns (Gibb, 1983; Pacione, 1995). Papers released under the 30 year rule reinforce the point that during the 1960s and 1970s central government expected and indeed planned for very severe contraction of employment and population in Glasgow City (Robertson, 1998; Levitt, 1997, 1999 and 2001). McCrone (1991) notes that Glasgow was one of the first cities in the world where population decline was a deliberate policy. Efforts to attract alternative employment through inward investment in growth sectors were targeted on the New Towns through large scale public investment and financial incentives to business.

Not surprisingly, Glasgow City's share of the total conurbation population fell sharply from 62 per cent in 1951 to 42 per cent in 1991. The highest rate of decentralisation coincided with the period of greatest job decentralisation, i.e. the 1960s and 1970s (Bailey et al, 1999). Since the 1980s population decline through outward movement from the city core has slowed considerably. The slowdown has been experienced both in suburbanisation and out-migration from the conurbation as a whole. Nevertheless, Table 4.1 shows that Glasgow City was still experiencing the highest rate of population decline of all the British conurbation cores in the first half of the 1990s (2.1 per cent or 3300 people a year on average), along with Liverpool. The continuing fall in population during this period once again contradicted the popular narrative of revitalisation and reversal.

Subsequently, the rate of decline fell by almost half during the second half of the 1990s, when the city was losing only 1800 people a year on average (1.5 per cent). The rate of improvement from 1991-95 to 1995-2000 was better than in most conurbations apart from London and Manchester. However, one should not read too much into this comparison since part of the improvement was due to a one-off adjustment to Glasgow's population figure in 1997-98 and it still has one of the fastest rates of decline in absolute terms (second only to Liverpool). Apart from this, the timing of the improvement and its coincidence with the change in economic circumstances suggests some connection between them. The fact that Glasgow's population was still declining should not be overlooked. It is clearly premature to refer to Glasgow having experienced a turn around in demographic terms. Continuing population loss remains a problem affecting large parts of the city beyond the Centre and West End (Glasgow City Council, 2002).

Table 4.1   Population change in British conurbation cores, 1991-2000

Local authority	*Population 1991 (000s)*	*Population change 1991-95* (%)*	*Population change 1995-2000 (%)*	*Shift 1991-95 to 1995-2000 (%)*
Greater London	6889.9	1.7	5.3	+3.5
Manchester	438.5	-0.6	1.6	+2.2
Glasgow	631.7	-2.1	-1.5	+0.6
Sheffield	529.3	-0.1	0.3	+0.4
Liverpool	480.7	-2.1	-2.9	-0.8
Birmingham	1006.5	0.2	-0.7	-0.9
Leeds	717.4	1.1	0.2	-0.9

Note: * Population change has been adjusted to exclude the effect of boundary changes. Some core conurbation authorities are more tightly bounded than others, which limits their strict comparability.

Source: Mid-year estimates published the ONS and GRO Scotland.

Bearing in mind that population change is the product of net migration and natural change, a better understanding of recent developments is obtained by considering these elements separately. They convey slightly different messages about Glasgow in the 1990s. Figure 4.6 shows the trends in net migration and Figure 4.7 the pattern of natural change. Looking at Figure 4.6, Leeds was the only city to experience net in-migration between 1991 and 1995. This was probably linked to its relatively strong employment performance (Turok and Edge, 1999). All the other conurbation cores lost population through net out-migration. The highest rate of loss was Liverpool, followed fairly closely by Manchester, Birmingham and Glasgow. These were by far the poorest performing city cores during the early 1990s in terms of net migration. They had been the worst performers during the 1980s (Champion, 1999), and they were also the poorest performers in terms of jobs, as noted earlier.

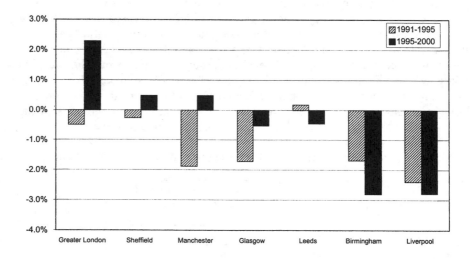

Figure 4.6   Net migration, 1991-1995 and 1995-2000

Figure 4.6 suggests that the situation had turned around in Greater London, Manchester and Sheffield by the second half of the 1990s. After several decades during which they lost population through net out-migration, these three cities were actually gaining people through net in-migration. In London's case this was solely attributable to immigration from abroad. Glasgow City was still losing population through net out-migration, although the trend was moving in the right direction and Glasgow's rate of improvement was the third highest among the conurbations. This may be related to the employment turn around slowing out-migration and increasing in-migration, as well as the winding up of dispersal policies. Improved residential opportunities may have played a part too since there was an increase in private house building in the city, particularly flats aimed at smaller households. Population retention has become a strategic priority of the City Council in recent years because of its impact on the budget and public services. For example, efforts have been made to identify parcels of land within its boundaries to accommodate private housing development, particularly for middle income families (Glasgow City Council, 2001b), and to relax planning constraints on private house building.

The pattern of natural change in Glasgow was negative and moving in the wrong direction. Figure 4.7 shows that Glasgow was the only conurbation core to experience a decline in this demographic component during the first half of the 1990s, i.e. more deaths than births. Moreover, the disparity with most of the other areas was quite marked. The excess of deaths over births increased further by the second half of the 1990s, and at a faster rate than in the other cities. The pattern in most cities contrasted with the trend of births exceeding deaths in other parts of Britain. The situation in Glasgow was apparently deteriorating, and in the second half of the 1990s natural change accounted for almost two thirds of Glasgow's population loss.

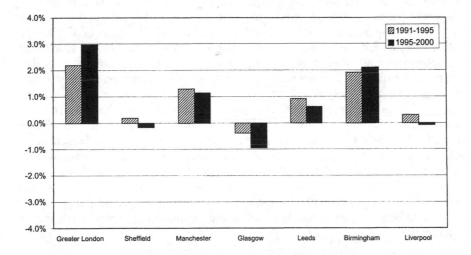

Figure 4.7   Natural change, 1991-1995 and 1995-2000

Both components of natural change (fertility and mortality) reflect socio-economic conditions as well as the age and sex structure of the local population. Glasgow has had a declining rate of natural growth since the 1970s (Webster, 2000b). The problem seems to stem from a steady fall in the birth rate without an equivalent compensating fall in the death rate (Freeke, 2001). Greater Glasgow's fertility has fallen much more than the rest of Britain and its mortality has been rising relative to Britain. The main reason for Glasgow's high mortality appears to be the level of poverty and worklessness. Shaw et al (1999) show that Glasgow has all six of the worst constituencies in Britain for premature death (people dying under the age of 65). They also show that unemployment and low income have strong effects on ill health and mortality. The link between deprivation and deaths from suicide, coronary heart disease, stroke and some cancers has been confirmed by McLaren and Bain (1998). They also show that 51 per cent of the population in the Greater Glasgow Health Board area was in the most deprived socio-economic categories in 1991, compared with only 18 per cent of Scotland's population. Research for the Scottish Executive has also shown consistently that the scale and intensity of poverty and deprivation in Glasgow are exceptional within Scotland (Duguid, 1995; Kearns et al, 2000). The most comprehensive and most recent study found that more than half (56 per cent) of Glasgow City's wards are in the most deprived 10 per cent of wards in Scotland (Social Disadvantage Research Centre, 2003). Using one indicator of low income from that study, 29 per cent of Glasgow's population were estimated to be poor compared with 16 per cent of Scotland's population as a whole.

The trends in natural change also diverge sharply across Glasgow, revealing growing social polarisation and residential segregation. The most deprived areas of the city have seen fertility falling fastest during the 1990s and no reduction in mortality (Freeke, 2001). The better off areas have seen least decline in fertility and most decline in mortality, in line with national trends. The connection between falling fertility and the poorest neighbourhoods indicates the likely influence of unemployment and poverty on fertility, through family breakdown, ill health, substance misuse and homelessness, although these relationships require further research since there may also be a positive aspect in the reduction of teenage pregnancies and lone parenthood. Poverty and unemployment factors also seem to have prevented any decline in mortality in deprived areas. In the Shettleston area of Glasgow's East End, average male life expectancy is 64, which is 13 years lower than the UK average. Although spatial trends *within* Glasgow City have not been addressed in detail in this paper, the stark contrasts between the relatively dynamic city centre and the run down areas of the inner core, and between the middle class suburbs and the working class estates on the periphery, clearly reinforce the point about the uneven and segmented character of Glasgow's turn around.

4.8   Conclusion

Greater Glasgow lost 197,000 full time manufacturing jobs between 1971 and 2001 and gained 145,000 full time equivalents in services. The overall situation has improved within the last decade, with half of the gains coming during this period. This is a significant change, particularly for the core city. It has taken total employment in the conurbation back to the level of 1981. However, the nature of the opportunities available has shifted radically, with most growth in white collar industries and occupations and negligible growth in opportunities that are accessible to blue collar workers. Only a quarter of the full time jobs left in the core city are manual, compared with a third in Britain as a whole. Working class residents of the core city have lost out from this shift in the composition of Glasgow's economy, while better qualified suburban commuters have prospered.

Consequently, the employment rate of Glasgow City residents is between 60-63 per cent, which is very low by national standards. To raise it to the Scottish rate would require over 40,000 additional local residents to get jobs. Most of the people who are workless in the City have moved onto 'inactive' benefits and are not registered as unemployed. Almost one in five of the City's working age population is on sickness or disability benefits. There is some debate about the real rate of unemployment in the City. One estimate puts it at 22.7 per cent, which is one of the highest in the UK. Getting a higher proportion of these people back to work will require further increases in labour demand, especially in industries and occupations that are accessible and suitable for them. It cannot be achieved through supply side measures focused on employability and skills alone. Greater flexibility in the benefits system also seems important.

The high level of unemployment and economic inactivity in Glasgow is reflected in demographic trends. The very high rate of population decline through net out-migration during the 1970s and 1980s slowed considerably during the 1990s as the economic situation improved. Nevertheless, the city is still losing population at a higher rate than most major UK cities. One of the City's most striking demographic features is its high rate of mortality. Glasgow has all six of the worst constituencies in Britain for premature death. This is linked to the high levels of worklessness and poverty.

The significant change in Glasgow's economic position within the last decade has not benefited the whole community. The city centre has been revitalised through substantial public and private investment, expansion of financial, business and public services, and increased consumer spending. However, many poorer parts of the city remain depressed and distressed. The imbalanced nature of Glasgow's turn around means that considerable human and physical problems persist. They undermine the image of transformation and could threaten investor and visitor confidence. They also constitute a profound challenge to the commitments of the UK government and Scottish Executive to deliver full employment and social justice for all. The major policy challenge is to broaden the composition and location of employment opportunities towards people and places that have hitherto been neglected. This will require sustained investment in derelict land improvement, new physical infrastructure and a supportive strategic policy framework at city-region and Scottish levels (Turok and Bailey, 2004).

Acknowledgements

The research on which this chapter is based was part of the Central Scotland Integrative Case Study under the ESRC Cities Programme (award number L130251040) with additional support from the Scottish Executive, Scottish Enterprise and Communities Scotland. Additional thanks are due to John Parr and David Webster for comments on an earlier draft and to Tony Champion for his assistance with Table 4.1. The usual disclaimers apply.

References

Alcock, P., Beatty, C., Fothergill, S., Macmillan, R. and Yeandle, S. (2003) *Work to Welfare: How Men Become Detached from the Labour Market*, Cambridge, Cambridge University Press.

Arlidge, J. (1996) 'Glasgow's fix of culture and couture', *The Observer*, 19 May, London, Observer Newspapers.

Arnott, J. (2001) 'The use of benefits data in estimating worklessness and unemployment', *Local Economy*, 16(4), pp.328-332.

Bailey, N. and French, S. (2004) 'Cities and financial services' in Buck, N. et al (eds.) *Changing Cities*, Palgrave (forthcoming).

Bailey, N., Turok, I. and Docherty, I. (1999) *Edinburgh and Glasgow: Contrasts in Competitiveness and Cohesion*, Glasgow, University of Glasgow.

Bailey, N., Docherty, I. and Turok, I. (2002) 'Dimensions of city competitiveness: Edinburgh and Glasgow in a UK context' in Begg, I. (ed.) *City Competitiveness*, Bristol, Policy Press.

Beatty, C., Fothergill, S., Gore, T. and Green, A. (2002) *The Real Level of Unemployment 2002*, Sheffield, Sheffield Hallam University.

Booth, P. and Boyle, R. (1993) 'See Glasgow, see culture' in Bianchini, F. and Parkinson, M. (eds) *Cultural Policy and Urban Regeneration: The West European Experience*, Manchester, Manchester University Press.

Business Strategies (2001) *Glasgow Economic Audit*, London, BSL.

Champion, T. (1999) 'Migration and British cities in the 1990s', *National Institute Economic Review*, 170, pp.60-77.

Danson, M. and Mooney, G. (1998) 'Glasgow: a tale of two cities?' in Lawless, P. et al, (eds) *Unemployment and Social Exclusion*, London, Jessica Kingsley.

Docherty, I., Bailey, N. and Turok, I. (2001) *Central Scotland Business Survey: Preliminary Report*, Glasgow, Department of Urban Studies, University of Glasgow.

Donnison, D. and Middleton, A. (1987) *Regenerating the Inner City: Glasgow's Experience*, London, Routledge.

Duguid, G. (1995) *Deprived Areas in Scotland*, Edinburgh, Central Research Unit, The Scottish Office.

Economist (1998) *Glasgow: Refitting on the Clyde*, 22 August, London, Economist Publications.

Fitzpatrick, S. (2000) *Social Inclusion Inquiry: Discussion Paper*, Glasgow, Glasgow Alliance.

Freeke, J. (2001) *Demographic Change in Glasgow City in the 1990s*, paper presented at the British Society for Population Studies Annual Conference, Leeds.

General Register Office for Scotland (GROS) (2002) *Comparisons with Previous Estimates and Implications for Revisions.* Edinburgh, GROS.

General Register Office for Scotland (GROS) (2003) *The Registrar General's 2001 Census Report to the Scottish Parliament.* Edinburgh, GROS.

Gibb, A. (1983) *Glasgow: The Making of a City*, Beckenham, Croom Helm.

Glasgow City Council (1998) *Glasgow Strategic Plan for Housing*, Glasgow, GCC.

Glasgow City Council (2001a) *Glasgow Economic Monitor: Spring 2001*, Glasgow, GCC.

Glasgow City Council (2001b) *Glasgow City Plan*, Glasgow, GCC.

Glasgow City Council (2002) *Current Estimates of Area Forum Populations and Expected Changes 2000-2010*, Report to Policy and Resources (Regeneration Strategy) Sub-Committee, Glasgow, GCC.

Glasgow Development Agency (1999) *Upbeat Glasgow*, Glasgow, GDA.

HM Treasury (2001a) *Productivity in the UK: 3 – The Regional Dimension*, London.

HM Treasury (2001b) *The Changing Welfare State: Employment Opportunity for All*, London.

Howard, R. (2001) 'Glasgow', *High Life*, British Airways, May 2001, pp.57-62.

Kearns, A., Gibb, K. and Mackay, D. (2000) 'Area deprivation in Scotland: a new assessment', *Urban Studies*, 37(9), pp.1535-1559.

Keating, M. (1998) *The City That Refused To Die*, Aberdeen, Aberdeen University Press.

Landry, C. (2000) *The Creative City*, London, Earthscan Publications.

Leadbeater, C. and Oakley, K. (1999) *The Independents: Britain's New Cultural Entrepreneurs*, London, Demos.

Lever, W. (1997) 'Glasgow: the post-industrial city' in Jensen-Butler, C. et al (eds) *European Cities in Competition*, Aldershot, Avebury.

Lever, W. and Mather, F. (1986) 'The changing structure of business and employment in the conurbation' in Lever, W. and Moore, C. (eds) *The City in Transition: Policies and Agencies for the Economic Regeneration of Clydeside*. Oxford, Clarendon Press.

Levitt, I. (1997) 'New towns, new Scotland, new ideology, 1937-57', *The Scottish Historical Review*, 76(2), pp.222-238.

Levitt, I. (1999) 'The Scottish Air Services, 1933-75 and the Scottish New Towns, 1943-75: a guide to the records at the National Archives of Scotland', *Scottish Archives*, 5, pp.67-82.

Levitt, I. (2001) *The National Archives of Scotland: Files for 2001 Press Preview*, mimeo, University of Central Lancashire.

McCarthy, J. and Pollock, A. (1997) 'Urban regeneration in Glasgow and Dundee: a comparative evaluation', *Land Use Policy*, 14(2), pp.137-149.

McCormick, J. (2000) *On the Sick: Incapacity and Inclusion*, Edinburgh, Scottish Council Foundation.

McCrone, G. (1991) 'Urban renewal: the Scottish experience', *Urban Studies*, 28(6), pp.919-938.

McLaren, G. and Bain, M. (1998) *Deprivation and Health in Scotland: Insights from NHS Data*, NHS in Scotland, Information and Statistics Division, Edinburgh.

Maver, I. (2000) *Glasgow*, Edinburgh, Edinburgh University Press.

Murray, C. (1996) 'The emerging British underclass' in Lister, R. (ed) *Charles Murray and the Underclass: The Developing Debate*, London, Institute for Economic Affairs, Health and Welfare Unit.

Office for National Statistics (ONS) (2001) *Local Area and Sub-regional Gross Domestic Product*, London, ONS.

Office for Public Health in Scotland (2001) *Constituency Health Report 2001*, Glasgow, OPHIS.

OECD (2002) *Urban Renaissance: Glasgow, Lessons for Innovation and Implementation*, Paris, OECD.

Pacione, M. (1995) *Glasgow: The Socio-Spatial Development of the City*, Chichester, John Wiley.

Paddison, R. (1993) 'City marketing, image reconstruction and urban regeneration', *Urban Studies*, 30(2), pp.339-350.

Peat, J. and Boyle, S. (1999) *An Illustrated Guide to the Scottish Economy*, London, Duckworth.

Registrar General for Scotland (2003) *Key Statistics for Council Areas and Health Board Areas in Scotland*.

Robertson, D. (1998) 'Pulling in opposite directions: the failure of post-war planning to regenerate Glasgow', *Planning Perspectives*, 13, pp.53-67.

Scotland on Sunday (2002) *No Means City*, 20 January, p.16.

Scottish Business Insider (2001) *Regional Report – Glasgow*, Insider Publications, September, pp.24-42.

Scottish Enterprise Glasgow (2000) *2020 Vision: Metropolitan Glasgow*, Glasgow, Scottish Enterprise Glasgow.

Scottish Executive (2001) *A Smart, Successful Scotland*, Edinburgh, Scottish Executive.

Scottish Executive (2002) *Review of Scotland's Cities: The Analysis*, Edinburgh, Scottish Executive.

Scottish Executive (2003) *Scottish Economic Report*, Edinburgh, Scottish Executive.

Scottish Office (1988) *New Life for Urban Scotland*, Edinburgh, Scottish Office.

Shaw, M., Dorling, D., Gordon, D. and Smith, G.D. (1999) *The Widening Gap: Health Inequalities and Policy in Britain*, Bristol, The Policy Press.

SLIMS (2001) *Glasgow Labour Market Statement*, Hamilton, SLIMS.

Social Disadvantage Research Centre (2003) *The Scottish Indices of Deprivation 2003*, Edinburgh, Scottish Executive.

Steinle, W.J. (1992) 'Regional competitiveness and the Single Market', *Regional Studies*, 26(4), pp.307-318.

Sunday Times (1996) *The Great Escape*, 1 June, p.1.

Turok, I. (1993) 'Contrasts in ownership and development: local versus global in Silicon Glen', *Urban Studies*, 30(2), pp.365-386.

Turok, I. (2000) *Inclusive Cities: Building Local Capacity for Development*, Luxembourg, European Commission.

Turok, I. and Bailey, N. (2004) 'Twin track cities: competitiveness and cohesion in Glasgow and Edinburgh', *Progress in Planning* (forthcoming).

Turok, I. and Edge, N. (1999) *The Jobs Gap in Britain's Cities: Employment Loss and Labour Market Consequences*, Bristol, The Policy Press.

Urry, J. (1990) *The Tourist Gaze*, London, Sage.

Webster, D. (1999) 'Targeted local jobs: the missing element in Labour's social inclusion policy', *New Economy*, 6(4), pp.193-198.

Webster, D. (2000a) 'Scottish social inclusion policy: a critical assessment', *Scottish Affairs*, 30, pp.30-50.

Webster, D. (2000b) 'The political economy of Scotland's population decline', *Fraser of Allander Institute Quarterly Economic Commentary*, 25(2), pp.40-70.

Technical Appendix

Employment data is drawn from the Annual Business Inquiry (ABI) and its predecessors, produced by the Office for National Statistics (ONS) and extracted from NOMIS. Full time equivalent (FTE) figures are used throughout, assuming one full time job is equivalent to two part time jobs. This source covers employees but excludes people who were self employed. In Scotland, between 1992-03 and 2002-03, self employment rose exactly in line with increasing employment so the proportion of people in work who were self employed remained at 9.8 per cent (figures derived from the Labour Force Survey).

Population data is taken from the General Register Office for Scotland's (GROS) mid-year population estimates, extracted from their website. The figures used here are based on the 1991 Census. While the mid-year estimates have been revised by GROS following the Census 2001 (see below), the previous figures are retained in order that they are comparable with other sources, notably LFS data.

GDP data is taken from ONS estimates for local areas (ONS, 2001). The ONS figures are an estimate of the GDP produced by the workforce of the area. To estimate GDP produced by the residents of the area, GDP figures are adjusted for net commuting flows (estimated from LFS data at the individual level). GDP per employee is estimated using the number of FTE jobs based on ABI figures. The 'employment rate' (employees per resident) uses the same FTE jobs figures and the mid-year population figures from GROS.

Labour Force Survey data is produced by ONS and extracted from NOMIS. Data is drawn from the Quarterly Labour Force Survey results for local authority areas, with data for four successive quarters averaged to reduce fluctuations due to small sample sizes and to remove variations due to seasonality. At the time of writing, LFS data had not been adjusted to reflect the changes in population estimates following the Census 2001. The figures used here are therefore consistent with the population and GDP figures used.

Impacts of the Census 2001

For the Census 2001, the ONS and GROS produced an estimate of the population adjusted for non response using the 'one number' methodology (GROS, 2003). This produced significantly different estimates of the population for some locations, compared with previous estimates achieved by 'rolling forward' figures from the 1991 Census by allowing for natural change and estimated migration (GROS, 2002). Scotland's estimated population was revised down by 1.1 per cent. Of the local authorities, Glasgow was by far the biggest 'loser' (revised down by 5.9 per cent), followed by North Lanarkshire and Renfrewshire (both down by 2.1 per cent). Dundee City, Moray and Argyll and Bute were all revised up by over 2 per cent.

ABI employment figures will be unaffected as they are based on a survey of employers. LFS figures are grossed up using estimated population figures. This will be revised in due course but it is difficult to say at the present time what the impact of the changes will be.

Chapter 5

Economic Change and Challenges in the Highlands and Islands

Stuart Black

5.1 Introduction

This chapter reviews recent economic trends in the Highlands and Islands, discusses the main challenges which the area continues to face and focuses on the response of the Highlands and Islands Enterprise (HIE) Network. The past ten years have seen a rapid rate of change in the Highlands and Islands with the establishment of the Enterprise Network in 1991, the European Union Objective 1 programme 1994-99, and the development of new industries in the area, notably in the Information and Communications Technologies (ICT) sector. In spite of overall improvements in the economy there remain problems of economic decline in some of the more remote parts of the region. While unemployment has reduced significantly, the region's GDP per capita tends to still lag behind the Scottish and UK averages and is also subject to significant variation around the region. Therefore while there has been undoubted progress over the past decade there remain major challenges to be overcome.

5.2 Demographic and Economic Trends

Between 1991 and 2001 the population of the Highlands and Islands increased by 0.8 per cent (General Registers Office (Scotland)). This compares to a decrease for Scotland as a whole over the same period and represents a slowdown from the 2.6 per cent growth achieved in the area during the 1980s. Within the region there has been a differential pattern of growth and decline with population losses in the Western Isles (-10.5 per cent), Lochaber (-3 per cent) Argyll and the Islands (-1.2 per cent), Caithness and Sutherland (-3.9 per cent), Shetland (-2.4 per cent) and Orkney (-1.9 per cent). In contrast, there has been growth in the other four local enterprise company areas in the Highlands and Islands. This has been the case in Inverness and Nairn (6.6 per cent), Moray, Badenoch and Strathspey (4.3 per cent), Skye and Lochalsh (3.2 per cent) and Ross and Cromarty (2.2 per cent). As the statistics show, in areas such as the Western Isles and parts of Argyll, and

Caithness the classic 'Highland problems' of out-migration and an ageing population remain.

The 2001 Highlands and Islands population of 433,745 represents about 8.5 per cent of the Scottish population spread over 50 per cent of the landmass. This gives the region a population density of only 11 people per square kilometre, making it one of the most sparsely populated parts of the European Union. The population density compares to 65.5 people per square kilometre for Scotland and 241 people per square kilometre for the United Kingdom. Sparsity of population remains an endemic challenge to economic success as it imposes additional costs on providers of goods and services.

Over the period 1998-2002 the numbers of people in employment grew slightly by around 1 per cent (Table 5.1). Employment in the primary sector, including the self employed, accounts for 9 per cent of all employment in the Highlands and Islands. Since 1998, however, there has been a 2.6 per cent fall in employment in the primary sector. Between 1998 and 2002 there was a 6.5 per cent fall in the numbers employed in manufacturing. This reflects the loss of employment in the oil fabrication industry which has largely disappeared from the inner Moray Firth area. In contrast, however, the biggest manufacturing employer in the Highlands, Inverness Medical (IML) which makes diabetes testing kits now employs 1200 people at its Inverness centre. IML started in 1997 with 30 employees in the city and its expansion has been a key feature of the growth of the Inverness economy over the past decade.

Table 5.1   Employment changes by industry in the Highlands and Islands

Industry (1992 SIC)	1998	2002	% change
Agriculture, fishing and forestry	5550	5400	-2.5
Energy and water	4050	3200	-21.0
Manufacturing	20400	19100	-6.5
Construction	12600	10300	-18.3
Distribution, hotels and Restaurants	48000	45500	-5.2
Transport and communications	9900	9350	-5.5
Banking, finance and insurance	12750	17350	36.0
Public administration, education and health	47650	52950	11.1
Other services	8650	7650	-11.6
TOTAL	169600	170800	0.7

Note: the figures are for employees only and exclude the self employed.

Source: ONS (NOMIS).

Within the service sector there has been a decline in retail and tourism employment of 5 per cent. This reflects several difficult years in the tourism industry in particular, including the impact of foot and mouth disease which caused a significant drop in tourism, notably from the US. There has been significant increase in employment in banking, finance and insurance of 36 per cent. This may reflect changes in definition but also the growth of the contact centre industry in the area, notably in the inner Moray Firth but also in Argyll at Dunoon and Bute.

The public sector is an important component of economic activity in the Highlands and Islands accounting for 31 per cent of employment, slightly above the national average. In the Islands, however, the public sector is more important, reaching as high as 37 per cent of employees in the Western Isles. Employee numbers in this sector have increased by 11 per cent since 1998, primarily due to increases in investment in the National Health Service and growth in local government.

5.3   Unemployment

Table 5.2 illustrates the trend in claimant count unemployment since January 2001 in the Highlands and Islands (HIE estimates), Scotland and Great Britain. Unemployment trends in the Highlands and Islands reflect the seasonal nature of the economy with unemployment peaking in January and reaching low points in July. This reflects the importance of tourism and also seasonal work in the primary sector and construction. This is most starkly illustrated in travel-to-work-areas such as Skye and Ullapool and Sutherland where the July rate can be half that in January.

Over the past three years the claimant unemployment rate has fallen from 4.5 per cent in the Highlands and Islands to the January 2004 rate of 3.2 per cent. As the unemployment rate has fallen the size of the seasonal peaks has also declined such that the differential in January unemployment rates compared to Scotland has narrowed significantly.

The incidence of unemployment, however, varies significantly around the Highlands and Islands. In some of the travel-to-work-areas such as Shetland, Dufftown and Orkney, the rates are well below the regional and national average. In contrast in Sutherland, Lewis and Harris, and Campbeltown, they are well above average. The incidence of long term unemployment also shows similar variation around the area. Long term unemployment in February 2004 stands at 24 per cent of the unemployed in the Highlands and Islands compared to 28 per cent for Scotland and 31 per cent for GB. In addition long term unemployment in the Highlands and Islands fell by 5 per cent over the previous 12 months, compared to an increase of 1 per cent in Scotland, and a fall of 2.1 per cent in GB.

Table 5.2   Unemployment in the Highlands and Islands, Scotland and Great Britain

	H and I, %	*Scotland, %*	*Great Britain, %*
January 2001	4.5	3.8	3.0
February 2001	4.4	3.8	2.9
March 2001	4.2	3.7	2.8
April 2001	3.6	3.5	2.8
May 2001	3.4	3.4	2.7
June 2001	3.1	3.3	2.6
July 2001	3.2	3.4	2.6
August 2001	3.2	3.5	2.7
September 2001	3.1	3.2	2.6
October 2001	3.2	3.1	2.5
November 2001	3.5	3.2	2.5
December 2001	3.7	3.3	2.6
January 2002	4.1	3.6	2.8
February 2002	3.9	3.6	2.8
March 2002	3.7	3.5	2.7
April 2002	3.3	3.4	2.7
May 2002	3.0	3.3	2.6
June 2002	2.9	3.3	2.6
July 2002	2.9	3.4	2.6
August 2002	2.8	3.4	2.6
September 2002	2.7	3.1	2.6
October 2002	2.7	3.0	2.5
November 2002	3.1	3.1	2.5
December 2002	3.3	3.1	2.5
January 2003	3.6	3.5	2.7
February 2003	3.7	3.5	2.8
March 2003	3.4	3.4	2.7
April 2003	3.1	3.3	2.7
May 2003	2.8	3.2	2.6
June 2003	2.7	3.2	2.6
July 2003	2.7	3.3	2.6
August 2003	2.6	3.3	2.6
September 2003	2.5	3.1	2.5
October 2003	2.7	3.0	2.4
November 2003	2.9	3.0	2.4
December 2003	2.8	3.1	2.4
January 2004	3.2	3.4	2.6

5.4   Incomes and Gross Domestic Product

In general, earnings in the Highlands and Islands tend to lag behind those in the rest of Scotland. The latest figures for earnings in the Highlands and Islands, for 2001, are set out in Table 5.3.

Table 5.3   Average gross weekly earnings, 2001

Employee type	Highlands and Islands	Scotland	H and I as % of Scotland
All full time	£366.70	£404.50	90.6
Full time males	£402.40	£448.50	89.7
Full time females	£319.50	£342.30	93.3

Source: ONS, *New Earnings Survey*, April 2001.

Table 5.3 shows that average earnings are typically seven to ten percentage points below the Scottish averages. There has been relatively little variation in these figures over time, although full time manual male rates were slightly above the Scottish average in the mid 1990s. These reflected higher levels of overtime pay due to longer hours worked and higher wages in the oil fabrication sector. Interestingly the survey shows relatively little variation in the differential across employee types.

The latest GDP per capita statistics for the Highlands and Islands, released recently by Eurostat, are for 2001. These show that GDP per head was 72.4 per cent of the EU15 average. This represents a fall since 1994-96 when the comparable figure was 76 per cent. This opens up the potential for a future programme of European regional assistance, following the end of the current Objective 1 transitional funding which covers the period 2000-2006. This is because although the ten new member states joining the EU in May 2004 have lower GDP per capita, the Highlands and Islands figures mean funds could still be available as one of the so-called Objective 1 'statistical effect regions'. In the absence of enlargement the region would have qualified and so there is likely to be a further package of assistance for regions which meet these criteria. The detail of any package will be subject of negotiations over the coming months.

5.5   New Business Formation

Statistics from the Committee of Scottish Clearing Bankers illustrate that the rate of new business formation in the Highlands and Islands is above that for Scotland as a whole. The number of new business bank accounts opened by branch at the four main clearing banks over the past three years is set out in Table 5.4.

Table 5.4   New business bank accounts

	2001	*2002*	*2003*	*Rate per 1000 population, 2003*
Highlands and Islands	1702	1650	2199	5.1
Scotland	16967	18518	21468	4.2

Source: Committee of Scottish Clearing Bankers.

In common with the rest of Scotland the HIE area has witnessed a growth in the number of new business starts over the past three years. The area, however, has retained its share of new business starts at c10 per cent compared to a population share of 8.5 per cent. The business start up rate in the area is consistently above the Scottish average partly reflecting the greater proportion of self employment. Individual local enterprise company (LEC) areas which are above the Highlands and Islands average rate include Skye and Lochalsh (7.7 starts per 1000 people), Ross and Cromarty (5.7) and Inverness and Nairn (5.6). The latter two rates reflect the buoyancy of the Inverness city economy in particular.

5.6   Problems and Opportunities in the Highlands and Islands Economy

The main problems in the region's economy relate to its continuing reliance on primary sector industries, the rundown of the oil fabrication industry, changes in tourism markets, and the current strength of sterling against the dollar. Producers of sheep and cattle have been affected by some of the poorest years for agriculture for several decades although there have been improvements in the past year or so. The main way in which this is being tackled has been by focussing efforts on the production of high quality products such as the 'Orkney Gold' premium beef brand.

The aquaculture industry is also under severe pressure with competition from the world's largest producers of Atlantic salmon, Norway and Chile. Currently costs of production of Scottish salmon are in excess of market prices. The industry has seen some bankruptcies among smaller firms, notably in Shetland. A period of consolidation is currently underway with firms aiming to move production towards more premium status such as organic production and the French 'label rouge'. In addition, companies are entering markets for new species such as cod and halibut which offer good opportunities given the decline in wild stocks. The current crisis in the white fish sector is also creating challenges in major fishing areas such as East Moray and Shetland.

The rundown in the oil fabrication sector was a feature of the late 1990s. This led to the loss of the Lewis Offshore yard in Stornoway which had employed up to 400 people in 1998, while the Nigg and Ardersier yards of BARMAC entered a care and maintenance period in mid 2000. The latter two yards had a peak workforce of around 5000 people as recently as autumn 1999, although as many as 50 per cent of these workers were from other parts of Scotland and the UK. The knock-on effect of the rundown has been estimated at between £80 and £100 million lost to the local economy, making it the largest redundancy situation in the UK at the time.

In 2003 the Lewis Offshore yard was redeveloped by Highlands and Islands Enterprise in a £12m refurbishment aimed at the renewables energy market. Although there have been setbacks, the prospects for this sector look good with major onshore and offshore facilities set for construction as part of the UK government and Scottish Executive targets for renewable energy. In early 2004 the Ardersier yard to the east of Inverness was put on the market by its owners McDermott's, while the Nigg Yard owned by KBR has recently had some minor successes in the renewables market but is no longer active in the oil sector.

In the tourism industry changes in holiday patterns among domestic visitors and the strength of sterling, notably against the dollar, have had a detrimental effect on tourism in rural Scotland. The 2003 season, however, was the best for many years and is leading to renewed optimism and investment. The Highlands and Islands are much more dependent on tourism than other parts of Scotland. The response to this challenge has been to improve the quality of the tourist experience through upgrading of facilities and attractions, and more staff training. European funding through two schemes operated by the HIE Network, HIE Standards and HIE Attractions, has been important in helping to co-finance the improvements in standards of accommodation and attractions. The development of e-commerce also offers opportunities for the tourism industry, while others have argued that more effort needs to be placed on marketing spend to bring visitors to Scotland, and rural areas in particular.

The recent announcement of the review of the Area Tourist Boards which will come under the aegis of VisitScotland has set an ambitious target to double tourism spend over the next five years. The Highlands and Islands aims to play its part through improved marketing and the upgrade of existing centres such as the Aviemore Highland resort. This is building on opportunities created by the new Cairngorm National Park and associated infrastructure investment such as the Cairngorm funicular railway. In addition cultural tourism is becoming a significant part of the region's marketing efforts. A major Year of Highland Culture 2007 will play an important part in this. It stems from the unsuccessful bid by InvernessHighland 2008 to become the European Capital of Culture in 2008. While that accolade went to Liverpool, 2007 will see the opening of the re-furbished Eden Court theatre in Inverness, following a £10m upgrade and a significant programme of events throughout the region and beyond.

One of the keys to increasing visitor numbers and spend is accessibility. In particular flights to Inverness airport are important in bringing visitors into the region. Low cost operators such as EasyJet have been crucial in increasing visitor numbers, as have improvements to connectivity in other airports in Scotland such as Ryanair flights to Prestwick. In March 2004 two important additions to flights to Inverness include a twice weekly service to Stockholm and a new daily service to

Heathrow. The Superfast ferry service from Zeebrugge to Rosyth has also been important in enabling European visitors to come straight to Scotland. Recent research has shown two thirds of continental visitors using the service have a final destination in the Highlands and Islands.

Over the 1990s the Highlands and Islands saw an increase in inward investment projects, notably involving ICT related developments. During 1998/99, the peak year, 1275 jobs were gained by the area from inward investment. These included significant new manufacturing capability such as expansion of the Inverness Medical Limited diabetes plant and the AGM Batteries operation in Thurso. Contact centre developments have been assisted by significant improvements to the telecommunications infrastructure of the area over the past ten years. Over this period HIE has been involved in projects totalling some £86m, with its investment of c£5m matched by European Regional Development Fund investment, through the Objective 1 programme, of over £8m and private sector investment of over £72m. The Highlands and Islands Telecommunications Initiative was the most significant investment by HIE and involved the provision of a digital ISDN network for the bulk of the area.

There are now around 20 contact centres operating in the Highlands and Islands with current employment of c3000 people. This is a remarkable rate of expansion for an industry which began with 20 employees in Thurso in 1992. Contact centre developments have tended to be located in Caithness, the Inner Moray Firth area and in Argyll, notably Bute and Dunoon. In addition contact centres and back office processing activities are becoming established in more remote locations such as the Western Isles. This includes a 20 person operation running HIE's financial functions from Benbecula. This is part of the drive to locate public sector employment away from the central belt. As already noted in Chapter 3, under this policy Inverness will benefit from the relocation of the headquarters of Scottish Natural Heritage from Edinburgh in 2007. The 250 posts which will relocate will provide a significant additional boost to the local economy.

Other opportunities in the Highlands and Islands relate to decommissioning, associated with the Dounreay nuclear facility, and the development of renewable energy. In relation to Dounreay it has been estimated that over the next 30-40 years over £4.3bn will be spent on the decommissioning of the facility which equates to over £100m per annum. Caithness and Sutherland Enterprise are developing a strategy to ensure as much of this expenditure is retained within the local economy. In addition there is the potential to develop expertise in nuclear decommissioning which has a global market place.

The renewable energy sector offers excellent opportunities for the area's economy. The Danish firm Vestas operates a 200 employee wind turbine manufacturing plant at Machrihanish on the Kintyre peninsula. The Scottish Executive target of 40 per cent of energy production from renewables means significant investment needs to be made in the energy grid if the wind and tidal energy resources of the Highlands and Islands are to reach markets in the central belt and beyond. Investment such the European Marine Energy Centre (EMEC) in Orkney is aimed at ensuring Scotland becomes a world leader in offshore tidal generation. Edinburgh based Ocean Power Delivery and Inverness based Wavegen are among the Scottish firms taking a lead in this new industry.

The University of the Highlands and Islands Millennium Institute (UHIMI) is a £100m project, partly funded by the Millennium Commission, to create a new higher education institution for the region. This project will be a key economic driver for the area, not only as a direct employer but also in terms of spinout companies and benefits from links with SMEs in the area. The University is expected to create some 800 jobs with an annual injection of £70m into the local economy. It is based on 13 institutions from the North Atlantic Fisheries College in Shetland in the north, to Lews Castle College in Stornoway in the west, to Perth College in the south and Moray College in the east. This new collegiate university will be based on an advanced telecommunications infrastructure and will also have a large number of outreach local learning centres. The latter are key to the future delivery of lifelong learning in the region. On current plans the UHIMI will have degree awarding status in 2007.

In addition research institutes such as the Dunstaffnage marine laboratory are key to creating new employment opportunities in marine biotechnology through the UHIMI. A new £12m upgrade and incubator facility is ensuring this facility is one of the most modern and attractive in the UK. The Inverness Medicentre project, which will be built on the grounds of Raigmore Hospital, adjacent to Inverness Medical's campus, aims to build on the biomedical expertise of these two operations. This project, along with Dunstaffnage, is part of the strategy to develop a life science sector in the region. These types of knowledge based jobs are essential if the income differential between the Highlands and other parts of Scotland is to be addressed.

Key to the development of the UHI has been the provision of high speed telecommunications. The delivery of a broadband to all parts of the Highlands and Islands is a strategic aim of HIE and the Scottish Executive. Broadband availability is being rolled out to main centres in the region by British Telecom and a number of other projects such as HIE's own HI-WIDE wireless broadband initiative aim to address the most remote communities. The pace of take-up is also a challenge in broadband enabled areas and grants for both conventional and satellite systems are being marketed to encourage adoption of the technology.

5.7   Conclusion

The chapter has shown that the Highlands and Islands faces a variety of challenges and opportunities over the coming decade. The establishment of the Scottish Parliament has led to an increased interest in the regions of Scotland. It has also led to a greater interest in rural affairs both through the establishment of the Rural Affairs Department and the parliamentary committee on rural affairs (considered further in Chapter 6). The Highlands and Islands is being viewed as a model for other parts of Scotland in terms of rural development policy. There is no doubt that while the region has approaches to share with other parts of Scotland there is also much to learn. In particular one of the major challenges for rural areas will be how to gain more bandwidth in the information economy. It is highly probable that this issue will require a solution for rural Scotland as a whole. Otherwise there is a real danger of a digital divide opening up between urban and rural Scotland, to the detriment of the country as a whole.

In addition, as the Census shows, people are seeking to move into many rural areas, particularly around the main centres of population. This is posing challenges for the planning system and particularly the delivery of affordable housing. If the Highlands and Islands, and rural Scotland in general, are to prosper there must be opportunities for people to live in these areas. In many locations high house prices and relatively low wages in the rural economy mean that young people can not afford to live there. The housing challenge is arguably one of the greatest facing rural Scotland over the coming years.

Chapter 6

The South of Scotland – Challenges and Opportunities

Douglas Scott

6.1   Introduction

The South of Scotland has a relatively low profile within Scotland. This chapter aims to increase awareness of the South of Scotland and examines the issues and challenges that are confronting the area. In particular comparisons are made with the treatment given to the Highlands and Islands, Scotland's other major rural area. The chapter considers the main economic and social issues and trends in the South of Scotland. It concludes with a consideration of future policy directions.

6.2   The South of Scotland

6.2.1   Definition

The former South of Scotland European Parliament constituency, which is also the area covered by South of Scotland list Members of the Scottish Parliament, includes Dumfries and Galloway, Scottish Borders, South and East Ayrshire, South Lanarkshire and East Lothian. However, the definition used in this chapter confines the South of Scotland to the local authority areas of the Scottish Borders and Dumfries and Galloway. The reasons for this are that:

- The other local authority areas, despite having relatively large rural areas, tend to have an urban or city conurbation focus. This is because of their large urban populations and their relative proximity to the cities of Glasgow and Edinburgh. The areas covering South, North and East Ayrshire, South Lanarkshire and East Lothian have population densities of around 100 people per square kilometre and over. This compares to a population density of 23 people per square kilometre for Dumfries and Galloway and the Scottish Borders.

- The Scottish Borders and Dumfries and Galloway form the 'rural strand' South of Scotland Objective 2 European Programme area for the purpose of assistance from European Union Structural Funds for the period 2000-2006.

6.2.2 *Differences and Unifying Features*

The South of Scotland extends from the Atlantic to the North Sea and encompasses the whole of Scotland's common boundary with England and embraces two distinct regions i.e. the Scottish Borders and Dumfries and Galloway. This distinctiveness is shown by differences in:

- Connectivity – the Scottish Borders connects closely with the Edinburgh area and the North of England whilst Dumfries and Galloway looks to the West of Scotland, Northern Ireland and the North of England.

- Institutions – both Scottish Borders and Dumfries and Galloway have their own local authorities, local enterprise companies, area tourist boards, health boards and further education bodies. Dumfries and Galloway also has its own police and fire services whilst in the Scottish Borders these responsibilities are shared with the local authorities in the Lothians.

- Primary sector and industrial structures – within agriculture, grain crops and oil seed rape predominate in low lying areas of the Scottish Borders whereas dairying predominates within Dumfries and Galloway. Forestry and wood processing is much stronger in Dumfries and Galloway. In manufacturing, textiles are a significant sector in the Scottish Borders despite major closures in the past, whereas much of the textiles industry in Dumfries and Galloway (with the notable exception of Langholm) has closed down. There are also former coal mining areas in Dumfries and Galloway.

Notwithstanding these differences there are remarkable similarities. The unifying features of the South of Scotland are its rurality which gives rise to considerable commonalties between both areas, and its perceived peripherality from the rest of Scotland. Both Dumfries and Galloway and the Scottish Borders have strong communities with rich cultural identities and each area has a long involvement in regional economic development.

6.2.3 *Scotland's Other Periphery*

In Kellas's *The Scottish Political System* (1973), there is only one regional chapter, entitled 'The Highland Periphery'. Interestingly, there is a footnote to this title that states that the 'Borders' are to some extent a second Scottish periphery. This description might be applied to the whole of the South of Scotland and indeed this is likely to be the area referred to by the author. In similar vein, Crichton (1999) calls Borders 'the land we all forgot' referring to the area as being on 'the fringe of the nation, geographically, historically, politically and now economically'.

It can be argued that this perceived isolation is more psychological than real given the South of Scotland's close proximity to the cities of Central Scotland and Northern England. Indeed there is an increasingly strong body of opinion that the Scottish Borders, especially its northern part, should be seen as part of the Edinburgh city region for planning purposes. The reasons for this are the connectivity of north/south transportation corridors with Edinburgh, the impact of commuting on local housing markets and the extent of travelling to Edinburgh for higher level services. This connectivity will be reinforced if part of the former Waverley railway is reinstated between Edinburgh and Galashiels (discussed further in Chapter 9).

The link with the North of England is also a significant one for the South of Scotland. For some parts of the South of Scotland, the main service centres are not Glasgow or Edinburgh, but are across the English border in Carlisle, Berwick and Newcastle. There are growing numbers of residents in Dumfries and Galloway commuting to work outside the area particularly to Central Scotland, Ayrshire and Carlisle.

6.2.4 Rurality

The South of Scotland has a high quality and distinctive environment. It encompasses one seventh of the land area of Scotland. It had a population of 254,710 at June 2002, a population density of 23 per square kilometre, the lowest outside the Highlands and Islands

Within the South of Scotland, there is no city or conurbation that forms a central focal point. The 2001 Census of Population showed that Dumfries with a population of 31,146 is the largest town and there are only three other towns with a population of over 10,000 inhabitants (Hawick, Galashiels and Stranraer). Over two thirds of the population live outwith settlements of 10,000 people. This compares with 28 per cent in Scotland as a whole. The small towns and villages scattered throughout the South of Scotland act as centres of economic activity, service centres and population holding points.

The area's rurality has a major impact on the cost of service delivery, inward investment potential, infrastructure provision and sustainability of local communities. It also results in higher costs of public transport because of longer journeys and higher costs of private transport because of the relatively high fuel prices and greater use of the car. The services provided in settlements are threatened by the increasing centralisation of both public and private services, the continuing leakage of consumer spending to major urban centres outside the South of Scotland and the increasing threshold levels for the provision of viable services.

6.2.5 People and Communities

There is a great deal of civic pride, energy and community spirit amongst the people and communities in the South of Scotland. There is also a wide and varied voluntary sector and research by the Scottish Council of Voluntary Organisations (SCVO) in 1998 showed that both Dumfries and Galloway and the Scottish Borders had above average numbers of voluntary organisations per 1000 people compared with other Scottish local authority areas. The potential of the community and voluntary sectors could be greatly enhanced by greater strategic co-ordination, closer partnership working with public agencies, more community capacity building actions and the availability of more sustainable financial resources.

Overall, the population of the South of Scotland is predicted to fall by 3.4 per cent between 2002 and 2018, compared to only a 2.4 per cent fall in the rest of Scotland. Within the area, it is expected that there will be a fall of population of 7.2 per cent in Dumfries and Galloway and a rise of 1.9 per cent in the Scottish Borders in the period 2002-2018.

There is a marked ageing of the population in the South of Scotland. According to the 2001 Census of Population, the Scottish Borders and Dumfries and Galloway local authority areas had amongst the highest proportion of people over 60 of any area in Scotland. In addition, the average age of the population of the two areas was 41.5 years, 2.5 years older than Scotland as a whole, and higher than all other parts of Scotland apart from the Western Isles. Population projections suggest that the numbers of people over 60 will increase by around a third in the South of Scotland between 2002 and 2018, compared to around a quarter in Scotland as a whole.

The needs of young people, especially those, who do not take part in higher education, are a major issue in the South of Scotland. According to Jones and Jamieson (1997), '19 year olds living in the Borders [are] the most likely of any in Scotland to rate local job opportunities as 'worse than average', and the most likely to have moved town to find work – by the age of 19 those still living in the Borders are most likely of any region to have experienced unemployment (42 per cent)'. Research by the Rowntree Foundation, using the Scottish Borders as a case study, provided further evidence of the difficulties faced by young people (who do not leave to go into higher education etc.) in accessing employment, transport and affordable housing (Pavis et al, 2000).

Both Dumfries and Galloway and the Scottish Borders have very high dependency ratios. In the 2001 Census of Population the numbers of children and young people under 15 and elderly people over 60 as a proportion of the working population was the second and third highest respectively of all the local authority areas in Scotland. This places a considerable care burden on younger adult age groups and on public services. This is intensified when company closures force people of working age to leave the area.

6.2.6   The Economy

The South of Scotland has been experiencing considerable economic difficulties. During 1998 and 1999 the Scottish Borders lost over 2,500 jobs, primarily in the textiles, electronics and agricultural sectors, representing over one twentieth of the workforce. In the same period Dumfries and Galloway lost around 2000 jobs.

The South of Scotland has a relatively low average GDP per head. The latest available figures are for 1998. These showed the Scottish Borders GDP per head at 78 per cent of the UK average and that of Dumfries and Galloway at 87 per cent. The Scottish figure stood at 95 per cent of the UK average. The severe industrial problems experienced in the area since 1998 along with falls in agriculture income (over one tenth of GDP stems from agriculture), especially as a result of the Foot and Mouth Disease outbreak, would suggest that there has been a significant decrease in GDP per head since 1997.

The Scottish Borders and Dumfries and Galloway are amongst the ten poorest paid areas in Great Britain. According to the 2003 *New Earnings Survey*, the Scottish Borders average gross weekly wage levels were 81 per cent of the Scottish average, the lowest of any region in Scotland while the Dumfries and Galloway figure was 87 per cent, reflecting the rurality and industrial structure of the South of Scotland. There is also a gender imbalance with women in general having a lower average wage than men. In 1996 investment per employee in manufacturing in the South of Scotland was around 40 per cent lower than the Scottish average.

The South of Scotland has a business base predominantly composed of micro businesses and the self employed. While 95 per cent of South of Scotland businesses employ fewer than 50 staff, which is in line with the Scottish average, the proportion of people employed by these small firms is much larger in the South of Scotland. According to *Scottish Economic Statistics 2002*, over half of workers in the South of Scotland were employed in firms of less than 50 staff, compared to only a third in Scotland as a whole. With respect to self employment, the 2001 Census of Population indicated a self employment rate of almost 11 per cent, compared to less than 7 per cent in the rest of Scotland.

The South of Scotland has a greater share of employment in the primary and manufacturing sectors. According to the 2001 Census of Population the farming, fishing and forestry sectors accounted for 8.7 per cent of employment compared to 2.4 per cent in Scotland. Dumfries and Galloway and the Scottish Borders had the second and fourth highest proportions of their workforce employed in these primary industries of any local authority area in Scotland.

Agriculture plays a major role in the economy, social fabric and the environment of the South of Scotland. This was very evident during the Foot and Mouth Disease outbreak of 2001, which directly affected Dumfries and Galloway and parts of the Scottish Borders and had a severe adverse impact on the local economy. In 1999 agriculture accounted for approximately 36 per cent of businesses in the South of Scotland.

Around one fifth of the Scottish forestry resource is located in the South of Scotland. There is also a significant fishing industry based in Eyemouth in the Eastern Borders and to a lesser extent in Kirkcudbright in Galloway.

Manufacturing in 2001 accounted for 17.3 per cent of employment in the South of Scotland compared to 12.7 per cent for Scotland. The key industrial sectors are textiles, with gross added value in 2000 of £90m, and food and drink, with gross added value of £82m.

As elsewhere the service sector provides the main source of employment in the South of Scotland. However, the area has a below average share of employment in this sector. In 2000 the South of Scotland's share of service sector employment was 70 per cent compared to the Scottish average of 78 per cent. Compared with Scotland, there is a below average proportion of employment in banking and finance. The public sector is a very important employer accounting for approximately 26 per cent in public employment in line with the Scottish average.

Despite its high quality and distinctive environment and its major potential, tourism is not strong in the South of Scotland. In 1999 hotels and restaurants accounted for around 900 businesses or 8 per cent of business stock which is marginally lower than the Scottish figure. Tourism employment, as portrayed by the hotels and restaurants sector, is around the Scottish average.

The South of Scotland experiences particular industrial problems when there are company closures and rationalisations because of its settlement pattern which is based on relatively small towns. City and conurbation areas have larger and more diverse economic and employment bases that can more readily cope with job losses. Due to their greater range and type of industries, cities are much less exposed to economic downturns in particular industrial sectors. In comparison, many towns and villages in the South of Scotland have only a small number of businesses and some depend for employment on only one major industry. The result is that when businesses undergo economic difficulties resulting in job losses, there are few if any alternative job opportunities for the unemployed.

6.2.7   Social Exclusion

Standard indicators that are used to measure poverty tend to have an urban bias and understate rural problems that are particularly prevalent in the South of Scotland. Until 2002, the *Revising the Scottish Area Deprivation Index 1998*, produced by the Central Research Unit, was the main official text for prioritising areas of deprivation within Scotland. This states that 'the index would be largely urban-centred and this is clearly borne out by the results' and that 'there needs to be a separate study of rural deprivation'. The use of this Index resulted in only a few priority areas being designated in the South of Scotland.

In 2003, the *Scottish Indices of Deprivation* were created. In compiling these, it was recognised that 'there is a particular need for indicators to capture the deprivation experienced by people living in rural areas'. Despite this recognition it is evident that the indices continue to ignore some of the key economic and social issues which cause disadvantage in households and communities within the South of Scotland and rural Scotland as a whole. These are:

- Population factors – linked to out-migration of young people and a relatively large proportion of elderly people.

- Economic factors – related to lack of capacity in the local economy, limited economic diversification, and market failure or lack of market interest in developing business sites and properties. These problems are intensified by the settlement structure of rural areas which is based on small towns and villages.

- Investment issues – related to low GDP and investment levels in industry.

- Labour market issues – linked to low wages, relatively low qualifications in the workforce and skill shortages.

In the South of Scotland, 71 per cent of the population live outside settlements of 10,000 people or more, compared to 28 per cent for Scotland as a whole. This means that socially excluded individuals and groups tend to be much less concentrated than in heavily urban areas such as West Central Scotland. For this reason spatial approaches underpinned by aspatial policies such as policies for social justice, young people, equal opportunities, sustainable development etc are required to tackle social exclusion in the South of Scotland.

The spatial focus has been recognised by the South of Scotland Objective 2 European Programme which is targeting resources on particular areas, such as the Wigtown and Upper Nithsdale areas in Dumfries and Galloway and the Hawick and Eyemouth and East Berwickshire areas within the Scottish Borders.

6.2.8   Education and Training

In the South of Scotland school attainment statistics at both Standard and Higher grade level are above the national average. There are relatively larger numbers of young people going into further and higher education but significantly lower levels of school leavers on training schemes or who have found employment. Adult participation rates in higher education are lower in the South of Scotland when compared to the Scottish average. There is a relatively low skill base within the working population. According to the 2001 Census of Population 40 per cent of the 16-74 age group residents in Dumfries and Galloway had no formal qualifications, compared to 34 per cent in the Scottish Borders and 33 per cent in Scotland as a whole.

To provide more higher education opportunities, university campuses have been established in the South of Scotland. Heriot Watt University took over the Scottish College of Textiles based in Galashiels and is focusing its attention on fashion textiles. The Crichton University campus at Dumfries now offers a unique multi-institute campus facility, with institutions including the Universities of Glasgow and Paisley, Bell College and Dumfries and Galloway College having a presence on the site. These developments offer significant opportunities for business development and growth, employment and diversification, quality jobs and the retention of young people, and postgraduate research student placements

6.2.9   Infrastructure

There have been some relatively significant information and communication technologies (ICT) investments in recent years in the South of Scotland. These have been related to the new university campuses in Galashiels and Dumfries. British Telecom has also been investing in its telecommunication network systems.

Scottish Enterprise Dumfries and Galloway and Scottish Enterprise Borders have supported significant broadband telecommunications investments.

It is hoped that access to broadband systems in the South of Scotland will be transformed by the Broadband Pathfinder Initiative. This is a joint project between Scottish Executive, Dumfries and Galloway Council, Dumfries and Galloway NHS, Scottish Borders Council and Scottish Borders NHS. It aims to connect broadband technology to public services throughout the area and a successful outcome will mean that every school, GP practice, dentist, pharmacy, library, Council and NHS office should have reliable access to internet services, video links and interactive learning environments. However, even with broadband technology there will remain a need to encourage a substantially greater use of ICT by businesses and local people and communities, to develop more ICT support services and to create a stronger software electronics sector.

Within the South of Scotland there is evidence of a lack of interest by the private sector in the provision of good quality business premises and business infrastructure. This has placed a considerable responsibility on local authorities and local enterprise companies to provide business sites and premises and to look at the opportunities for setting up joint ventures with the private sector.

There are transportation and communication problems in the South of Scotland. These are due to the need to maintain and improve an extensive road network, a relative lack of rail investment, the need to develop a strategic public transport system, and the need to improve remote rural roads for the extraction of forestry.

A number of specific transportation and communication issues need to be addressed in the short and medium term. These include the reinstatement of the former Waverley railway line between Edinburgh and Carlisle that passes through the Central Borders and the upgrading and dualling of the A75 trunk road in Dumfries and Galloway, a key international transportation route to Northern Ireland. There are also cross-border transportation issues such as the need for the dualling of the A1 and for further improvements to the A68 and A7.

Waste management is also an important infrastructure issue as the capacities of refuse tips in the South of Scotland are extremely limited.

Initial appraisals of market burghs in the Scottish Borders have revealed a considerable need for town centre properties in private ownership. There are similar problems in Dumfries and Galloway.

The Scottish Executive's review of Scotland's cities, *Building Better Cities* (2003), identified the future strategic role of the six cities and led to the creation of a City Growth Fund of £90m. This type of strategic thinking and investment is also needed for the towns of rural Scotland.

6.3   Comparisons with the Highlands and Islands

There is a strong view within the South of Scotland that it has been disadvantaged in development policy terms. To understand the basis for this view, a brief comparison will be made of the development policy history of the South of Scotland with the Highlands and Islands, Scotland's other major rural area. The

Highlands and Islands has similar issues and challenges, albeit of a more serious nature in its western and northern areas and islands caused by physical remoteness combined with a very low population density and the relatively poor quality of agricultural land.

6.3.1   The 1960s and 1970s

The White Paper, *The Scottish Economy 1965 to 1970* (1965), provided the basis for the production of the Central Borders plan in 1968 and the South West Scotland (i.e. Dumfries and Galloway) plan in 1970. In the Eastern Borders the Development Commission created its first Special Investment Area in Scotland. The entire South of Scotland area was also designated an Assisted Area for the purpose of regional aid. In the Highlands and Islands, the Highlands and Islands Development Board (HIDB) was established in 1965 with an economic and social remit and a range of industrial intervention powers, including financial assistance.

During the 1970s development activities in both areas were strengthened by local government reorganisation in 1974 and the establishment of Regional and Island authorities. These were given strong strategic development powers in relation to roads and transportation, planning and economic development, water and sewerage, and education. In the South of Scotland there were two Regional authorities, Borders Regional Council and Dumfries and Galloway Regional Council.

In the Highlands and Islands there were two Regional authorities, Highland Regional Council and Strathclyde Regional Council (which included Argyll and the islands of Arran and Cumbrae), and the Islands Councils for the Western Isles, Orkney, and Shetland. The establishment of these Councils in the Highlands and Islands, alongside the powerful and wide ranging development and advocacy role of the HIDB, greatly strengthened the institutional base of the area and provided an extremely effective tool for lobbying purposes.

The South of Scotland benefited from the establishment of the Scottish Development Agency (SDA) in 1975. Until the change of government in 1979 the SDA had an interventionist philosophy that led to significant company and industrial property investments being made in the South of Scotland, especially in the Scottish Borders. Also the designation of Assisted Area status enabled the South of Scotland to gain infrastructure assistance from the European Regional Development Fund (ERDF) from the late 1970s onwards. Similar assistance was also available to the Highlands and Islands.

6.3.2   The 1980s

In 1982 Assisted Area status was withdrawn from much of the South of Scotland. This also meant the loss of access to infrastructure assistance from ERDF and under the Local Employment Act 1972. The only part of the South of Scotland that had access to these forms of assistance were the Galloway travel-to-work-areas (TTWAs) which remained Intermediate Areas. The result was a 'drying up' of significant inward investments into the area during the 1980s and 1990s.

During the 1980s the SDA focused on the leverage of private sector investment and intervention to deal with tightly defined market failures, primarily in large urban areas. This disadvantaged the South of Scotland as it resulted in advance factories no longer being constructed, equity assistance no longer being provided to companies, and rural areas being given a low priority. The SDA put a special emphasis on the work of its Small Business Division in rural areas but this service had limited staff resources. In addition, urban areas in the South of Scotland had difficulties in accessing Urban Aid. This form of assistance was the basis for supporting many innovative community regeneration projects in Scottish cities.

Meanwhile during the 1980s the Highlands and Islands was protected from the loss of Assisted Area status by the HIDB. Also, significant European support began to flow into the Highlands and Islands from the Western Isles Integrated Programme, the National Programme of Community Interest, and the Objective 5b Programme. The only area in the South of Scotland to qualify for Objective 5b status was Galloway.

With the HIDB in mind, there was a debate in the 1980s as to whether a social remit should also be given to the SDA. However, the Chief Executive of the SDA argued that 'the best social development flows from economic development' and accordingly the reference to economic and social development in the 1965 (Highlands and Islands) Act should be treated as two facets of the same objective rather than two separately identifiable objective (Scottish Affairs Committee, 1984-85).

6.3.3   The 1990s

In the 1990s the South of Scotland benefited from the establishment of local enterprise companies in both Dumfries and Galloway and the Scottish Borders. This led to additional 'ringfenced' development resources being provided to the area. Also the whole area became eligible for Objective 5b status in 1994. During local government reorganisation in 1996 both Dumfries and Galloway and the Scottish Borders were successful in retaining local authorities for their areas. These successes were the result of strong lobbying.

Meanwhile the Highlands and Islands achieved a great deal more resource allocation for its development activities by the achievement of EU Structural Funds Objective 1 status in 1994. According to the Arkleton Centre (2000), the Highlands and Islands received £287m in Structural Funds, around £780 per capita. During the same period, the Scottish Borders and Dumfries and Galloway were awarded £22m and £34m respectively from their Objective 5b designations, a total of £56m or £224 per capita.

It is should however be noted that in Objective 1 areas, Objective 5a measures including the relatively expensive Hill Livestock Compensatory Allowances are incorporated in the regional programmes and financial package, whereas this is not the case in Objective 5b areas. Thus, of the £287m for the Highlands and Islands Objective 1 Programme, £68.7m was devoted to the primary sector and food processing, most of which represented Objective 5a spending in lowland Scotland (i.e. the rest of Scotland outside the Highlands and Islands).

In the period 1994-99 the Highlands and Islands gained Assisted Area status at the highest category of aid. In addition the region received considerable funding support for the establishment of the University of the Highlands and Islands. The stronger lobbying ability of the Highlands and Islands also enabled significant investments in ICT by British Telecom and other providers which provided an additional stimulus for inward investment.

6.3.4   The Present Situation

For the period 2000-2006 the South of Scotland has been designated an Objective 2 Programme for purpose of assistance from EU Structural Funds. According to the Arkleton Centre (2000), the South of Scotland will receive £44m from this Programme which amounts to £174 per capita (1998 population figures). On the other hand the Highlands and Islands has been designated a special transitional programme area, which is worth £194m in EU funding or £526 per capita (1998 population figures). Moreover, in comparing the Highlands and Islands and South of Scotland figures, it should be noted that agricultural policy spending of £27m is included in the Highlands and Islands Transitional Funding.

For the 2000-2006 period, the Highlands and Islands was given Assisted Area status although at a lower level than previously (at around 30 per cent) and covering a lower proportion of the population (around 70 per cent, due mainly to the exclusion of Inverness). However, those areas not covered will still be eligible for aid from Highlands and Islands Enterprise. In the South of Scotland the population coverage was improved significantly, to 44 per cent in the Scottish Borders and 28 per cent in Dumfries and Galloway, although at a maximum rate of 15 per cent grant equivalent to assisted enterprises. The South of Scotland thus remains disadvantaged vis-a-vis the Highlands and Islands in terms of both population coverage and the level of aid.

The Arkleton Centre (2000) found that Highlands and Islands Enterprise had a budget of 1999-2000 of £78 million, around £212 per capita. In addition, HIE has greater freedom in decision making over spending, as a greater proportion of HIE spending is discretionary compared to that of Scottish Enterprise. The budget for Scottish Enterprise Dumfries and Galloway and Scottish Enterprise Borders was estimated to be a total of £18 million in 1999-2000, around £71 per capita, just one third of the figure for HIE.

Finally it should be noted that agriculture in the South of Scotland receives substantial resources from the EU's Common Agricultural Policy (CAP). In 1999, agricultural policy payments to farmers in the South of Scotland amounted to some £105m or over £420 per capita, CAP transfers over the period 2000-2006 being more than ten times the value of Structural Funds per capita per annum. These subsidies for farmers in the South of Scotland are however likely to be reduced significantly as a result of the reform of the CAP in 2003.

6.3.5   The Highlands and Islands Convention

In 1996 the government announced the establishment of the Highlands and Islands Convention as a forum to bring together the key players in the economic and social development of the Highlands and Islands. Before the formation of the Scottish Parliament, the Convention was chaired by the Secretary of State for Scotland. In 2000 the Convention was re-established by the Scottish Executive and is now chaired by the First Minister. The Convention acts as a very important lobbying and policy formation vehicle as its meetings require the attendance of Scottish Executive Ministers. The Scottish Executive also has a Minister for the Highlands and Islands, which is the only regional position. This post gives considerable regional policy weight to this area, a fact recognised at the 2003 Convention by First Minister Jack McConnell when he said the Convention 'allows local leaders to communicate their ideas and concerns directly to Ministers'.

6.3.6 *The South of Scotland Alliance*

Following the example of the Highlands and Islands Convention, a South of Scotland Forum was established in 1998, at the instigation of Dumfries and Galloway Council and Scottish Borders Council, to discuss the serious economic problems affecting their areas. The sectors experiencing most difficulties were agriculture, textiles, electronics, and plastics. The Scottish Office Minister for Business and Enterprise was invited to chair the Forum. It met on two occasions.

Since the Forum's last meeting in 1999, the two Councils and local enterprise companies have been meeting informally. They are of the view that co-operation between Dumfries and Galloway and the Scottish Borders should be further developed because of the commonality of economic, social and environmental issues across the South of Scotland. This feeling has been reinforced by the ongoing work on the South of Scotland Objective 2 European Programme.

In 2001, the Forum was renamed and launched as the South of Scotland Alliance and since then has aimed to raise the profile of the South of Scotland. The Alliance which continues to involve the two Councils and local enterprise companies is concentrating its efforts on a number of key themes of a common lobbying or advocacy front, with the recognition that development solutions for the South of Scotland must be long term and involve sustained funding. The themes are to:

- Raise the political and marketing profile and image of the South of Scotland within Scotland by carrying out a 'Look South' campaign.

- Rectify market failure and tackle market restructuring.

- Tackle inclusion by promoting parity of opportunities.

- Ensure sufficiency of funding.

- Be outward looking and build international links.

It is evident from the above analysis that there have been considerable differences in the political and public policy treatment of the development of the Highlands and Islands compared to the South of Scotland. This has led the Highlands and Islands to be allocated much higher levels of resources. This imbalance is still evident today.

6.4   General Policy Issues

Within market economies, city regions are key generators of wealth, income and employment. In Scotland, Gross Domestic Product (GDP) per head is above average in Aberdeen, Edinburgh and Glasgow. Rural areas tend to have a below average GDP per head. The development focus in rural areas such as the South of Scotland must therefore be on creating sustainable local economies. To carry out this task the private sector, local communities and voluntary organisations in rural areas need the support of local authorities and local development bodies, the government and the European Union. To enable the creation of more sustainable local economies in the South of Scotland there is a need to tackle a number of important policy issues.

6.4.1   The Lack of an Effective Regional Development Policy in Scotland

As alluded to above, many books on Scotland have only one regional chapter i.e. the Highlands and Islands. For example, *Scotland in the 20th Century* (Devine and Finlay, 1996) has a chapter entitled 'The Scottish Highlands: From Congested District to Objective One' but has singled out no other region in this way. As mentioned above, the only area recognised as important enough by the Scottish Executive to have a regional Minister is the Highlands and Islands. Yet Scotland is characterised by its diversity as evidenced in different dialects (and languages), cultural attributes, land use categories, settlement patterns and industrial structures.

In national policy terms it can be said that the Highlands and Islands is now the only region of Scotland that is recognised. The rest of Scotland is more and more referred to as lowland Scotland, which reflects the boundaries of Scottish Enterprise but not the regional diversity within the area. An example of this is the Scottish Objective 3 European Operational Programme for Lowland Scotland. The danger of this reductionism is that there will be a tendency for the regional issues of central Scotland to predominate and those relating to the South of Scotland to be ignored. A spatially balanced approach to the economic development of Scotland is needed to make the most effective use of its resources and to spread economic growth to all parts of Scotland.

In response to the Consultation Paper on Regional Policy issued by the Department of Trade and Industry (DTI) in March 2003, the South of Scotland Alliance stated that:

> The outputs of a Regional Policy for Scotland should be that the inhabitants of each region should have a standard of living as close to the Scottish average as possible and that the regions make an effective as possible contribution to the development

of Scottish economy. These outputs would be achieved in a sustainable way taking account of the needs of social justice and the environment. The scope of a Regional Policy for Scotland would comprise the various elements of the development process required to meet these outputs. The links between these elements would require an integrated approach. The elements would involve interventions related to businesses, people, communities, place and natural resources. This would translate into development instruments involving business development, education and training, community development, regeneration and infrastructure, and strong linkages to the developments in agriculture, fishing, mining and the harnessing of other environmental resources.

6.4.2 The Lack of a National Economic Development Strategy to Inform an Effective Regional Development Policy

To implement a regional economic policy that would benefit areas such as the South of Scotland, there is a need for an effective national economic strategy. There has been no national economic development strategy for Scotland since the White Paper on the Scottish economy in 1965. National economic strategies have proved very effective in small countries such as Finland and Ireland and have been an important focus for regional development. A national economic development strategy would not mean simply combining the economic strategies of Scottish Enterprise and Highlands and Islands Enterprise.

In response to the DTI Consultation Paper on Regional Policy, the South of Scotland Alliance stated that:

> A Scottish Economic Development Framework was unveiled in 2000 by the Scottish Executive, which was an important step in the direction of a national economic strategy. It is considered that the Scottish National Economic Development Framework should be revisited and revamped with much greater stakeholder involvement and ownership and extended to provide guidelines for the preparation of regional economic development plans for the whole of Scotland. This approach should also be based on a better understanding of the relationship between rural and urban economies.

6.4.3 The Lack of a Strong Rural Policy for Service Delivery and Community Development

The South of Scotland has been fortunate in that there are coterminous boundaries for Councils and other agencies both within the Scottish Borders and Dumfries and Galloway and there are effective partnership mechanisms which are being supported through the community planning processes (discussed further in Chapter 11).

However, there are concerns about the robustness of service delivery in the South of Scotland and other rural areas within Scotland and the adverse effects of the standardisation and centralisation tendencies within both public and private national organisations in Scotland. This has led to the centralisation of services in fewer towns along with closure of village shops, bank branches and the area offices of major utilities. Some of these general service issues were highlighted by the

Scottish National Rural Partnership (2002) as well as more specific service issues relating to postal services, retailing and financial services, the provision of information and advice, and childcare.

The Scottish Executive's office relocation policy, discussed in Chapter 3, is a positive step in reducing the impact of these trends by providing high quality service jobs in rural areas. Whilst this policy has benefited the Scottish Borders with the relocation of the Scottish Public Pensions Agency to Tweedbank near Galashiels, it has not yet provided any office jobs in Dumfries and Galloway.

The Scottish National Rural Partnership (2002) has highlighted the importance of vibrant communities and a strong voluntary sector for an effective approach to rural development. To achieve this end there is a need to provide long term sustainable assistance to enable communities and voluntary groups to fulfil their own potential, to assist communities to engage with public and private bodies, and to carry out community development. However, there are apparent differences within Scotland in the approaches to supporting local communities for the purpose of rural development, particularly between the Highlands and Islands and the rest of Scotland. It is recommended that 'further research is needed on the Highlands and Islands experience and the perceived variations in support for service delivery elsewhere in rural Scotland' (Scottish National Rural Partnership, 2002). It is considered that these rural service and community development issues can only be addressed by a strong and effective Scottish rural policy.

6.5   Future Policy Directions for the South of Scotland

The main challenges facing the South of Scotland are as follows:

- Dealing with the major restructuring issues in the agricultural and manufacturing industries, and supporting economic diversification, particularly the attraction of higher paid service and research and development jobs.

- Ensuring that its companies, communities and people fully benefit from the knowledge economy and the opportunities arising from e-commerce and the new broadband technology.

- Growing existing and new companies.

- Maximising the opportunities presented by the region's high quality natural environment.

- Encouraging a more balanced population structure, which is important in terms of support for the care sector and the development of a diverse range of economic and social activities.

- Establishing stronger and positive economic linkages (in terms of business, tourism, higher education, and research and development) with the urban areas to the north in central Scotland especially Edinburgh, to the west in Northern Ireland and to the south in northern England.

- Improving the economic and social viability and physical fabric of town and villages in the face of changing service delivery patterns and efficiency thresholds.

- Providing more opportunities for young people in terms of quality jobs with good conditions and a career structure, and better access to transport and affordable housing.

- Making the most of the higher and further education facilities being developed in the area, especially to provide more lifelong opportunities and to support company spinoffs from research and development.

- Tackling social exclusion using both a spatial approach (involving towns and wider areas) supported by aspatial policies (prioritising support for groups such as young people, women, the elderly, the unemployed and isolated households living in remoter areas).

- Building on the strength of communities, the voluntary sector and the private sector by increasing their capacity, encouraging more partnership working with public bodies, supporting community activism, the establishment of stronger business associations, and enhancing support to the voluntary sector and to volunteering.

- Advocating the needs of the South of Scotland in terms of infrastructure, employment and service requirements and for public institutions and services to continue to be administered locally rather than elsewhere.

Hunter (1999) has argued that the Highlands and Islands 'has attributes, which are scarce in today's world: an attractive natural environment, a unique set of cultural attributes, and a high quality of life. That combined with the extent to which new communications technologies are making it easier to do business in places formerly thought remote is why the area is doing as well as it is and has the potential to do a whole lot better'. These same arguments apply if anything with greater weight to the South of Scotland because of its closer proximity to major cities and transport routes.

Moreover, Fairley (1999) has argued that:

> It is possible now for the elected politicians, the institutions, and the active citizens of rural Scotland to engage with this new level of activity, and in so doing, provide a more effective 'voice' for rural Scotland and gain a greater prominence and influence within the Scottish polity. However, it is equally possible that the failure

to so engage will lead to the continued or even increased marginalisation of rural
society and its concerns, in a Scotland, where the dominant culture is, in Professor
Smout's view, 'emphatically an urban culture', and where the national media is
largely based in the main urban centres and focused on Edinburgh.

The implications of the arguments of both Hunter (1999) and Fairley (1999) are
that the South of Scotland is right in pursuing and developing its co-operative
policy agenda through the work of the South of Scotland Alliance. From a practical
point of view this agenda is being pursued through the implementation of the South
of Scotland Objective 2 European Programme, complementing the economic
strategies of the Scottish Borders and Dumfries and Galloway Economic Forums,
and addressing the common issues of rurality that are apparent across the South of
Scotland. It is enabling co-operative working on issues such as infrastructural
investment, transport, e-commerce, tourism, research and development, community
development, business development, and economic intelligence.

The work on the Objective 2 European Programme is also informing the
development of the policy agenda of the South of Scotland Alliance, by raising the
profile of the South of Scotland and highlighting issues of concern to the area. In
the future the South of Scotland Alliance may look to develop into the model of the
Highlands and Islands Convention.

In addition, the Border Visions forum established in 2000 is providing a
platform for the South of Scotland to work with its neighbours in Cumbria and
Northumberland. A debate is currently ongoing as to how joint working may help
address issues of common concern. There is also a need for the Scottish Borders to
recognise the reality of the developing city region of Edinburgh but for the Scottish
Borders to benefit fully there must be a mature two way relationship between the
city and surrounding areas.

The Scottish Executive and its agencies are beginning to take steps from a
policy perspective to recognise that the rural nature of the Scottish Borders and
Dumfries and Galloway is similar to the Highlands and Islands. The best example
of this is the Broadband Pathfinder Initiative. In addition, when in 2003
Futureskills Scotland, a joint operation of Scottish Enterprise and Highlands and
Islands Enterprise, introduced its study of rural labour markets by defining 'rural
Scotland as the Highlands and Islands, Scottish Borders and Dumfries and
Galloway', it was the first time an official study had recognised the Highlands and
Islands and the South of Scotland as being the two main rural areas in Scotland.

To support the ongoing work in the South of Scotland it is also important that
there are strong national economic and regional policies, with an effective rural
dimension. The regional dimension should recognise the strong community
planning and inter-agency partnerships working in the South of Scotland, which
has been the result of the coterminous administrative boundaries for Councils, local
enterprise companies, Area Tourist Boards and Health Boards in both Dumfries
and Galloway and the Scottish Borders. It is important that these bodies continue to
have the policy and funding discretion to target local and regional concerns and not
simply implement a set of national policies at a local level.

The South of Scotland – Challenges and Opportunities 87

References

Arkleton Centre for Rural Development Research (2000) *Raising the Profile of the South of Scotland: Development Policies and Issues. A Report for the South of Scotland Partnership*, unpublished report, University of Aberdeen.
Crichton, T. (1999) 'The land we all forgot', *Sunday Herald*, 14 March.
Devine, T. and Finlay, R. (eds) (1996) *Scotland in the 20th Century*, Edinburgh University Press, Edinburgh.
Fairley, J. (1999) *Scotland's New Democracy – New Opportunities for Rural Scotland?*, paper presented at conference on 'The Scottish Parliament and Rural Policy: What Room for Manoeuvre?', University of Aberdeen, 3 November.
Hunter, J. (1999) 'Balance of power could shift to the Highlands and Islands', *The Scotsman*, 11 November.
Jones, G. and Jamieson, L. (1997) *Young People in Rural Scotland: Getting Out and Staying On*, CES Briefing 13, Centre for Educational Sociology, University of Edinburgh.
Kellas, J. (1973) *The Scottish Political System*, Cambridge University Press, Cambridge.
Pavis, S., Platt, S. and Hubbard, G. (2000) *Young People in Rural Scotland: Pathways to Social Inclusion and Exclusion*, Joseph Rowntree Foundation.
Scottish Affairs Committee (1984-85) *Highlands and Islands Board: Volume 1 Report and Proceedings of the Committee*.
Scottish Executive (1999) *Making it Work Together*, Scottish Executive.
Scottish National Rural Partnership (2002) *Implementing Services in Rural Scotland: A Progress Report*, Scottish Executive.
South of Scotland Alliance (2003) *Position Paper on the Future of European Regional Policy*, South of Scotland Alliance.
South of Scotland European Partnership (2000) *The South of Scotland Objective 2 Programme 2000-2006*, Consultation Document, South of Scotland European Partnership.

Chapter 7

Economic Development: A Crowded Landscape

Mike Danson

7.1 From Regional Problem to Institutional Thickness

In recent times, there has been a movement away from the traditional forms of intervention in the economy towards more enabling programmes and policies. The postwar consensus of supporting problem regions through grants and loans to manufacturing companies, the nationalisation of industries which were significant to the north and west of Britain, the subsequent persuasion of these corporations to invest in these poorer communities and the application of automatic stabilisers to secure more balanced growth and development of the national economy overall all came under scrutiny in the period after 1977. Privatisations, and their regional aftermath (Gripaios and Munday, 1999), entry to the European Union and the consequent restrictions on the ability to support industries directly and the general displacement of Keynesian demand management by supply side economics all adversely affected the depressed regions of the UK in the first instance. Partly as a result of the increased disparities across the country induced by such changes, and partly reflecting the apparently convincing performance of the development agencies in addressing these forms of divergent development, the 1980s and 1990s experienced a time of new types of intervention in the economy based on area specific institutions (Halkier and Danson, 1997).

In the case of Scotland, the effects of these policy changes and the associated restructuring of the economy and industrial base were as severe as anywhere in the UK. Out of these changes came a redrawing of the policy landscape with new players, enhanced powers and activities for existing agencies, and a vast expansion in the range and forms of initiatives and interventions in the economy. The dislocation to traditional ways of influencing forces of supply and demand should not be underestimated, with actions moving down the spatial scale, increasingly being applied at the urban rather than the regional level. This period also witnessed the transmogrification of the interventionist Scottish Development Agency and Highlands and Islands Development Board into the more market oriented Scottish Enterprise and Highlands and Islands Enterprise (Danson et al, 1990 and 1991), with training and business development activities being merged as a result.

By the time the Scottish Parliament had been re-established in 1999, the infrastructure landscape for economic development in Scotland had become somewhat crowded. Over the previous quarter century, local authorities had been steadily expanding their role in local economic development as their respective areas collapsed into crisis (Lloyd and Rowan-Robinson, 1987; McQuaid, 1993). In parallel, two networks of a combined twenty three local enterprise companies (LECs) had been created to lead activities across the country from the perspective of the two regional development agencies – addressing market failures in labour, capital and property markets within their particular fiefdoms. As well as local authorities and LECs, enterprise trusts, chambers of commerce, area tourist boards, higher and further education institutions, and a host of other agents with a legitimate role to play in the economy were also vying for influence and resources.

Not unconnected with the development of this competitive institutional landscape, the Scottish partnership approach to economic development (Danson et al, 1999) had evolved to rationalise the complex nature of this mosaic of institutions and had subsequently been adopted throughout the European Union on the back of this perceived success. Regional structural plan teams (Roberts, 1997) and the European Partnerships (Cameron and Danson, 1999) were therefore also significant players in the Scottish support structure for training and business development in 1999 when the new Enterprise and Lifelong Learning Committee (ELLC) of the Scottish Parliament sat down to deliberate on its priorities for the first year. Despite an academic literature which places institutional thickness and capacity at the heart of the analysis of the economic development process (Macleod, 1997), almost inevitably the Committee expressed concern at the potential and real duplication and overlap between this myriad of agencies in Scotland. The ELLC therefore resolved to make its initial inquiry an examination of the degree to which public resources were being wasted and efforts undertaken inefficiently through this configuration of actors in local economic development. The Committee commenced its work in autumn 1999 and aimed to complete this study by spring 2000. An implicit objective of the inquiry was to assess the extent of disparity in the delivery of economic development activities across Scotland through the exploration of the effectiveness of different models of support in the context of this crowded institutional landscape. This chapter reports on the mapping exercise of that inquiry, the element which laid out for the first time the range of key players within each area in Scotland. Although similar reviews were initiated around this time by the local authorities through the Convention of Scottish Local Authorities (COSLA), by Scottish Enterprise, and by the Scottish Executive, while the European Partnerships funded under the 1996-1999 programmes were also faced with ad hoc and post hoc evaluations, the ELLC report represents the only truly independent research of the position at the end of the century.

The chapter is organised in the following way. In the next section the concepts of institutional thickness and capacity are introduced as background to the analysis of the position in Scotland. In section 7.3, the methodology of the ELLC research is outlined before the 'map' of Scottish economic development support is described. An exploration of the European partnerships and other players' activities is undertaken in section 7.4 along with a brief account of the COSLA audit of development activities to broaden out the information available for the research. The regional specific aspects of the *Framework for Economic Development in Scotland* (Scottish Executive, 2000) and the *Smart, Successful Scotland* policy for the regional development agencies (Scottish Executive, 2001) are reviewed in section 7.5 as a prelude to the discussion of the evidence of disparities in the delivery of economic development support across the nation.

7.2   Institutional Capacity and Thickness in Regional Economic Development

Since the late 1980s, it has been argued that regional economic development can be promoted through regional learning and intelligence embedded in the agents and governance structures of an area. This reasoning can be traced back to the 'notions of industrial districts, clustering and system areas and it is also associated with the themes of innovation strategies, institutional thickness and the embeddedness of development' (Kafkalas and Thoidou, 2000, p.115).

Much of the work of endogenous growth theorists also suggests that knowledge and innovation are significant factors in accounting for unexplained growth differentials between nations and regions (Boltho and Holtham, 1992; van der Ploeg and Tang, 1992; Scott 1992; Doeringer et al, 1987). These ideas have tended to displace the focus on the industrial structure of the region, its export base, and the availability and costs of the factors of production in explaining differential rates of economic development. The institutional framework is taken to be critical in the application of knowledge, including both the formal organisation, such as the regional development agency, and the informal, which by operating through 'tradition, custom or legal constraint, tends to create durable and routinised patterns of behaviour' (Hodgson, 1988, p.10). As much of this knowledge, by its very nature, is *tacit* and so not easily transferable, it is argued that the benefits of improved human resource development and networking will tend to accrue to the region where they are delivered and nurtured.

Morgan (1997), Cooke and Morgan (1998) and Lundvall (1992) have stressed the significance of relationships between agencies or partners in enhancing the effectiveness and successful adoption of local knowledge strategies in those processes of raising competitiveness, performance and innovation. The role of untraded interdependencies (such as labour markets, local conventions, norms, values, public or semi-public institutions) are highlighted as key in these processes. Much attention has been focused on the application of these concepts to regional innovation and enterprise, in particular by the New Regionalists (Amin and Robins, 1990), while they are also deemed to be relevant to the creation of capabilities and attitudes to economic development which are considered to underpin the enhanced capacity of successful economies and communities.

Confirming the spatial and community focus of these processes of human resource development, Gregersen and Johnson (1997, pp.481-482) make a distinction between 'the production of knowledge and the utilization of knowledge', and stress how the learning process becomes endogenous to the region. Similarly, Lundvall and Johnson (1994) and Storper (1995) identify the importance of communication between government, firms and others and the need for trust and co-operation between the economic actors if a strategy based on the knowledge or learning region is to be promoted effectively. The associated interactions between government, agencies and the other key partners are essentially in and of the community in which they are located, and so central to the establishment and nurturing of trust and co-operation. The success of strategies based on the notions of the knowledge economy and the learning society, and of the promotion of co-operation between agencies to avoid unnecessary overlap and duplication, therefore is inextricably dependent on the institutions specific to the region, and inevitably their effectiveness must involve an understanding of their respective roles and capabilities.

Against this theoretical background, the Enterprise and Lifelong Learning Committee embarked upon its 'Inquiry into the delivery of economic development, post-school vocational education and training (excluding higher education) and business support services at the local level in Scotland'. One particular area of focus was the co-ordination of services provided by different agencies at the local level, and the degree of overlap and duplication between organisations, with the objective of identifying the potential to improve the effectiveness of these services. For the different regional and local economies across Scotland, there is a range of structural and competitive forms characterising each area. The economies of the different regions of Scotland are described and analysed elsewhere in this book, especially in the detailed case studies in Chapters 3-6. In brief, in many LEC areas, non indigenous companies represent the core of many sectors and have a critical role to play in realising the potential for growth and development locally. This suggests the encouragement of competitiveness here will require specific policies and interventions which recognise this. In others, established and new small and medium enterprises have a greater role to play, suggesting a different balance of support services.

Despite these differences, the institutional capacity is often stressed in such strategies, and Scotland has a particularly rich landscape of organisations which work in partnership to the advantage of the economic community. The Committee was therefore required to audit business support services at the local level and to examine in some detail the provision of the core generic services within selected geographic areas if it was to identify examples of good practice in Scotland.

To ensure the future competitiveness of all the areas of Scotland requires that resources are applied efficiently in the delivery of support services. Having considered the specifics, this meant analysing the strategic framework, partly through consideration of the experiences of comparator areas through the establishment of the grid of services, and partly through an examination of a number of generic service types within particular areas. This would allow a better identification of the best practices and the capturing of synergies, as well as the elimination of wasteful duplication. In turn, the conclusions of the ELLC and the associated Department should promote actions in support of local economic growth and suggest methods to generate a strategy to realise the benefits of the policy environment.

7.3   Mapping the Economic Development Landscape

To allow the Enterprise and Lifelong Learning Committee to undertake a description and analysis of the degree of duplication and overlap within areas of Scotland, a *mapping exercise* involving the cataloguing of local economic development services in Scotland, was carried out in early 2000 based on eighteen areas covering the country. This exercise defined the area, the development agency responsible for the area, any European Union Structural Fund designation and assisted area status, the key organisations at core and subsidiary levels, and the key issues facing the economy. Descriptions of the principal activities, partnerships and strategies were presented. These were based on the submissions to the Committee Inquiry, the Written Reports, the case study visits made by the Committee, and such other material as it was possible to collect and collate in the time available. The areas selected were based on either the territory of the local enterprise company or the local authority, or some combination of the two. In a number of cases, the boundaries of the LEC and local authority were coterminous: Shetland, Orkney, Western Isles, Fife, Borders, Dumfries and Galloway, Glasgow. In others, a limited number of local authorities with a significant degree of cohesion nested into the relevant LEC territory with no appreciable difficulties: Grampian, Lothian, Ayrshire, Lanarkshire. A few areas in the Highlands and Islands had boundaries which overlap in terms of Highlands & Islands Enterprise (HIE) and Scottish Enterprise (SEN) LECs and/or local authorities, though this did not appear to create major difficulties: Highland, Argyll and Bute, Moray, Badenoch and Strathspey. In the three remaining areas, there were a number of local authorities with perhaps less internal cohesion: Renfrewshire, Dunbartonshire and Forth Valley. In all cases, the territory defined offered the greatest coherence in terms of the actual delivery of economic development activity, though this will have sacrificed detail at the margin. Where there were important local initiatives specific to a local authority area within a LEC area, for instance, these were identified separately in the profile.

The second element of the report to the ELLC incorporated a *detailed discussion* of a number of generic areas of activity. This covered business development, general business development, innovation and product development, export and trade development, property and managed workspace, training for young people, training provision for the unemployed and social inclusion, and provision for workplace training. These reflected the main programmes and activities of the key players in local economic development. In each case, case study material was used to illustrate the wider picture with significant differences drawn out.

Finally, a *grid* of direct, advisory, financial and other forms of support delivered by agencies at the European, UK, Scottish and local levels was compiled.

The ongoing negotiations over the new EU Structural Fund area designations and the redrawing of the assisted areas map made some of the detail in that section preliminary and incomplete. What the grid highlighted, however, was the large range and forms of support available across most of Scotland although there was little uniformity with local and regional initiatives abounding.

Thus, the primary source of information for this analysis and for the ELLC report were the submissions to the inquiry, with other sources utilised where time and resources permitted. The period and the forms of consultation allowed ample opportunity for contributions to be made and so to be included in the deliberations of the Committee. This would have suggested a rich vein of material to draw upon in compiling this map of the economic development landscape. However, what offered itself as a simple exercise in reality was unique. Although the information submitted to the Committee was incomplete, there had been no previous attempts to undertake this sort of mapping before and the picture undoubtedly has continued to evolve since. In response to this, some of the initial feedback received perhaps indicated a divergence between what is perceived and what is actually happening in the field, accounting for some of the questions raised over the interpretation of service delivery locally across Scotland. Undoubtedly, for many agencies there is a belief that their activities are critical in promoting economic development, but this is often not the full story. Believing that the particular organisation is at the centre of the economic development universe locally is natural but there are many perspectives over this landscape. Without a mapping exercise, it is tempting to adopt the perspective of Copernicus, with similar outcomes for the author?

Although the mapping exercise produced a comprehensive description of the key players and projects across all parts of Scotland, the precis of the report (ELLC, 2000-01) identified the significance of the local enterprise company and the local authority in the typical area in all fields and at all levels of policy and practice. Table 7.1 confirms their leading roles throughout the activities of the economic development landscape. Partnerships dominate as a mode of operating in this context, with other players typically tending to be involved as appropriate in a standard manner across the country. More detailed work on the delivery of, for instance, support for business startups, revealed more diverse practices across Scotland but with a growing consensus over the benefits of adopting a co-ordinated facility within and between areas. There is a high degree of standardisation of provision, therefore, with the recommendations of the ELLC paralleling the conclusions of the reviews of the enterprise networks carried out by the Enterprise and Lifelong Learning Department and the agencies themselves.

Subsequent to these analyses, Careers Scotland has been created as an all-age nationwide service, working in association with Scottish Enterprise and Highlands and Islands Enterprise. Local Economic Fora (LEFs) were introduced by the government in response to the arguments in the research for the Inquiry so realising the potential of the *Joint Economic Strategy; Economic Forum* in the typical Scottish area model.

Table 7.1   Economic development: the typical Scottish area model, responsibilities of key players

Local Enterprise Company (LEC)	Joint Economic Strategy; Economic Forum; Training and Learning Forum; Business Development; General Business Development; Innovation and Product Development; Export and Trade Development; Property and Managed Workspace; Training for Young People; Training for the Unemployed and Social Inclusion; Provision for Workplace Training
Scottish Enterprise National (SEN)	Some depending on area; Innovation and Product Development
Local Authorities (LAs)	Joint Economic Strategy; Economic Forum; Training and Learning Forum; Business Development; General Business Development; Innovation and Product Development; Export and Trade Development; Property and Managed Workspace; Training for Young People; Training for the Unemployed and Social Inclusion
Chamber of Commerce	Economic Forum; Training and Learning Forum; Business Development; General Business Development; Export and Trade Development
Enterprise Trusts (ETs)	Business Development; General Business Development
Area Tourist Boards (ATBs)	Economic Forum; Business Development
Careers Company	Training and Learning Forum
Employment Service	Training and Learning Forum; Training for the Unemployed and Social Inclusion
Training Providers	Training for Young People; Provision for Workplace Training
Non Departmental Public Bodies (NDPBs)	Economic Forum
Scottish Trade International (STI)	Export and Trade Development
Prince's Scottish Young Business Trust (PSYBT)	Business Development
Higher Education Institutions (HEIs)	Economic Forum; Training and Learning Forum; Innovation and Product Development
Further Education Colleges (FE)	Economic Forum; Training and Learning Forum; Training for Young People; Provision for Workplace Training
Scottish Council Development and Industry (SCDI)	Export and Trade Development
Employers/private sector	Economic Forum; Training and Learning Forum; Property and Managed Workspace; Training for Young People
Trades Unions	Economic Forum; Training and Learning Forum
Voluntary sector	Training and Learning Forum; Training for the Unemployed and Social Inclusion
Community sector	Economic Forum; Training and Learning Forum; Training for the Unemployed and Social Inclusion

7.4   Other Players in Business Development, Vocational Education and Training

Although it is clear that there is a growing preference to adopt partnership working as the model approach to overcoming duplication and overlap, as will become apparent below some of the most significant partnerships were only marginally covered in the mapping and descriptive exercises. The European Partnerships in Strathclyde, Highlands and Islands, the South and the East of Scotland have all been instrumental in the promotion of enhanced co-operation across agencies and organisations. The modes of working in these partnerships has engendered an atmosphere of trust and co-operation in the action groups and programme monitoring committees which determine policies and ensure their efficient implementation. By involving a wide range of partners in the development and implementation of common strategies and frameworks over a number of years, there has been a building of respect and common agendas. In turn, this has led to improved levels of skills and capacities in partnership working, greater understanding of the linkages and objectives of other agencies, and so an appreciation of how further co-operation could lead to synergies, efficiencies and economies.

The European partnerships have been critical, therefore, in bringing together economic development agencies and so in making further partnership possible, productive and non threatening. As long term relationships are established, so organisations are less likely to adopt short term payoffs and are increasingly exposed to the benefits of joint working. The partnership model also becomes a vehicle for the dissemination and promotion of good practice.

The mid term evaluations of the regional European Partnerships across Scotland and of the nationwide Objective 3 ESF programme confirmed the significance of the Structural Funds to the development of businesses, communities and human resources, and to economic and social cohesion. Anticipating enlargement, concerns over the future funding of such interventions in the Scottish economy are beginning to be raised as the end of the traditional Structural Fund support approaches in 2006 (Bachtler et al, 2002). Impacts are likely to be felt most in the Highlands and Islands and in Strathclyde, where many training initiatives and intermediate labour market projects have been financed over the years and continue to provide essential training and employment opportunities. The withdrawal of general and significant EU support will tend to lead to some renationalisation of regional policy (HM Treasury et al, 2003) so that business development and investment may not be affected so critically. These changes, therefore, may have differential effects across Scotland, and make economic and social cohesion and human resource development both more difficult to promote and yet have to be resourced more through specifically Scottish budgets than hitherto.

Similar to the European Partnerships, the Structure Plan teams from the former regional councils have played a critical role in establishing a framework for the development of economic strategies at the regional and lower levels. By encouraging the key players to address the impacts of certain forms of activity from the perspective of other parts of a region, they have been instrumental in creating the environment where regional economic strategies can be forged. The structural plan team directly and in their wider consultations can ensure that strategic sites for industrial or business development, the provision of related infrastructure, the linkage of education and training initiatives across the region and to other activities, and the delivery of joint projects for levering EU money can all be developed more effectively. Technical, economic, business and joint policy studies have been organised through and with structural plan teams, while the Common Economic Development Perspective which has so enhanced the single programming document for Strathclyde was developed through these offices.

Nevertheless, there have been instances where institutional rivalry and lack of partnership working have undermined the formation and implementation of regional strategies, with the history of the redevelopment of the Clyde being an obvious example of such obstacles to consensus progress.

In a number of the case study areas across Scotland and in several of the submissions it was clear that two technical areas deserve further consideration: economic and labour market intelligence and information; and the development of regional and local economic strategies, frameworks and fora. Both of these issues are linked to the activities of the European Partnerships and the Structure Plan teams. There were many informed requests through the submissions to the ELLC, paralleling the COSLA/Scottish Enterprise best practice guide *Working Together in Partnership*, for a Scottish economic development framework to be constructed. It was argued that this would allow joint economic strategies to be developed by partners within regions of Scotland which were competent, consistent and compatible with what was being proposed at higher levels. The Scottish Executive subsequently launched such a top down process and this is discussed below.

The second and related issue concerns some of these essential materials and the provision of information and intelligence on the local, regional and national economy in particular. In recent times, the Strathclyde Labour Market Information Service, Fife Labour Market Information Service (developed from Fife Vocational Education and Training Strategy), and the Eastern Scotland Labour Market and Economic Intelligence Project (LMEIP) have provided an information service for areas across central Scotland. Indeed, apart from the south of Scotland, Grampian and the HIE area there is the promise of a consistent approach already, while these latter regions also should be well able to play a similar role in overcoming market failures. There is a degree of potential duplication too, however, with sub regional projects in several areas replicating the same basic groundwork and much use of consultants to interpret publicly available data.

Scottish Enterprise, Highlands and Islands Enterprise and the Scottish Executive conducted a study into 'mapping existing labour market information activity in Scotland' which aimed to: build on existing and previous work, such as the LMI audit and recent evaluations and reviews of existing LMI systems; identify good practice; review the formalisation of LMI systems through remits, quality standards and standard output agreements; and suggest a suitable approach and method by which to deliver LMI in future, which meets (and can continue to develop to meet) changing customer needs. Following this study, a Scottish labour market intelligence unit was announced in early summer 2000 and launched as Futureskills Scotland in 2002. As with the proposal to construct a Scottish national economic framework, with complementary regional and local joint economic strategies (discussed below), so it could be argued that the supporting labour market and economic intelligence requirements are correctly being addressed and made consistent across Scotland through this initiative.

In many areas and across many aspects of business and economic development, a rich mixture of community, voluntary and trades union bodies provide a series of often critical support mechanisms to the main players. However, these are often hidden and so not fully appreciated as crucial to the effective and efficient operation of economic development. The Scottish Low Pay Unit, for instance, is frequently contacted by SMEs for information on such topics as minimum wage rates, hours of work and statutory rights. These sectors are explicitly recognised in certain parts of Scotland as key players, with Highlands and Islands Enterprise both duty bound to incorporate their views, but also willing to draw on their local expertise, experience and capacities to involve the community. In Social Inclusion Partnership (SIP) areas, the involvement of local people is both an objective of the programme but also an essential part of the process of inclusion and empowerment. ACAS, the Health and Safety Executive, the Inland Revenue and other public agencies likewise tend to be the first or early port of call for many new firms, SMEs, and other actors in the economy who only rarely encounter the need for information and advice. Similarly, the specialist expertise and experience contained in these organisations is frequently invaluable to the core players in economic development.

Many of the most successful task forces, partnerships and strategies have been developed with the full co-operation and involvement of the STUC and trade unions. The Prestwick Task Force, Caterpillar Working Party, and the Fife Redundancy Advisory Group, for instance, have all demonstrated the advantages of such co-operation. Elsewhere in Europe, it is seen as essential to involve all the social partners in the development of strategies and frameworks and this approach has been adopted in Ayrshire, Dumfries and Galloway and the Borders with a good impression of success. The adoption of a more pro-active approach to dealing with potential redundancies has been best practice in North America for many years. The forward planning of US defence establishments must incorporate any possible exit strategy, including the generation of new enterprises and a consideration of the impact of withdrawal on SMEs. The Canadian RISK programme to address large scale redundancies through a federal task force and partnership model has been successful in encouraging labour markets to adjust more effectively, timeously and efficiently than where markets are left to their own mechanisms. The need for good intelligence and intervention at an early stage characterises these interventions in the market. The examples of co-operative working in Scotland in the Borders, Prestwick and elsewhere similarly support a wider use of co-ordinated efforts to plan strategically to meet the challenges of local and regional economic change.

One instance where it is commonly suggested that there could be wider involvement in Scotland is tourism, with a clear need expressed by many that area tourist boards should be incorporated more directly into economic development strategies and fora. The resolution of this continues to be a problematic area in Scottish local economic development, reflecting difficulties within this sector as much as complications with partnership working and the other attributes of the industry.

The advantages of involving a wide range of partners also stresses the need to consider economic development in broad terms and not simply as business development. Regional strategies across the developed world which have defined the policy area narrowly have tended to be much less successful than those which consider the linkages between the varied elements of economic development in a holistic way. The logic of social inclusion, European and other partnerships confirms this need to address all the opportunities and challenges in particular localities as well as in Scotland as a whole.

As a corollary, the essential roles that local authorities play in delivering many services, and in investing in and maintaining infrastructure must be recognised in the analysis of local and regional economic development. Ensuring that they have the capacities and resources to fulfil these roles is significant. Their experiences of working with the socially excluded and their management of the services which most affect the lives of people in SIP areas also means they have a clear role to play in addressing this part of the overall economic development agenda. The creation of Communities Scotland, from elements of Scottish Homes – the Housing Agency for Scotland – and of Scottish Enterprise was an attempt to improve linkages between housing and economic development. The transfer of Glasgow's housing stock to the Glasgow Housing Association (GHA) was similarly justified in part by such thinking. However, success with each of these changes is unproven as yet, confirming that institutional change alone is insufficient to address economic and social exclusion.

A survey of the economic development activities of local government in Scotland (EKOS 2000) confirmed that Scottish local authorities were indeed significant players in this field. Direct economic development expenditure was estimated at £92m in 1998/99, with a further £20m of EU funds approved for relevant projects under their sponsorship. This compares with the annual budgets of Scottish Enterprise £455.2m and Highlands and Islands Enterprise £78m at that time. The consultants argued that since unitary authorities were introduced after local government reorganisation in 1996, there has been greater joint working between departments and rationalisation of procedures within authorities against a background of Best Value and Community Planning. Nevertheless, they believe the degree of integration 'remains patchy'. Most councils now have explicit economic development strategies and are involved formally in economic development plans and partnerships with other local players, particularly the LECs, with LEFs now confirming such links. Indeed, the majority claim that their priorities match those of their partner LEC. However, the consultants argued that there was room for improvement and especially that effective strategy development was the 'key to a more consistent and joined up approach to Councils (sic) economic development activities' (EKOS, 2000, p.ii).

A measure of the significance of local authorities' activities in Scotland can be gained from the average expenditure on economic development per head of population. This was estimated to be £18.12 in 1999, and contrasts with a 1998 Audit Commission review of the position in England and Wales which suggested that only £4.21 was spent on equivalent activities elsewhere in Britain. This affirms the important role local government plays in Scotland, even with the more comprehensive economic development institutions existing here anyway. From Table 7.2, it can be seen also that, in a period of restricted resources, although local authorities continue to intervene across a range of areas of activity, they are devoting more to non physical and business oriented programmes. Expenditure on human capital development and inclusion are becoming more prominent along with support to the operations of other agencies, which is suggestive of partnership working and networking. Especially within the context of the ELLC inquiry, the report also stresses the essential and progressive role of partnership, with broadly positive feedback from local authorities and an embracing of the need for increased joint working and shared economic development strategies.

Table 7.2   Economic development expenditure, 1997-1999 (£000)

	1997/98	*1998/99*	*Change, %*
Business competitiveness	15,189	14,809	-2.5
Physical business infrastructure	17,084	16,189	-5.2
Training and human resource development	10,520	11,185	+6.3
Economic inclusion/CED/area initiatives	7,294	7,554	+3.6
Generic area and tourism promotion	17,149	13,952	-18.6
Core funding to other local development organisations	4,030	4,375	+8.6
SUB TOTAL	71,266	68,064	-4.5
Professional and support staff	22,865	23,811	+4.1
TOTAL	94,131	91,875	-2.5

Source: Table 1.1, EKOS (2000).

7.5   Framework for Economic Development in Scotland and Smart Successful Scotland

According to the *Framework for Economic Development in Scotland* (FEDS) (Scottish Executive, 2000), balanced economic development is one of the regional objectives of the Executive. However, while the undertaking of economic activity in more peripheral regions is seen to be less problematic with better communications alone, FEDS identifies disparities and growth inequalities in Central Scotland with some concern. In particular, differences between the prosperous Edinburgh economy, with its increasing developmental pressure over the coming years, and the struggling regions and communities in the old industrial areas are highlighted. In a significant contrast with the philosophy which established the regional development agencies in the 1960s and 1970s, the dynamism of the leading areas is to be protected and promoted through the strategies of the Executive and its agencies. Planning and other regional instruments of economic development, therefore, are to work with market forces, with spillover effects encouraged to capture these benefits within Scotland and to address constraints on further growth.

Thus, it is argued that it would be 'inappropriate to seek to resist the implications of these economic forces insofar as they impact on regional and community prosperity for better or for worse' (Scottish Executive, 2000, p.65). In the traditional industrial areas of the west of Scotland and the more peripheral regions of the north and south, disparities are to be faced through mainstream top down supply side policies; it is highly questionable whether these on their own can address the needs of these shattered economies. The underpinnings of the knowledge economy, lessons from the successful regeneration of deindustrialised communities, and the rationale for establishing regional development agencies (Cameron and Danson, 1999) all suggest that market failure will continue and these areas will not benefit from trickle down or trickle across growth. Explicit intervention in the economy will continue to be necessary as a prerequisite for sustainable economic growth.

Perhaps in an acknowledgement that the aspirations in FEDS would be difficult to fulfil, partly because the Scottish Executive has such limited leverage over the Scottish economy (Newlands 1999), increased attention has been paid to the role and responsibilities of the development agencies. *Smart, Successful Scotland* established an updated agenda for Scottish Enterprise and Highlands and Islands Enterprise in 2001 (Scottish Executive, 2001). However, with LEFs coming into existence, a centralisation of several LEC functions into their respective headquarters, the creation of Futureskills Scotland, Careers Scotland, Communities Scotland, trans-Scotland approaches to business development and trade and export promotions etc, it is understandable that the organisations have struggled to establish a clear idea of their status in the economic development field.

Burdened with expectations, functions, responsibilities and partnerships, SE and HIE often have appeared overwhelmed. The concentration of so many powers on unelected quangos which are heavily scrutinised by Parliament, government and public alike does not seem an efficient way to deliver their many services in Scotland. The slow take-up of EU funds for business development support by Scottish Enterprise and the need for integration within and across the new elements of these quangos has undoubtedly diverted their attention, resources and energies. Whether the anticipated long term efficiency gains are secured remains to be seen.

7.6   Conclusion

Within a crowded institutional landscape, the dominant partnership approach to regional and local economic development in Scotland can be seen as a way to address the problems of duplication and overlap between agencies and organisations. However, although it appears to satisfy this particular public policy objective, other aspects of the delivery of services to the community have been neglected. In the context of the New Regionalism, but also more generally, there is a danger of ossification of the agencies and their initiatives across Scotland if the same standard package of measures is imposed throughout the land. The need to be aware of good practice and best value in supporting indigenous and inward investment cannot be denied but the loss of the benefits of customised and tailored solutions to local problems is threatened by the introduction of national gateways to small and new business support, standard export partnerships etc. Yet, it could be argued that, what appear from the map of economic development activities to be bottom up partnerships, in reality are increasingly structures and modes of delivery which are determined from above. The community of SMEs, local employers, trade unions and elected representatives are being progressively removed from the arena in favour of professionalisation within a nationalised regional framework.

Recent analysis of institutional changes elsewhere suggests that other nations are addressing such problems by diverting functions away from RDAs or by creating dedicated smaller agencies with specific tasks and a good deal of autonomy (Brown and Danson, 2003). There is a real sense that the institutional landscape in Scotland is ossifying with limited institutional and corporate learning and innovation, in contrast with former times. It could be argued that there is indeed a forgetting of what works.

Economic disparities in Scotland require a disparate set of local priorities and programmes rather than the top down imposition of Scottish wide one-size-fits-all packages. Questions over the optimal size of the LEC areas appropriate for different geographies within Scotland, their funding regimes and the extent to which they should be in competition with each other as much as in enforced co-operation remain unanswered, and often unasked. The confluence of New Regionalism and supply side, market oriented policies (Webb and Collis, 2000) perhaps has made this approach most attractive but that does not guarantee success. This chapter has suggested that there is a great array of institutions and agencies, mostly but not exclusively local and national state organisations, operating within each area of Scotland. That we have such a rich landscape of institutional thickness and capacity and yet continue to face the disparities identified already suggests that there are wider issues for the Scottish Executive and Enterprise and Lifelong Learning Committee (now the Enterprise and Culture Committee) and Scottish civic society to consider than the standardisation of the delivery mechanisms of economic development policies. The quality of the institutional capabilities in the West of Scotland is especially poignant given their endemic economic problems. Returning to an analysis of the underlying structural constraints and potentials of the regions of Scotland recommends itself as a more fruitful task for the Parliament and Executive than the perceptions of overlap. Examination of the dislocations to traditional markets and linkages and the failure of the economic strategies of the last two decades to embed sustainable growth deserves to be raised up the research and policy agenda before more tinkering with the infrastructure is offered as a panacea.

References

Amin, A. and Robins, K. (1990) 'Industrial districts and regional development: limits and possibilities' in Pyke, F., Becattini, G. and Sengenberger, W. (eds) *Industrial Districts and Interfirm Co-operation in Italy*, Geneva, pp.185 –219.

Bachtler, J., Josserand, F. and Michie, R. (2002) *EU Enlargement and the Reform of the Structural Funds: The Implications for Scotland*, scotecon, University of Stirling.

Boltho, A. and Holtham, G. (1992) 'The assessment: new approaches to economic growth', *Oxford Review of Economic Policy*, 8(4), pp.1-14.

Brown, R. and Danson, M. (2003) *Regional Development Agencies: Breaking the Mould?*, RSAI British and Irish Section 33rd Annual Conference, St Andrews, 20-22 August.

Cameron, G. and Danson, M. (1999) 'The European partnership model and the changing role of regional development agencies. A regional development and organisation perspective' in Danson, M., Halkier, H. and Cameron, G. *Governance, Institutional Change and Development*, Ashgate, Aldershot, pp.11-36.

Cooke, P. and Morgan, K. (1998) *The Associational Economy: Firms, Regions and Innovation*, Oxford, Oxford University Press.

Danson, M., Fairley, J., Lloyd, G. and Newlands, D. (1990) 'Scottish Enterprise: an evolving approach to integrating economic development in Scotland' in Brown, A. Parry, R. (eds) *The Scottish Government Yearbook 1990*, Edinburgh, Edinburgh University Press.

Danson, M., Fairley, J., Lloyd, G. and Turok, I. (1999) 'The European Structural Fund Partnerships in Scotland – new forms of governance for regional development?', *Scottish Affairs*, 27, pp.23-40.

Danson, M., Lloyd, G. and Newlands, D. (1991) 'The Scottish Development Agency, economic development and technology policy' in Ter Heide, H. (ed) *Technological Change and Spatial Policy*, Royal Netherlands Geographical Society, Amsterdam, pp.179-190.

Doeringer P., Terkla, D. and Topakian, G. (1987) *Invisible Factors in Local Economic Development*, New York, Oxford University Press.

EKOS (2000) *Survey of the Economic Development Activities of Local Government in Scotland*, Report to COSLA, Edinburgh.

Gregersen, B. and Johnson, B. (1997) 'Learning economies, innovation systems and European integration', *Regional Studies*, 31(5), pp.479-490.

Gripaios, P. and Munday, M. (1999) 'Regional winners and losers from recent trends in utility rationalization', *Regional Studies*, 33(8), pp.769-778.

Halkier, H. and Danson, M. (1997) 'Regional Development Agencies in Western Europe: a survey of characteristics and trends', *European Urban and Regional Studies*, 4(3), pp.243-256.

HM Treasury, the Department of Trade and Industry and the Office of the Deputy Prime Minister (2003) *A Modern Regional Policy for the United Kingdom*, London.

Hodgson, G. (1988) *Economics and Institutions*, Cambridge, Polity Press.

Kafkalas, G. and Thoidou, E. (2000) 'Cohesion policy and the role of RDAs in the making of an intelligent region: lessons from the Southern European periphery' in Danson, M., Halkier, H. and Cameron, G. *Governance, Institutional Change and Development*, Ashgate, Aldershot, pp.115-137.

Lloyd, M.G. and Rowan-Robinson, J. (1987) 'Local authority economic development activity in Scotland: further evidence', *Local Economy*, 2(1), pp.49-54.

Lundvall, B.A. (ed) (1992) *National Systems of Innovation*, London, Pinter.

Lundvall, B.A. and Johnson, B. (1994) 'The learning economy', *Journal of Industry Studies*, 1(2), pp.23-42.

MacLeod, G. (1997) '"Institutional thickness" and industrial governance in Lowland Scotland', *Area*, 29, pp.299-311.

McQuaid, R. (1993) 'Economic development and local authorities: the Scottish case', *Local Economy*, 8(2), pp.100-116.

Morgan, K. (1997) 'The learning region: institutions, innovation and regional renewal'. *Regional Studies*, 31(5), pp.491-503.

Newlands, D (1999) 'The economic powers and potential of a devolved Scottish Parliament: lessons from economic theory and European experience' in McCarthy, J. and Newlands, D. (eds) *Governing Scotland: Problems and Prospects. The Economic Impact of the Scottish Parliament*, Aldershot, Ashgate, pp.11-24.

Roberts, P. (1997) 'Sustainability and spatial competence: an examination of the evolution, ephemeral nature, and possible future of regional planning in Britain' in Danson, M., Hill, S. and Lloyd, G. (eds) *Regional Governance and Economic Development*, European Research in Regional Science, 7, London, Pion, pp.7-25.

Scott, M. (1992) 'A new theory of endogenous economic growth', *Oxford Review of Economic Policy*, 8(4), pp.29-42.

Scottish Executive (2000) *Framework for Economic Development in Scotland*, Edinburgh.

Scottish Executive (2001) *A Smart, Successful Scotland: Ambitions for the Enterprise Networks*, Edinburgh.

Storper, M. (1995) 'The resurgence of regional economies, ten years later: the region as a nexus of untraded interdependencies', *European Urban and Regional Studies*, 2, pp.191-221.

Van der Ploeg, F. and Tang, P. (1992) 'The macroeconomics of growth: an international perspective', *Oxford Review of Economic Policy*, 8(4), pp.15-28.

Webb, D. and Collis, C. (2000) 'Regional development agencies and the 'new regionalism' in England', *Regional Studies*, 34(9), pp.857-864.

Chapter 8

Vocational Education and Training

John Fairley

8.1 Introduction

Vocational education and training (VET) was devolved before the creation of the Scottish Parliament. The process began with administrative changes in the 1970s, in anticipation of devolution (Anderson and Fairley, 1983). In the early 1990s, training policy was devolved as part of the then Prime Minister, John Major's 'taking stock' initiative. The establishment of the Parliament created the potential for democratic oversight and accountability for VET. The first enquiry by the Parliament's Enterprise and Lifelong Learning Committee[1] included an examination of aspects of work-based learning, while the second focussed on lifelong learning[2] (ELLC, 2002).

The Parliament's responsibility for VET is one of the features which makes it more powerful than the German Länder (Leonardy, 1998). However, during the first years of the Parliament, VET did not appear to be high in the Executive's priorities. Indeed, as we shall see, the main VET initiatives were more clearly identified with the office of the Lord Chancellor than with Scottish institutions.

There is little difference between Scotland's political parties on VET though, as we shall see, there may be emerging differences between Scotland, England and Wales. In general, the statements on VET which are made by the main political parties seem to reflect Scottish support for a quite remarkable international consensus which has two main aspects. The first asserts that the coming together of 'globalisation' and the 'knowledge economy' require that nations which wish to remain 'competitive' must 'invest' heavily in VET, and in education more widely, and that individuals take responsibility for their own 'lifelong learning'. This set of propositions appears to be driving VET policy internationally.

The second area concerns the policy response to unemployment, and reflects a strong consensus between the USA and the UK. There are, in summary, two main aspects of this argument. The first is that unemployment is not a problem of insufficient jobs. Rather it is that the unemployed lack the appropriate skills, attitudes and behaviours to be able to get and keep the available jobs. VET is the appropriate supply side response to unemployment. The second aspect is really a

---

[1] The author was an Adviser to the enquiry.
[2] The author contributed to the background research for this enquiry.

restatement of Say's Law, arguing that an improved supply of skilled labour will somehow lead to job generation and increased levels of employment.

This is not the place for a thorough review of these theories and the available critiques. However, the strength of the consensus is perhaps demonstrated in the fact that, while critiques are emerging[3], they appear to be having little impact on policy formation.

8.2   The Characteristics of VET

Perhaps the first characteristic worthy of comment is that VET is little discussed. It attracts little research effort.[4] Less is known about VET than mainstream parts of education such as schooling and the universities. Indeed it is not possible to say how much public expenditure supports VET in Scotland (Fairley and McArthur, 1999; Blake Stevenson, 2001), and there are no reliable data on spending by employers.

A second characteristic is that employer participation in VET is almost entirely voluntary. Despite the fact that a tradition of voluntarism has consistently failed to produce sufficient training at higher skill levels, the main political parties seem to be committed to this principle. There are only three economic sectors – construction, engineering construction, and sea fishing – where VET organisations have statutory powers to raise training levies[5] from employers (Fairley and McArthur, 1999). This is regarded as a symptom of VET weakness in these sectors, in that levy powers have been retained because employers have proved unable or unwilling to bring forward adequate voluntary arrangements. There is simply no critical discussion of the limits of voluntarism (Streeck, 1998).

The third most important characteristic is the profusion of institutions involved in VET. The main Executive Department is Enterprise and Lifelong Learning (ELLD). In 2001/02 ELLD had a budget of more than £2,150m. Some 70 per cent of this went to further education (FE) and higher education (HE). Around £455m went to the Enterprise Networks and an estimated 21 per cent of this went in training programmes (Fairley, 2003). However other parts of the Executive play substantial roles in VET and lifelong learning. As an example, the recently created NHS Education for Scotland spends nearly £200m per year on lifelong learning for health care workers. The Scottish Prison Service funds the VET associated with

---

[3] Grant (1998) and Gray (1998) offer critiques of 'globalisation'. Ashton and Green (1996) offer a critique of the relationship of VET to the economy. Paterson (1999) and Warhurst and Thompson (1999) offer elements of a critique from Scottish perspectives. There is a tradition of critical literature on the role of VET in tackling unemployment, stretching back to the early 1980s. In the contemporary debate, see in particular Turok and Webster (1998), Turok and Edge (1999) and Webster (2000). Fairley (1998a) offers a critique of the New Deal for young unemployed people.

[4] A recent comprehensive account of Scottish education (Bryce and Humes, 1999) has over 1,000 pages and 112 chapters. However, only one, 11 page chapter is devoted to VET (Weir, 1999). The second edition (2003) gives VET more attention.

[5] In construction and engineering construction, the levy is based on payroll costs, while in sea fishing it is based on the weight of the catch.

rehabilition of prisoners (Blake Stevenson, 2001). We return to the issue of 'fragmentation' below.

In the delivery of VET there is a bewildering range of organisations of different types. There are 47 FE colleges, Sector Skills Councils (until recently National Training Organisations), 22 Local Enterprise Companies, the 32 local authorities, and others. VET is funded through EU Structural Funds and programmes, ranging from fishing and agriculture, to urban regeneration. Social Inclusion Partnerships, urban regeneration partnerships, rural development partnerships, and 23 New Deal partnerships are all concerned with VET. Some universities have substantial VET activities.

Given the degree of institutional complexity, it is perhaps not surprising, that 'strategy' for VET in Scotland has tended to be very weak (Fairley and Paterson, 1999). In recent times 'strategy' has consisted primarily of exhortations to employers to do more. The Advisory Scottish Council for Education and Training Targets (ASCETT) set annual targets for VET and for skills levels. However, after five years when it became clear that this attempt at 'moral suasion' had had no measurable impact on VET, the ASCETT targets were quietly discontinued. It may be that VET is simply so fragmented that the capacity for stronger approaches to 'strategy' is not present (Fairley and McArthur, 1999).

VET has long been characterised by a plethora of initiatives and programmes which are generally only poorly co-ordinated, if at all, which sometimes compete, and which are often discontinued after a short period of implementation (Fairley, 1989). Commenting on the situation in the late 1990s, Lowe (1999) pointed to the tenuous nature of the links between initiatives and strategy.

The preferred approach to governance issues prioritises partnership and consensus (Fairley, 1998b). Even where central government hoped that its reforms would lead to greater competition, successful efforts have been made to ensure co-operative forms of working. For example, while in England there is considerable competition between FE colleges and across the FE-schools divide, in Scotland the situation is characterised by co-operation (Finlay, 1996).

One relatively new and unique characteristic of VET for the unemployed, which has been introduced by the Westminster Labour government, is compulsion (Fairley and Paterson 2000). Unemployed people who refuse to take part in the New Deals for the young and the older unemployed suffer loss of benefits, with the sanctions being applied at 100 per cent. Jarvis (1997) has argued that there is consensus support for compulsion across the political parties at Westminster. However, the all party Scottish Affairs Committee criticised this aspect of the New Deal for young people and urged the UK government to think again (Fairley, 1998a).

A second characteristic of contemporary VET, which is also the result of Labour policy, and something of a paradox, is that the key initiatives underway are being driven by Westminster. Modern Apprenticeships (MA), the now abandoned Individual Learning Accounts (ILA), Scottish University for Industry (SuFI), the Trade Union Fund for Learning (TUFL), and the New Deal (ND) all have their origins at Westminster. In a policy area which appeared to be wholly devolved, the years after 1997 saw a strong centralisation of control at Westminster. Indeed it was not until the ELLC Enquiry of 2001-02, that the Parliament began to really exert itself in this policy area.

8.3 The Institutional Framework

In policy and funding terms, the most important part of the Executive is the Enterprise and Lifelong Learning Department (ELLD) (Fairley 2003).

In delivery terms, VET seems to be even more fragmented than the more discussed case of local economic development. At the time of writing, there are 47 FE Colleges, the FE sector being by far the most important provider of Vocational Qualifications (VQs). 43 of these colleges became incorporated bodies following their removal from local authority control in 1993. Two are trusts, and the colleges in Orkney and Shetland remain with their local councils. The network of colleges is the basis for the University of the Highlands and Islands, one of the most ambitious educational initiatives of recent years which is widely expected to bring economic benefit to the area (Newlands and Parker, 1998). In July 1999, FE was given its own Funding Council. In 1999-2000, the FE sector enrolled 434,435 students on a wide range of courses from vocational training to higher education.

Almost 90 per cent of FE courses are vocational, and more than 80 per cent are part time. The evolving nature of FE made the sector strategically important to a number of government priorities including VET and work based learning; access for communities, older students and women; and the expansion of higher education, more of which was being delivered by FE. The sector also played a central role in New Deal and Modern Apprenticeship (see Scottish Office, 1999a). Research carried out for the Scottish Office by Raab (1999) showed that over 90 per cent of those resident in Scotland lived less than 30 minutes drive from a college. Comprehensive data and information are readily available for the FE sector. In 2001-02, the Further Education Funding Council (FEFC) budget was some £418m (Fairley, 2003).

There are 22 local enterprise companies (LECs) which are controlled by Scottish Enterprise (SE) and Highlands and Islands Enterprise (HIE), which in turn report to ELLD. The LECs have enjoyed responsibility for the centralised 'volume' VET programmes for the unemployed, although the arrival of New Deal changed this somewhat (see section 8.5). The LECs also fund some VET through business development packages, though there are no reliable data on this (Fairley and McArthur, 1999). Public funding for Modern Apprenticeship is channelled through the LECs which have some policy discretion, e.g. whether or not to fund older entrants to apprenticeship. This may restrict access for groups who enter the labour market later in life, for example women returners. Again data on the funding of apprenticeships are not in the public domain. The LECs are entitled to representation on the boards of incorporated colleges, the government having rejected a recommendation by the National Audit Office (1998) that the right to automatic representation be ended.

In 2000, there were 71 National Training Organisations (NTOs), most of which operated across Britain. The NTOs were approved and loosely regulated by the then Whitehall Department for Education and Employment (DfEE). In Scotland they were co-ordinated by the Scottish Council of National Training Organisations (SCONTO). The DFEE required the NTOs to consider Scotland in their forward planning though many of the smaller ones lacked the capacity to do this effectively.

Most of the NTOs were small, and most depended on public funds to some degree, although it is not at all clear how much public funding supported NTO operations in Scotland (Fairley and McArthur, 1999). Some of the NTOs were quite large and experienced, having evolved from the statutory Industrial Training Boards of the 1960s. Three retained statutory training levies, although not all of these published data on levy impact and grant activity in Scotland. These three were executive Non Departmental Public Bodies of two Whitehall Departments and therefore potentially accountable to the Scottish Parliament for their activities north of the border.

The NTOs had a range of responsibilities including the provision of 'voice' in relation to VET for employers, Modern Apprenticeship, developing new learning initiatives, and providing labour market information. Most of the NTOs were sectoral, some were focussed on occupations, and a few, e.g. the NTO for e-commerce, were rather generic in nature.

The NTOs were 'business plan led' which means that they tended to concentrate their efforts where public expenditure was available and, more importantly in those areas where most of the membership was located. This could of course create difficulties for an enterprise seeking to access NTO expertise but finding itself simply in the wrong place. Highlands and Islands Enterprise tried to ensure that the key NTOs were engaged with the area and that enterprises were not disadvantaged, in this respect, by location.

The LEC-NTO interface was clearly important to ensuring that local, sectoral and occupational approaches to VET developed in ways that were consistent and complementary. The number of agencies involved was bound to create some difficulties. The role of the NTO-LEC relationship in Scottish Enterprise's new strategy of developing economic 'clusters' (Botham, 1999; Botham and Downes, 1999) appeared not to have been considered. However, some leading experts in FE were optimistic that appropriate, cluster focused approaches to VET would evolve from practice (Leech, 1999).

However, criticisms of over-fragmentation led to a review of the NTOs by the Ministers for Lifelong Learning in the four UK territories, and to their replacement by a smaller network of Sector Skills Councils and other agencies. In time this may simplify the interface with LECs. However, there have also been some examples of confusion regarding the role of Britain-wide agencies in devolved Scotland.

8.4   VET and Social Division

It is widely acknowledged that access to higher education disproportionately favours young people from the middle classes. VET is, by contrast, focused on young people leaving school with low (or no) qualifications, people in work, and the unemployed. VET is quite widely separated from the world of 'mainstream' education. There are points of contact, vocational studies will be more important within schooling after the implementation of Higher Still,[6] some apprenticeship programmes are being recognised for access purposes by some HE institutions, a unified qualifications system is emerging but nevertheless the worlds of 'vocational' and 'academic' education remain a long way apart.

The progressive rhetoric of Scottish education talks of a 'unified' system and 'parity of esteem' within it. However, these aspirations are a long way off. The vocational-academic gap is perhaps the largest division of all.

There are also divisions within VET. These are well known to professionals and practitioners. However, the poor availability of data for VET (and for local labour markets), compared with mainstream education, has always made it difficult to discuss these important issues. Perhaps the largest division is that the quality of VET provision for people who are unemployed is often poorer than for those in work and there are few 'bridges and ladders' to facilitate movement for unemployed people once they have been trained. Furthermore, unemployed people are the only post-16 group who are *compelled* to take part in VET. This last issue raises concerns that are more to do with human rights and social justice than with VET per se.

Resources for VET remain focused on school leavers and young people and comparatively little is available for older people. This is also a clear factor in post school education and some commentators (see Lowe, 1999) regard it as a serious obstacle to the development of lifelong learning. Research commissioned by the Parliament (Blake Stevenson, 2001) also demonstrated that those most in need of education and/or training seem to attract the least resources and that funding streams are complex and lack transparency.

In the case of some 'task force' type responses to large industrial closures, there seems to have been a tacit acceptance that older, male manual workers have been in a relatively hopeless situation and so job replacement strategies have not prioritised their VET needs. However, in some cases, notably in the HIE area, strategic intervention seems to have protected male manual workers in situations of cyclical downturn in their sector. In addition, the UK government continues to develop schemes for specific age groups or social groups and the resulting programme fragmentation is widely thought to obstruct the development of integrated strategies for lifelong learning.

Another extremely important dimension of division within VET is gender, which has recently been researched in Scotland (Powney et al, 2000). The issues, and their complexity, have been recognised for some time. Evidence for this is provided by the fact that the European Social Fund has provided finance for women only VET initiatives since the early 1980s, something which the more entrepreneurial Scottish District Councils[7] exploited to help fund VET for women and to overcome their own inadequate legal powers in this regard. Again,

---

[6] The new school leaving certificate, being implemented from autumn 2000.
[7] A number of District Councils followed Edinburgh's lead and set up women only technology training centres in the 1980s, sometimes against opposition from the Regional Councils and their FE Colleges.

comprehensive data are not available, with SE suggesting to the ELLC Enquiry that it had never been required to produce such data. It does appear that some schemes are very skewed. In Modern Apprenticeship for example, the proportion of training places taken up by women varies by LEC area, from 4 per cent in the Western Isles to 27 per cent in Glasgow (Blake Stevenson, 2001).

Scotland is a highly urbanised society. However, a significant number of people live in rural communities and quite a number live in remote areas. Some thirteen local authority areas are officially designated as rural. Clearly, access and choice in VET are likely to be more restricted for citizens of rural and island Scotland. A number of issues are underway to try and address this problem. These include the higher education initiatives in the Highlands and Islands, and in Dumfries and Galloway, and the online learning systems being developed by a number of NTOs. An initiative by SE and HIE, Futureskills Scotland, aims to improve labour market intelligence.

It is also likely that Scotland's minority communities – the minority ethnic groups, religious minorities, and those with disabilities – face restrictions on choice and access, wherever they live. Once again, the data do not exist to say very much about these problems.

Finally, sometimes public policy contributes to, or exacerbates, social division. In the 1990s, the Scottish Office developed a preference for funding VET systems which had rather crude performance management 'targets', a strong element of 'output budgeting' or 'payment by results', and sub-contracted delivery. SE and HIE and the LECs are contractually bound into this approach to public policy. At the centre this approach appears to provide focus of purpose, control and the 'capacity to deliver' (Fairley and Peterson, 1995). However, the effects may be quite contrary to what is intended.

There are several potential difficulties that arise from bringing managerialism into any aspect of education in these ways (Fairley and Paterson, 1995). However, there are two main problems for VET. The first is that inappropriate, unhelpful or wrong targets may be selected. The Scottish Executive's grant-in-aid to Scottish Enterprise for VET focuses on targets in just three areas: trainee numbers, the number of SVQs achieved, and the number of trainees who get employee status. These are the matters on which SE must focus and this leaves little scope or incentive for trying systematically to use VET to overcome divisions in society.

The second difficulty is that this sort of target setting sends out the wrong signals to VET sub-contractors. They feel pressure to recruit trainees who will quickly succeed in achieving qualifications, particularly if payment comes with results. The approach to recruitment that results is known as 'creaming'; the applicants who are perceived to be 'best' are recruited and any who do not 'fit the mould' are filtered out at this stage. It is difficult to look at the 4:1, male:female ratio in Modern Apprenticeship and not consider the possibility that such processes may be operating.

The Scottish Affairs Select Committee (1995) was critical of 'creaming' in its review of Scottish Enterprise. However, that advice was ignored and the Scottish Executive and its executive arms seem to be more committed to output budgeting than ever. There is an unfortunate irony in this, given the Executive's strong rhetorical commitment to promoting 'social inclusion'.

8.5   The Main VET Initiatives in Scotland

The highest profile initiative is the New Deal for young people aged 18-24. The architecture of this scheme is complex and this has been critically discussed elsewhere (see Fairley, 1998a).

The scheme aims to end claimant unemployment for young people. It seeks to do so, not by creating jobs, but rather by making young people more 'employable' or 'job ready'. The scheme is underpinned by the belief that an improved labour supply will somehow of itself improve the supply of jobs. At the time of its introduction in Scotland, in 1998, there were fewer than 11,000 in the client group, and about £250m was available over a four year period (Fairley, 1998a).

The New Deal was a manifesto, 'flagship' policy for New Labour in the 1997 UK general election. This meant that it had to be implemented quickly, and in a uniform manner across the UK. The only implementing machinery available for the purpose was the Employment Service (ES). This was controversial in Scotland for a number of reasons. The use of the ES, and the explicit link with welfare reform, meant that New Deal was driven by the UK government, even although most of the scheme's content is VET, which is a fully devolved area of policy. Second there were doubts as to whether it was realistic to expect the ES to rapidly 'reinvent' itself, from a benefits 'police force' to a caring agency that was capable of supporting disadvantaged young people. And third, the use of the ES appeared to be an attempt to bypass Scottish institutions and in particular to undermine the lead role of the LECs in VET for the unemployed. This ignoring of Scottish institutions came as Scottish Enterprise was beginning to advocate an alternative, 'lifelong learning' approach to assisting the unemployed (Scottish Enterprise, 1997).

Negotiations between the Scottish Office and Whitehall provided a compromise solution. In Scotland New Deal is implemented in 23 areas, the 22 LEC areas plus West Lothian, rather than the ES districts. And the Scottish Office devised an implementation scheme which guaranteed a clear role for each of the major 'partners' – the LECs, the ES, local government, and the voluntary sector – at the risk of reduced operational flexibility.

The scheme was widely welcomed, as it brought 'new money' (raised by means of a one-off windfall tax on excess utility profits) and appeared to herald a return to a more active employment policy. Less noticed, or perhaps conveniently overlooked, was the fact that the New Deal built on, and considerably extended the punitive welfare provisions of the Conservative's Job Seeker's Allowance (JSA), provisions that Labour had attacked when in opposition. Several of the major institutions of Scottish 'civic society', to their discredit, conveniently overlooked the coercive nature of New Deal, when 'new money' was made available for implementation (Fairley, 1998a).

Under New Deal, young people who have been on JSA for six months (and others who are at risk) are brought into the Gateway, an individually focused assessment of VET need. After the Gateway, they may go straight into jobs or into one of four labour market or educational options. Three of these options are for six months, while the educational one is for up to a year. Employers who participate by offering subsidised jobs are under no obligation to keep young people on at the end of their six months on New Deal.

One welcome innovation in this, the second Labour New Deal[8] for young people, is that the government has committed resources to monitoring and to achieving 'continuous improvement'. By mid 1999, this was already beginning to produce internally generated criticisms, and recommendations for action to improve the New Deal (New Deal Task Force, 1999a and 1999b). Early internal criticism included the acknowledgement that marketing had highlighted potential business benefits while downplaying business responsibilities and that the scheme plan had seriously underestimated the level of support that young people need in the workplace.

8.6   Modern Apprenticeship (MA)

MA seemed to be simply a matter of policy continuity, with Labour taking forward and extending an initiative of the Conservatives. When the Conservatives announced their intention to implement MA, the response from Scotland was decidedly lukewarm. There were a number of reasons for this: Scottish Enterprise was already offering its own standards and employment based youth training which was being marketed as 'Skillseekers' and it did not want to have two competing schemes with the same objectives. Second, MA was a Conservative initiative at a time when Scotland was very self consciously not a Conservative country. And third, the often present 'not invented here' factor in Scottish policy making was undoubtedly present. The low key Scottish response meant that the NTOs became more centrally involved in MA and that MA was implemented within the Skillseekers framework. Skillseekers cost some £79.5m in 1998/99 (National Audit Office, 2000). In 2002 the ELLC recommended that Skillseekers be phased out in favour of the MA programme which in turn should be improved.

At the time of Scotland's general election in 1999, the Scottish Office (1998, p.50) had announced a target of 15,000 MAs by 2002. There was no evidence of labour market demand or employer preferences to support this target and it was quite widely believed to be too high. During the election campaign, the Chancellor, Gordon Brown, announced a new 20,000 target for Scotland. There is no plan for occupations or sectors. Funding is a matter for LECs in the light of local short term demand.

There is no publicly available strategy for achieving the new Scottish target. In general, the National Audit Office (2000) criticised the lack of clear links between

---

[8] In the 1970s Labour launched the Youth Opportunities Programme as a 'New Deal' for young people.

training for 18-24 year olds and economic development needs. The lack of such links means that MA will be developed opportunistically, perhaps in those sectors where supply is easiest to vary, which may not be the industries that are most important to the economy or which are most capable of sustaining the employment of skilled workers. In September 1999, the Modern Apprenticeship Implementation Group announced that 69 MA frameworks had been endorsed for use in Scotland, which represented rapid growth. The MA system was intended to grow to cover all of the labour force which did not have access to initial training accredited at this SVQ level.

8.7   Individual Learning Accounts (ILA)

The ILA initiative was piloted as ADVANCE in the Grampian area, by the LEC. It was initially intended that 2000 workers, aged 18-64, take part in the pilot. The ILA was a virtual account[9] for an individual worker, to which the individual, the employer and the LEC could contribute. The individual could then use the account to fund access to learning, the assumption being that active learners would be better motivated workers.

The ILA was not a new idea. It probably had its origins in views put forward by the UK CBI in the mid 1980s; that funding for work based training should be effectively privatised and moved onto a credit based system. While there is a widely accepted need to simplify funding systems (Fairley and McArthur, 1999; Lowe 1999; Blake Stevenson, 2001), there was little critical discussion of the ILA concept and of the limits of this kind of voluntarism. The target was to achieve 100,000 ILAs in Scotland, at a public expenditure cost of £22m (Scottish Office, 1999b) and, once again, the target appeared to define the strategy.

The ILA system may simply have been expanded too quickly or it may be that appropriate management systems were not implemented. In 2002, difficulties in accounting for some expenditure led to ILAs being abandoned, first south of the border, then in Scotland.

8.8   LearnDirect – The Scottish University for Industry (SUFI)

LearnDirect Scotland is the 'brand name' of the Scottish University for Industry. Again this is closely associated with the Chancellor of the Exchequer although it will need to evolve differently in order to interface with specifically Scottish institutions. LearnDirect is essentially a brokerage service, helping learners, employers and providers to establish effective contacts. ICT and e-learning are seen as priority areas. Some £16m will be spent over three years on the setting up of LearnDirect.

---

[9] The commercial banks showed little interest in the scheme.

SUFI is intended to 'boost competitiveness and individual employability' (Scottish Office, 1999b, p.10) by acting as a broker, putting employers and individuals in touch with appropriate VET suppliers. While efficient brokerage could help to bring some coherence to VET, there is also the danger that another institution is added to the already crowded landscape and that fees charged to cover costs could take money out of the system.

8.9   The Trade Union Fund for Learning (TUFL)

This was set up in 2000 by the Scottish Executive, following a report by the Trade Union Working Party on Lifelong Learning, which was chaired by the Enterprise Minister (Fairley, 2003). TUFL is based on a scheme implemented earlier in England. It allows trade unions to bid for resources to train or reskill their members. A range of projects is underway (Blake Stevenson, 2001). £400,000 has been made available annually for 4 years.

8.10   The Future of VET in Scotland

It appears to be a matter of cross party support that VET should in future be planned within a lifelong learning context. This marks a significant break from the traditional British view which has, since the 1970s, favoured age specific schemes, from the Youth Opportunities Programme to the current New Deal. This new approach has come from the work of the Scottish Parliament's Enterprise and Lifelong Learning Committee.

In July 2001, the ELLC began its enquiry into lifelong learning. It began by 'mapping' existing provision and funding (Blake Stevenson 2001). It took written evidence from 120 organisations and individuals, and oral evidence from 58 organisations. Members of the cross party committee toured Scotland visiting case studies, and examining what was actually happening on the ground. In April 2002, the ELLC hosted a Lifelong Learning Convention (inspired in part by the Irish Education Convention held in the mid 1990s). Following the most comprehensive review ever of lifelong learning, including VET, the ELLC issued its final report in October 2002.

The Report (ELLC 2002) contained 79 recommendations (Fairley, 2003). These would see a radical shake-up of education and training in Scotland. It recommended much closer working between FE, HE, VET and community education.

However, its most radical recommendation concerned the remodelling of lifelong learning on the principle of entitlement, in effect moving the comprehensive principle post-16. The ELLC wished every citizen to be entitled to 720 credits, which typically would equate to two years of post-compulsory schooling plus four years of higher education. Within this system the learner would have much more freedom and choice as to when, where and how to study. In turn this would require more flexibility and cooperation between the four providing sectors.

The Scottish Executive responded in 2003 with its own strategy (Scottish Executive, 2003). This was broadly in support of the ELLC recommendations, advocating an approach which was firmly 'people centred'. Clearly, at the time of writing, it is too early to discuss the implementation of this strategy. However, it is equally clear that the Parliament has produced a broadly consensual strategy which provides a framework in which the Executive may take forward a more distinctively Scottish approach to lifelong learning.

8.11   Conclusions

VET in Scotland is fragmented and is often separated from other parts of the broader educational system. It is based on a firm commitment by government to voluntarism. In 2003, it was still being driven by UK priorities although this is an entirely 'devolved' policy area. Attempts to provide 'strategy' have to date at best been very weak. And the data available for VET are inadequate, although improving with the Scottish Executive Education Department now producing annual reports (2002).

The Scottish Executive has published its own strategy to modernise VET in a lifelong learning framework. The strategy has been developed in response to a comprehensive analysis and consensual report by the ELLC, one of the Parliament's more effective Committees. There will remain powerful forces in favour of common provision across the UK – party politics, and the need for labour mobility, for example. Nevertheless, it is possible that from 2004 aspects of VET will be more obviously 'made in Scotland' by Scottish institutions.

References

Anderson, M. and Fairley, J. (1983) 'The politics of industrial training in the UK', *Journal of Public Policy*.

Ashton, D. and Green, F. (1996) *Education, Training and the Global Economy*, Edward Elgar, Cheltenham.

Blake Stevenson Ltd (2001) *Mapping of Lifelong Learning Provision in Scotland*, Scottish Parliament Information Centre, September.

Botham, R. (1999) 'What can Scotland learn from Austin, Texas?', *Scottish Affairs*, 29, pp.43-58.

Botham, R. and Downes, B. (1999) 'Industrial clusters: Scotland's route to economic success', *Scottish Affairs*, 29, pp.59-72.

Bryce, T. and Humes, W. (eds) (1999) *Scottish Education*, Edinburgh University Press, Edinburgh.

Bryce, T. and Hume, W. (eds) (2003) *Scottish Education – Second Edition, Post-Devolution*, Edinburgh University Press, Edinburgh.

Enterprise and Lifelong Learning Committee (2002) *Report on Lifelong Learning*, October, Scottish Parliament, Edinburgh.

Fairley, J. (1989) 'An overview of the development and growth of the MSC in Scotland' in Brown, A. and Fairley, J. (eds) *The Manpower Services Commission in Scotland*, Edinburgh University Press, Edinburgh.

Fairley, J. (1998a) 'Labour's New Deal in Scotland', *Scottish Affairs*, 25, pp.90-109.

Fairley, J. (1998b) 'Stakeholders and partners in vocational education and training in Scotland' in Finlay, I., Niven, S. and Young. S. (eds) *Changing Vocational Education and Training – An International Comparative Perspective*, Routledge, London.

Fairley J (2003) 'The Enterprise and Lifelong Learning Department (ELLD) and the Scottish Parliament' in Bryce, T. and Humes, W. (eds) (2003) *Scottish Education – Second Edition, Post Devolution*, Edinburgh University Press, Edinburgh.

Fairley, J. and McArthur, A. (1999) 'The public funding of vocational education and training in Scotland', *Scottish Affairs*, 29, pp.84-103.

Fairley, J. and Paterson, L. (1995) *Scottish Education and the New Managerialism*.

Fairley, J. and Paterson, L (2000) 'Social justice in Scottish education', *Education and Social Justice*, 2(3), Summer.

Finlay, I. (1996) *Bridges or Battlements? Current Relationships Between Colleges, Schools and Education Authorities*, Scottish School of Further Education, University of Strathclyde, Glasgow.

Grant, W. (1998) 'Perspectives on globalisation and economic coordination' in Hollingsworth, J.R. and Boyer, R. (eds) *Contemporary Capitalism – the Embeddedness of Institutions*, Cambridge University Press, Cambridge.

Gray, J. (1998) *False Dawn – The Delusions of Global Capitalism*, Granta, London.

Jarvis, T. (1997) *Welfare-to-Work: The New Deal*, Research Paper 97/118, London, House of Commons Library, 12 November.

Leech, M. (1999) 'Clusters and training policy', *Scottish Affairs*, 29, pp.78-83.

Leonardy, U. (1998) *Memorandum to the Enquiry into the Operation of Multi-layer Democracy by the Scottish Affairs Committee*, HC 460-ii, Stationery Office, London.

Lowe, J. (1999) 'Lifelong learning: from vision to reality' in Hassan, G. and Warhurst, C. (eds) *A Moderniser's Guide to Scotland – A Different Future*, Centre for Scottish Public Policy and The Big Issue in Scotland, Glasgow.

National Audit Office (1998) *Corporate Governance and Financial Management in the Scottish Further Education Sector*, Report by the Comptroller and Auditor General, HC 682, 1997-98, Stationery Office, London.

National Audit Office (2000) *Scottish Enterprise: Skillseekers Training for Young People*, Report by the Comptroller and Auditor General, laid before the Scottish Parliament, 28 February.

New Deal Task Force (1999a) *Lasting Value: Recommendations for Increasing Retention Within the New Deal*, July.

New Deal Task Force (1999b) *Bridges to Work: New Directions for Intermediaries*, September.

Newlands, D. and Parker, M. (1998) 'The prospects and potential of a new university in the Highlands and Islands', *Scottish Affairs*, 21, pp.78-94.

Paterson, L. (1999) *Education, Training and the Scottish Parliament*, Conference Paper, Skills for Scotland Conference, Glasgow, 15 April.

Pountney, J., McPake, J., Edwards, L. and Hamilton, S. (2000) *Gender Equality and Lifelong Learning in Scotland*, Equal Opportunities Commission, Glasgow.

Raab, G. (1999) *The Distribution of Further Education Provision in Scotland*, Scottish Office Education and Industry Department, Edinburgh.

Scottish Affairs Select Committee (1995) *The Operation of the Enterprise Agencies and the LECs*, HC 339, Stationery Office, London.

Scottish Office (1998) *Opportunity Scotland: A Paper on Lifelong Learning*, Cm 4048, Stationery Office, Edinburgh.
Scottish Office (1999a) *Further Education in Scotland 1998*, Stationery Office, Edinburgh.
Scottish Office (1999b) *Skills for Scotland – A Skills Strategy for a Competitive Scotland*, Stationery Office, Edinburgh.
Scottish Enterprise (1997) *Submission to the Department for Education and Employment*, Education and Employment Committee, HC 263, The New Deal, Stationery Office, London.
Scottish Executive (2003) *Life Through Learning, Learning Through Life: the Lifelong Learning Strategy for Scotland*, Stationery Office, Edinburgh.
Scottish Executive Education Department (2002) *Education and Training in Scotland – National Dossier*, Stationery Office, Edinburgh.
Streeck, W. (1998) 'Beneficial constraints: on the economic limits of rational voluntarism' in Hollingsworth, J. and Boyer, R. (eds) *Contemporary Capitalism – The Embeddedness of Institutions*, Cambridge University Press, Cambridge.
Turok, I. and Edge, N. (1999) *The Jobs Gap in Britain's Cities: Employment Loss and Labour Market Consequences*, Policy Press, Bristol.
Turok, I. and Webster, D. (1998) 'The New Deal: jeopardised by the geography of unemployment?', *Local Economy*, 12(4), pp.309-328.
Warhurst, C. and Thompson, P. (1999) 'Knowledge, skills and work in the Scottish Economy' in Hassan, G. and Warhurst, C. (eds) *A Moderniser's Guide to Scotland – A Different Future*, Centre for Scottish Public Policy and The Big Issue in Scotland, Glasgow.
Webster, D. (2000) 'Scottish social inclusion policy – a critical perspective', *Scottish Affairs*, 30, pp.28-50.
Weir, D. (1999) 'Vocational education' in Bryce, T. and Humes, W. (eds) (1999) *Scottish Education*, Edinburgh University Press, Edinburgh.

Chapter 9

Transport

Tom Hart

9.1 Introduction

This chapter considers how transport relates to disparities in Scotland and the role of transport related policy in reducing disparities. It concentrates on demands, opportunities and needs for access involving the physical movement of persons and goods. The approach adopted is to consider the theory of transport and economic development and relate this to the practical and political situation. Actual changes within and between Scottish regions are then examined in the context of global competitiveness and local pressures. Finally, there is comment on the extent to which policy and policy instruments relating to transport and access can reduce economic disparities while also advancing social objectives. This includes reference to a 'package' approach and the importance of decision making structures, funding and monitoring.

9.2 The Theory of Transport and Economic Development

Numerous authors and government reports have speculated on the links between transport and development. Recent examples include the Standing Advisory Committee on Trunk Road Assessment (SACTRA) Reports on *Transport and the Economy* (1998 and 1999) and their influence on the 2001 and 2003 versions of *Scottish Transport Appraisal Guidance* (STAG) (Scottish Executive, 2001 and 2003c). The key concept is that real cuts in the unit cost of transport relative to quality have made a substantial contribution to the scale and pattern of economic development. Classic writing provides a view of how lower transport costs – by using natural and artificial waterways and by wheeled vehicles replacing pack animals – allowed expansion of trade, competition and urbanisation *within regions* and *between regions* (Von Thunen, 1826 and 1850; Christaller, 1933; Dupuit, 1844). This process was taken further by the use of new power sources in transport and in refrigeration. Yet this did not imply an equality of growth between regions. Some performed far ahead of others, both in terms of total population growth and incomes per head. With rising real incomes and more sophisticated markets, quality took on an increasing importance as in the development of passenger liners, the motorised car and lorry, air mail and more generalised air travel. People and businesses became able and willing to pay more for travel and for a widened range of supplies and consumer products as real incomes rose. This increase in demand, and increased supply bolstered by population growth as well as technical advances, also contributed to large cuts in costs per unit of passenger or tonne mile at higher levels of quality – reinforcing growth.

These situations linked transport with increased disparities between regions. Attempts to block such disparities were seen as reducing overall economic growth. Within regions, transport improvements accelerated the shift from rural to urban living. It was in towns and cities that the majority of the jobs growth – in the service and manufacturing sectors – was concentrated. This unevenness also had an interregional dimension. Some regions, including Britain and the north eastern USA became the great nineteenth century centres for service and manufacturing activity, using transport to pull in the necessary supplies and to distribute outputs in their heartlands and to wider markets. Other commercial regions began to specialise in agricultural products, more transiently in mineral production and, more recently, in mass tourism. In Scotland, the Central Belt had greatly increased its population share by 1914 with urban incomes well in excess of rural. Most of the Highlands had begun to lose population, though to a much lesser extent than Ireland, but – apart from some 'congested districts' characterised by poverty – incomes in the 'commercial' Highlands moved closer to the Scottish average with marked urban growth at nodes like Inverness and Oban.

Since the eighteenth century, *transport intensity* has grown, i.e. the physical volume of movement has risen more rapidly than either population or real incomes per head. Economies became more transport intensive yet this is not to say that transport has been the main cause of growth. Extra use of transport, especially personal movement, has been an effect as well as a cause of economic growth. Theory has sought to isolate the causative impact of transport yet it is hard to disentangle this from the many other factors influencing growth. Transport's largest economic impact came from the 1750s to 1914 when it was part of the modernisation of Europe and its influence on the wider world. Yet this situation was changing by 1914.

Throughout the advanced world by 1914, the prior improvement of transport had lessened its future ability to influence economic growth. The main subsequent changes were network adaptations to suit motorised road vehicles (and vehicle ferries), aircraft, container and bulk cargo ports and, on some corridors, high speed passenger railways. The speed and nature of such change was often still seen as a means of improving regional competitiveness but most competition was now between regions heavily involved in manufacturing and services or able to use links to Europe to increase foreign penetration of European and North American markets e.g. the Japanese car and electronics industries. Strong remnants remained of a tradition of using infrastructure projects as a means of promoting growth; indeed, this tradition was reinforced by the growing role of the state in total spending and by the influence of Keynesian policies. Motor roads (offering extra capacity and higher quality) assumed the earlier developmental mantle of railways and ports yet, by the 1970s, actual results were often disappointing and there was increased concern at levels of taxation and public borrowing. While there was a continuing consensus that improved roads and vehicle ferries could play an important part in reversing population decline and stagnant incomes in the Highlands and Islands (population began to rise appreciably from 1961), doubts increased about the impact on national and regional growth of skewing road spending towards depressed industrial regions and their external links (Leitch Report, 1978; SACTRA, 1998 and 1999). Such policies could deflect attention, and limited resources, from more effective means of area regeneration and, at worst, could expose ill prepared regions to greater competition. Under the impact of the car, higher incomes and changing urban forms, *passenger intensity* continued to rise in the 20th century yet *freight intensity* weakened i.e. increases in freight movement began to lag rises in national income. In part, this reflected shifts in economic structure and a growth of both internal and external trade with a larger value added and service element. With respect to personal movement, the intensity of car use relative to income also came under pressure – especially from the 1980s – as air travel and some aspects of rail travel expanded.

Modern interpretations of the role of transport in overall and area development have become more cautious and selective, seeing transport as part of a more complex pattern of economic and social change. Despite high profiles for some projects, there is a reduced emphasis on new infrastructure and more concern to raise quality and align transport with sustainable economic development. 'High value added', conservation (of energy, materials and habitat) and recycling are becoming more prominent features of economic growth with both goods and car movement in the advanced world falling relative to national incomes (McKinnon, 1999/2000b; Hart, 1994; Hart and Doar, 1999). The changing factors in economic growth suggest *reductions in transport intensity* i.e. economies will grow more than increases in physical movement with the theoretical possibility of absolute cuts in overall movement. SACTRA doubted the feasibility of the latter but did accept that, in congested areas, policies reducing growth in road traffic could be more helpful to economic growth than former rates of increase. In other areas, SACTRA and STAG argued that extra movement could be a consequence of policies promoting regeneration with transport improvements only incorporated to the extent that they offered an added regeneration benefit without prejudice to national economic objectives i.e. there is a need for more analysis of both personal and spatial 'winners' and 'losers' from transport projects.

9.3   The Practicalities and Politics of Transport

Perceptions can be so strong that they become the realities of politics, especially in areas where the press sees an opportunity to play to the public and where politicians have an eye to what might influence votes in the next election. If anything, the coming of the Scottish Parliament has exaggerated this tendency though, in time, the Parliament may bring a more disciplined approach to funding priorities (see further at section 9.6). For the present, the press tends to highlight the iniquities of road fuel prices, stealth taxes on motorists and the superimposition of bridge tolls, direct road pricing (as in Edinburgh or, more widely, on Scottish motorways) and extra charges for workplace and retail car parking. The wish list of road schemes being pushed by business, many MSPs, local government and the public remains longer than lists for other transport projects and well beyond available funds given Scottish Executive commitments to concentrate the restricted funding of the Scottish Parliament on health, education and, in transport, public transport.

These perceptions clash with the evidence that most new roads give such small time savings as to have no discernible impact on business competitiveness. The transport costs of delivering goods to customer outlets is normally 2 per cent to 3 per cent of final prices with less than half of these costs being actual movement. In these circumstances, the 2 to 5 minute savings in trip times offered by current works to extend the A1 dual carriageway to Dunbar and the M77 to Kilmarnock cannot have any significant impact on haulage with any slight gains more than cancelled by increases in congestion in Edinburgh, on the Edinburgh Bypass and in Greater Glasgow. McKinnon (1999/2000a) has also pointed out that only 23 per cent of delays in deliveries relate to congestion with most delays being in the control of management. Rather than opposing tolls and road pricing, major lorry operators have become advocates of pricing and lorry lane priorities as a means of improving reliability by cutting delays and by providing the extra funds needed for selective transport investments. Though hauliers and bodies such as the AA and RAC differ on priorities for the use of congested road space, they are now more favourable to road pricing provided that arising funds are earmarked, ringfenced or otherwise hypothecated for transport. However, there is the fear that if only one area made moves to road pricing and/or workplace parking charges, it could immediately lose out to competitors with further losses coming as business and property developers switched planning applications to surrounding areas, or alternative regions, free of pricing.

Another important perception concerns the disparity between road taxation and road spending. This reflects a failure to distinguish between charges relating to the total costs of road provision and use and taxes levied on road users eg VAT, an energy tax or varied licenses to reduce emissions and improve fuel efficiency. In 1994, the *Eighteenth Report* of the Royal Commission on Environmental Pollution (RCEP) expressed the view that total UK road costs (excluding congestion) were about balanced by road taxation. The RCEP recommendations included direct regulations to reduce emissions, congestion pricing (subject to cost-benefit analysis) and a Fuel Tax Escalator which would double the real cost of fuel, promoting fuel conservation but raising tax take above assessed costs. This 'surplus' tax was to be used to reduce other taxes, including National Insurance. Unfortunately, the RCEP approach confused the principles of fair taxation with those of fair charging to cover costs. Resolving this conflict has not been helped by a devolution settlement under which the Treasury retained full control over road taxation but gave the Scottish Parliament jurisdiction over road charging – interpreted as charges additional to road taxation.

Staying with the practicalities of devolution, external air and shipping issues remain a matter for Westminster but with the Scottish Parliament having powers to 'pump prime' projects – including the Air Route Development Fund launched in

2003 – so long as this is not seen as interfering with EU pro-competition and anti-subsidy rules. Competition policy is a reserved Westminster issue though subject to EU constraints which are also now substantial in the areas of safety and emissions control. Rail policy is a 'grey' area where further change is likely. Alistair Darling, UK Secretary for Transport, finally conceded early in 2004 that the railway structures established in the mid 1990s were dysfunctional and required early review (see section 9.6).

The present '*melange*' is completed by a range of special funds (e.g. Rural Transport, Public Transport, Rail Passenger Partnerships, Rail Infrastructure Grants, Freight Facility Grants, Lottery Funding and Scottish Enterprise/HIE/LEC assistance) and an emphasis on partnership working. Downsides include considerable delays in agreeing projects, clouded objectives and debates relating to risk transfer and 'best value' with respect to Private Finance Initiatives (PFIs) or Public-Private Partnerships (PPPs). PFIs and PPPs involve substantial annual commitments of public funds over the life of partnerships which can eat into the funds available for other purposes. As well as the toll-related Skye Bridge, PFIs currently apply to the M77 extension and rural M74 but may be extended to include the £500m plus urban M74 project and plans for through rail services under Edinburgh Airport. It is in this context that the Scottish Executive is facing the task of securing joined-up thinking and effective delivery within limited funds of objectives for sustainable development, competitiveness and social inclusion (involving both spatial and interpersonal aspects of policy relating to narrowed economic disparities).

9.4   Transport and Intra-regional Disparities

Some 90 per cent of the Scottish population live within travel-to-work-areas where it is feasible to use the car for commuting and access to major centres in not more than one hour yet these areas contain large minorities (ranging from 40 per cent to 80 per cent of local populations) with no direct access to cars and facing severe penalties in access to work and training opportunities, shopping, health and other social and recreational services. Local facilities have been eroded by a rise in car use which has also aggravated economic disparities with the harshest impacts falling on those without a car (normally on lower incomes) and on those with low incomes forced into car use by the lack of adequate alternatives. There is a Hobson's choice between low paid local work or unemployment and access to better paid work at travel costs biting hard into income or requiring lengthy periods away from home and eventual migration. Diet and health can also be affected by the lack of access to a reasonable food range at competitive prices. A secondary problem is that of substantial localised depopulation, increasing the level of dereliction (or sometimes hiding it via the growth of holiday homes and a lack of housing for locals) and increasing the unit costs of maintaining the residual population.

The need to address such personal disparities in access to jobs and other facilities within regions has become a prominent aspect of the Executive's social inclusion and social justice agenda. This has been backed by growing UK research on accessibility standards and related programmes to deliver improvement. Higher spend in this area has been accepted but this has been conjoined with an interest in ensuring better results from unco-ordinated existing levels of spend by different bodies ranging from local authority departments to community trusts and NHS organisations. Social justice priorities have also led to some pressure to return to a more regulated approach to buses and stronger links with taxi type services. One problem here is the extent to which essentially commercial bus companies can be loaded with social obligations without detrimental effects on their core routes and financial outcomes. An overall rise in financial support for buses from public funds seems inevitable within either the present framework (which permits social support for services not competing with commercial services) or a reformed framework including area bus franchises or more extensive bus quality contracts (as permitted in the Transport (Scotland) Act 2001).

In addressing these personal disparities in access to facilities, it has to be accepted that some differences are inevitable while some may be tackled other than through transport policy. For example, the growth of population in parts of rural Scotland outwith a one hour commuting range to major centres and the comparatively young populations of some island areas suggests that both native inhabitants and incomers below retirement age prefer to live in such areas even if incomes are lower than in city regions. Scottish islands have increased their share of the Scottish population since 1981 though with wide variations between particular islands (census results quoted in *The Herald*, 29 November 2003). Work or self employment opportunities exist in or near the home avoiding the need for lengthy commuting while making the most of high value added outputs and internet options – including home shopping, home leisure and home training. Medical advances can allow delivery of some services locally rather than through visits to major hospitals while increased support for local shops and post offices, and information centres may give better community value than a large increase in direct support for transport services and reduced fares allowing the disadvantaged to access facilities further afield. In more urbanised areas, however, improved bus and taxibus transport is likely to be more feasible than efforts to bring jobs and other facilities closer to where people live. It is simply not practical for every area to have a full range of facilities or to expect that local people will necessarily opt for local jobs. There are also arguments that targeted training, general programmes for job creation and selective support for area renewal, community revival, health and fitness and local shops may be more effective in tackling income and health disparities than specific transport programmes. Nevertheless, there are transport elements which deserve integration in social justice programmes. These vary with local circumstances but can include:

* assistance to obtain a driving licence and a 'first car' (such schemes have been pioneered in Fife in areas where it would be expensive to raise public transport to the levels required for convenient commuting, especially for shift work or unusual hours).

- help in developing schemes to encourage car owners to give regular lifts to non owners as well as to share with other owners.

- modification of public transport service patterns and fares to make commuting and other travel by public transport a more feasible option for those without cars (and also capable of attracting car users to public transport, easing traffic and parking problems). Such modification needs to reflect moves away from a focus on those within one hour or 30 minutes by car from key facilities to the range of jobs and facilities which can be reached by public transport in similar timescales. Those without cars are still at a substantial disadvantage and effectively marooned in their immediate localities or forced to consider to moving elsewhere in Scotland or beyond.

- revised funding and regulations to encourage Green Travel Plans by major employers and business parks (with particular attention to hospitals, universities and colleges, and major public offices; funds from parking charges could be recycled within Green Travel Plans, including payments towards guaranteed taxi links outside normal working hours – as pioneered at Dutch hospital sites).

- use of land use strategies and conditions in planning applications to encourage settlement patterns favouring public transport use (and local access on foot or by cycle) and to require lower levels of parking and lower levels of access by single occupant cars – helping to ease congestion or avoid potential congestion. See National Planning Policy Guidance (NPPG 17) on *Transport and Planning* (Scottish Office, 1999), the successor Consultation Draft Scottish Planning Policy (SPP 17) on *Planning for Transport* (Scottish Executive, 2004) and current consultations on replacing *Traffic Assessments* of proposed developments with *Transport and Access Assessments* (Scottish Executive, 2003a).

A new Scottish Planning Bill is currently in preparation and will offer opportunities to integrate a revision of traditional land use planning with new strategic and regional approaches to planning and transport and a particular emphasis on community planning at local level. Plans and decisions have the potential to reduce present social and personal deprivation without significant economic damage. Nevertheless, there is some conflict between the separate objectives of social inclusion and encouraging modal shifts from car use. At another level, there is conflict between the potential for brownfield area renewal and the scope (often emphasised by business and housebuilders) for greater emphasis on elements of greenfield development within sustainable transport corridors allied with improved access to greenspace with recreational and amenity potential.

In certain cases, sustainable land use strategy may justify phased contraction of unsuitable settlements (e.g. poorly located former mining communities and some rural villages with surplus, low grade dwellings and declining prospects for the retention of local facilities). Such decisions have been taken in several Structure

Plans and Local Plans, sometimes with a low profile because of the controversy over the 'destruction' of communities. There is also a case for reconsidering decisions to zone business sites or industrial estates and related access roads in places where there is little prospect of substantial development i.e. political pressures can militate against workable strategies combining local support with realistic financing. On the other hand, abandoned sites – such as the Ravenscraig Steelworks and the Linwood Car Factory – or underused zones on the fringes of city centres can offer major opportunities. Greenfield sites have frequently been pressed forward as means of attracting jobs and reducing local unemployment. Access to such sites is clearly important yet past practice has focused on access by car and lorry, neglecting the need for good public transport access from an early stage of development (as recommended in NPPG17), including access from areas with high levels of unemployment. It is here that more skill and determination is required to develop the urban regeneration potential of the perceived stability of rail networks (with the bonus of increased frequency) and stabilised high frequency bus networks (as in the *Glasgow Overground* established by First Glasgow in August 1999). Additional funding is needed to ensure that such networks mesh with planning objectives at an early stage of area development or regeneration. Though policy now recognises the advantages of stability and high quality in core bus networks, there are still arguments that the full impact of buses (and taxibuses) in encouraging shifts from car use and improving access to facilities will not be gained without increases in public funding and greater use of *quality contracts* as distinct from either non statutory or *statutory partnerships*. Relevant powers are contained in the Transport (Scotland) Act 2001 but have not so far been used. Despite issues of capital cost control, there is also increasing awareness of the importance of *tram* or *light rail projects* in backing urban regeneration and development zone objectives in major cities. Edinburgh and Glasgow are now following many continental cities and Manchester, Sheffield, the West Midlands, Nottingham, Croydon and the London Docklands in tram projects utilising both street running, existing rail formations and new construction.

Such intra-regional policies are important aspects of programmes for employment growth and lessened disparity yet they raise wider issues involving a Central Belt and Scottish dimension. Without a strong lead from the Scottish Executive, there is a continuing risk of employment shifts rather than overall growth due to intensified inter council competition for shopping and leisure expansion and business parks often on greenfield locations. This can lead to duplicated efforts and shifts to car use. Yet other options can bring demonstrable reduction in disparities and modal shifts away from car use increasing the efficiency and enhancing the social benefits of transport and urban structures (as argued in NPPG17 and the draft update SPP 17).

9.5   Inter-regional Transport and Scottish Economic Disparities

Back in the 1960s, the *Central Scotland White Paper* (Scottish Office, 1963) gave the impression of linking development policies with greatly expanded transport programmes including a motorway network for Central Scotland and accelerated completion of a continuous A74 dual carriageway to Carlisle. This impression was repeated in the 1970s when the then HIDB placed great emphasis on completion of a reconstructed A9 from Perth to Inverness and the subsequent bridges over the Beauly, Cromarty and Dornoch Firths. In the 1990s, the Scottish Office made completion of the M74 motorway to Gretna a symbol of Scottish regeneration. In analysing the impact of such schemes, however, it is apparent that the regeneration of the Scottish economy which gained pace from the 1960s owed more to changes in grant assistance, training, research and enterprise than to road programmes. The latter, though having positive impacts, were only part of a broader based increase in public spending in the 1960s which gave Scotland an edge compared to most other UK regions. Subsequent pressures for 'value for money' and restraint in public spending downgraded the road programme (*West Central Scotland Plan*, Joint Steering Committee, 1974) yet managed to maintain a narrowing of the unemployment gap between Scotland and England. These changes coincided with some major road schemes but, as Scottish Transport Appraisal Guidance (STAG) (Scottish Executive, 2001 and 2003c) points out, it would be wrong to conclude that such schemes were the main contributors to overall Scottish growth. Similar but more spectacular changes in rates of growth were affecting the economy of the Republic of Ireland from the 1970s – despite per capita road spending in the Republic being far below the high spending which the UK government lavished on the roads of Northern Ireland. By the 1990s, Irish growth was producing stronger justification for road (and public transport) spending, notably around Dublin, but roads had not been the cause of growth. In the case of the Highlands and Islands, no monitoring of transport schemes has been published but there is a strong likelihood that population revival in many parts of the west owed far more to tailored grants, vehicle ferries and related road improvements than to the more spectacular A9 reconstruction. Jobs growth (and labour shortages) in Lochaber have increased despite little change on the transport front while, in Skye and Lochalsh, strong population growth was well established years before completion of the Skye Toll Bridge. In retrospect, business has also been critical of the even more ambitious reconstruction of the uncongested A74 as a three lane rural motorway involving £25 million a year PFI payments which could have given better value on other projects. More recently, similar arguments have been deployed in relating to the comparative results of diverting the planned £500m expenditure on completing the urban M74 to other projects and a sharper focus on road demand management at peak periods.

Despite some mistakes, Scotland has undoubtedly gained from stronger development policies than applied elsewhere in Britain. Quite apart from the impact of North Sea oil (which, in any case, has been less positive since the later 1960s), these policies have speeded the restructuring of the Scottish economy into areas of growth potential which will themselves need nurturing if global competitiveness is to be maintained in a scenario when the relative prosperity of Scotland – though with an overall population now in decline – works against former levels of funding from EU and UK sources. What is transport's role to be in this changing world?

In essence, the policies of the former Scottish Office encouraged newer types of employment by providing a range of sites, often on greenfields accessible to motorways and dual carriageways, from which developers could make their selection. Though there were nudges in favour of zones of higher unemployment, strategy favoured developer choice (not least because developers might opt for other countries) with some crumbs of area development projects in an effort to combat sharp falls in local employment or meet the demands of the rural agenda. This laissez-faire attitude allows for significant shifts in employment patterns, converting industrial estates to more flexible categories for business use. Greenfield business parks became more favoured than greenfield housing. The combination of more new housing on brownfield land and on dispersed sites with the changing employment pattern increased commuting to more dispersed locations often ill served by public transport. The underlying – and flawed – assumption here is that employment take-up can be maximised by combining a more highly educated population with longer distance commuting, mainly by car.

Despite the stronger emphasis placed by the Scottish Executive on sustainable development patterns, shifts from car use and more equitable access to facilities, the legacy of the former Scottish Office has a continuing influence. In the early years of the Scottish Executive, UK policy constrained public funds available to the Executive while it chose to put a particular constraint on transport spending. As the new Chief Executive at Scottish Enterprise, Robert Crawford endorsed this approach in a revised strategy which focused on topics of critical importance for the Scottish economy (*The Herald*, 30 March 2000). The *Smart, Successful Scotland* theme included a strong emphasis on promoting enterprise and maximising opportunities in higher value electronics, the communications and internet revolution and bio-engineering (see also Scottish Executive, 2000 and 2002b). Local area development was seen as a second level issue with scope for merger of LEC and local council responsibilities with congestion charging emerging as a new instrument to tackle particular city problems. Transport investment was not seen as a topic of overarching Scottish importance. This reflected business views that the internal Scottish transport system was in reasonable shape compared to competitor regions. The fundamental objective was to focus government activity in ways best fitted to stimulating the overall economy while also meeting social needs.

However, with the relaxation of public spending from 2002 and mounting business and council concerns about particular points and corridors of road congestion, added impetus was given to re-expansion of a road programme which included a 'pipeline' of developed projects relating to the A1, M77, urban M74, A80/M80 and A8/M8 plus various local schemes. In contrast, institutional and legal problems beset both road pricing plans in Edinburgh and efforts to expand programmes for integration of fares and information and improved rail and bus service delivery relating to social inclusion objectives and the aspiration to stabilise road traffic over the years to 2021 announced in Wendy Alexander's transport delivery document *Scotland's Transport: Delivering Improvements* (Scottish Executive, 2002a).

While the Executive has announced its determination to tackle these institutional problems and to ensure reduced congestion and a raising of public transport to 70 per cent of total transport spend by 2006, there are alternative views that significant expansion of road traffic is inevitable and, indeed, desirable, as part of realistic programmes to promote economic growth in Scotland underpinning an increased population and the funding of social programmes. In contrast to a focus on relatively compact cities, these alternative views favour more dispersed work and housing within the Central Belt and around cities such as Aberdeen and Inverness – continuing the pattern of increasing length in car trips (Allander Lecture by Professor Edward Glaeser of Harvard University quoted in *The Herald*, 10 February 2004). They also imply a 'hands off' approach by government to using transport to promote shifts in the balance of regional growth – leaving government to concentrate, if intervening at all, on measures to promote enterprise and competition.

This raises the issue of the extent to which transport policies can make significant contributions to reducing disparities in economic growth between regions. Historically, it has been shown (section 9.2) that transport can promote higher overall growth by widening disparities but this situation can change with respect to conditions for competition between more advanced economies. In the revised policies adopted by Scottish Enterprise under Robert Crawford, transport policy was still seen as having important roles in:

- improving the quality and range of external links, notably by air and sea (ongoing work is concerned with research and marketing to develop the value to Scotland of existing external links and opportunities for new routes)

- special studies of sectoral transport needs in relation to in-tourism, total quality and logistics, energy efficiency, air freight and the scope for more competitive rail freight, including piggyback services and Channel Tunnel services (i.e. issues relating to 'soft' factors rather than infrastructure)

- evaluation of the potential benefits of major international container transhipment hubs at locations such as Hunterston and Scapa Flow

- internal priorities paying greater attention to reduced congestion, city regeneration and reliable access to major ports, airports and railheads.

Subsequent actions have included start-up aid for the direct Rosyth-Zeebrugge ferry and funding via Scottish Enterprise and HIE for air route developments offering economic gains but allowable within EU 'state aid' rules. Campaigning has also started for greater use of EU powers to grant Public Service Obligation (PSO) protected status for regional air access to international hub airports. The White Paper on *The Future of Air Transport* (Department for Transport, 2003) supports moves in this direction. There is also an Executive interest in improving the existing rail link to Prestwick Airport and providing rail links for Edinburgh and Glasgow Airports by 2010.

Turning to inter-regional disparities in Scotland, this is primarily a matter for the Scottish Executive and for HIE (due to its special role in relation to the Highlands and Islands). In the past, much transport spending in the Highlands and Islands has been related to regional development while similar claims have been made for transport proposals affecting the north east, the Borders, Ayrshire and Dumfries and Galloway. Proof of actual impact has been more difficult due to other economic factors and the reality that road and ferry spending allocations are often based on social grounds rather than regional economic benefit assessments. In discussions on use of the new powers to specify the ScotRail passenger franchise and assist with freight shifts from road to rail or water, regional benefits have also been mentioned. The closest approach to a Scottish transport strategy for shifting economic benefits outwards from a prospering Edinburgh have been specifications seeking shorter rail trip times and improved frequency on routes linking Aberdeen and Inverness to Central Scotland – carrying on an emphasis found in previous programmes for road improvement. Due to the improved frequency and lower costs of Anglo-Scottish flights and the relatively long distances between London and Scotland, the Executive has shown less interest in assessing the possible benefits for Scotland of high speed (200mph) links to the south on the continental model. This issue may gain greater momentum due to airport congestion, CO^2 targets and stronger interest in high speed rail links within England north from the Channel Tunnel to London St Pancras route, due to open in 2007.

Examples of 'activist' views of inter-regional transport can be found but it is less certain that the Executive has a genuine belief in the ability of a centrally determined strategy (including transport elements) to influence the distribution of jobs and earnings within Scotland. Social factors and measures to improve overall job and population prospects in Scotland have greater priority. Official projections (which are open to some influence from policy change) suggest Scottish population falling below 5 million by 2015 though with local council areas varying from 5 per cent to 15 per cent growth around Edinburgh to falls over 10 per cent in the Western Isles, Dundee and Inverclyde (*The Herald*, 31 January 2004). Parallel projections of estimated incomes per head are not available – partly due to technical problems relating to places of work and residence being in different areas and to the political problems of differential forecasts of income growth. Experience has shown that both area job forecasts (of net gains) and of jobs related to specific firms or transport projects tend not to be fully realised in practice. The David Simmonds Consultancy (Simmonds, 2003) has undertaken work in this area with cautious results. Starting from a suspect fixed forecast of Scottish jobs growth, David Simmonds concluded in evidence to the urban M74 Public Inquiry that this scheme, by 2030, might have shifted 20,000 jobs from the Edinburgh area to Clydeside (though with losses, not gains, for areas such as West Dunbartonshire, Inverclyde and Ayrshire). This figure is only 4 per cent of Glasgow and Clyde Valley Structure Plan aspirations for 500,000 extra jobs by 2020. It needs to be compared with opportunities for alternative use of the £500m estimated M74 cost and with the possibility than future airport plans could shift jobs from Clydeside to Edinburgh.

There is also the issue of whether transport projects will move jobs or residence. The Borders Rail Project, for example, is seen as boosting the central Borders population but with a lesser impact on jobs – due to greater commuting to Edinburgh. Similarly, improved transport could allow more Edinburgh area jobs to be taken by Clydeside residents as well as allowing Edinburgh residents to work in Clydeside. With an appropriate package of policy instruments, however, there is potential for transport policy to influence some relative shift in the balance of both population and jobs from Edinburgh to Clydeside, the Upper Forth, Dundee, Fife and the Borders. Policy could also improve prospects further north through a better range of direct links – of which some can make specific contributions to inward tourism over a longer season as well as providing links attractive to business. Whether there is a strong desire for substantial, inter-regional modification is more arguable. The recent controversy over the high cost of relocating Scottish Natural Heritage from Edinburgh to Inverness has drawn attention to closer appraisal of the effectiveness of policies directed towards inter-regional shift and potentially drawing funds away from measures which could better promote overall growth in the Scottish economy.

Nevertheless, the political agenda is likely to involve some support for dampening growth in the hotspot around Edinburgh and acting to slow, or reverse, decline in areas with low incomes and projected population decline e.g. Western Isles, Islay, lower Kintyre, Inverclyde, Glasgow and Dundee. The issues here are, firstly, shifts from firefighting and perceived short term political advantage to longer term strategy maximising overall benefits for Scotland and, secondly, the nature of the transport component within strategy. This transport component also requires consideration of the balance between inter-regional and intra-regional policies and funding (see 9.6). The remainder of this section deals with inter-regional issues.

Since inter-regional road links are, for the most part, of good quality with significant spare capacity, an extensive upgrading is unlikely to fit policy objectives. Best value is likely to come from a shift from trunk road investment (apart from measures aiding safety and environmental quality) to improved maintenance and reliability, filling selective gaps and upgrading the quality of inter-regional rail services e.g. by improved passenger frequency, shorter trip times (requiring relatively modest investment) and improved freight facilities. These developments will come more quickly if allied with structural change devolving more rail powers to Scotland and improving delivery mechanisms (Scottish Executive, 2003b and 2003d).

There will be debate on which projects merit inclusion in a more selective list of infrastructure schemes. Airport access and air services policy is certain to attract attention and controversy. While the development case for direct overseas air services and improved Highlands and Islands air services (with lower fares) is strong, the case for further substantial expansion of direct British services from other Scottish airports is weaker. It is in central Scotland that the greatest opportunities exist for a more strategic use of air to promote overall access to Scotland in association with feeder rail services i.e. inclusion of these airports in the rail network rather than the provision of short shuttles to city centres. There is a significant opportunity here to combine improved airport access (increasing the effective catchment area) with an enhanced yet more economical range of flights to and from overseas destinations – including continental hub airports.

Despite doubts from Glasgow, Scotland as a whole is likely to be best served, as the Aviation White Paper proposes, by expanded terminal capacity at Edinburgh, diversion of rail services through the airport and safeguarded land for a second parallel runway. In final decisions next decade, it remains possible that developments in high speed rail plus higher environmental charges for air travel may further delay any requirement for an additional runway. Rather than invest heavily in controversial new runways, the White Paper also indicates a preferred way forward for the west of Scotland through some relative shift of expanding business direct flights to a more accessible Edinburgh coupled with fuller use of Glasgow Airport and spare capacity at Prestwick for a combination of business and leisure flights. Air transport is affected by the private ownership of most airports and airlines yet scope for state aid towards route development and surface access is higher in Scotland. A potential package could match potential job losses for the west arising from an emphasis on Edinburgh as Scotland's 'business' airport with aid placing both Glasgow and Prestwick Airports on the Scottish rail network – i.e. including through services across Glasgow – plus support towards expanded air freight and aircraft maintenance in the west of Scotland. As well as aiding airport access, through rail services from Edinburgh, Dundee and Aberdeen to the south and west of Glasgow would improve access to Ayrshire, Renfrewshire and Inverclyde while easing problems of congestion on the M8 and inner M77. There is a need to evaluate such proposals in the light of the SACTRA and STAG recommendations for assessments of overall gains and the spatial incidence of 'winners' and 'losers'. Similar assessments may justify earlier progress towards reduced rail trip times and improved frequencies from Inverness, Aberdeen and Dundee to Edinburgh and Glasgow.

9.6   Policy Aims, Frameworks and Instruments

As indicated in section 9.3, current policy aims suffer from a lack of clarity aggravated by frameworks which appear chaotic and contradictory. There is wide agreement on the need for a simplified rail structure with infrastructure powers devolved to Scotland and a stronger Executive lead on overall transport and land use strategy. It is now likely that this will see a transfer of rail infrastructure, as well as passenger franchising, powers to the Scottish Executive while also introducing larger elements of a regional devolution of transport powers in Wales and England. Changes in the present roles of the Strategic Rail Authority (SRA) and of the Office of the Rail Regulator (ORR) and Rail Safety regimes are also expected, creating a simpler structure and assisting improved planning and delivery. At the lower end of the 'pyramid of powers', Nicol Stephen, Scottish Minister for Transport, sparked off a debate on the future Scottish balance between Executive, regional and local government powers in transport with the publication of the *Scotland's Transport* consultation paper (Scottish Executive, 2003d). This could involve either an Executive agency, *Transport Scotland*, or an internal review of ministerial and civil service functions to improve delivery. At the regional and local level, however, there are unresolved tensions between the Executive, potential Regional Transport Boards and traditional local government organisation.

The issues here are, not only the balance between inter-regional and inter-regional transport strategy, but also integration with other government objectives, notably for sustainable economic development, area economic priorities and social inclusion in terms of personal training and access to facilities. Seeking perfection in 'joined up' thinking is a dangerous illusion but the Scottish Executive and Parliament must show that it can reduce fragmented thinking and loose partnerships creating their own delays and bureaucracy. How might this be done?

It is suggested that the principal need is to gain political acceptance of a framework within which integrated policies, including transport, can be considered with fuller consultation on longer term options and improved delivery of broadly supported five year programmes for delivery and monitoring. Three levels of framework seem essential:

a) factors external to Scotland but capable of being influenced by Scottish policy

b) Scottish wide policy and inter-regional issues

c) intra-regional and local issues.

With respect to a), there has to be acceptance of the limited ability of the Scottish Executive (even in an 'independent' Scotland) to influence international developments impacting on Scotland. That being so, it becomes possible to focus on the Scottish policies most likely to influence the situation e.g. training and enterprise initiatives, selective financial aids and rebates (within EU/UK rules), inducements for in-tourism, international business access, in-migration, higher birth rates. In tourism, for example, the economy has suffered not only from Scots holidaying abroad on an increasing scale but also from shifts away from Scotland by English and overseas tourists. Hence the emphasis on developing in-tourism niche markets (including transport adjustments) and in encouraging residents to take more short breaks within Scotland.

With respect to b), the Executive needs to develop a closer relationship with Parliament in setting forth its Scottish wide and inter-regional objectives together with arrangements for consultation, research, delivery and monitoring. Again, transport should be expected to have a limited role in impacting on the economy, though important at critical points in packages aiding sustainable development, social inclusion and the needs of particular problem areas. Key transport issues will include:

• targets for the contribution of transport to cumulative cuts in greenhouse gas emissions, reduced social costs, improved air quality and reduced noise (including review of Scottish and local targets for road traffic reduction)

- setting forth policies for fares and road pricing on a Scottish base with respect to all services receiving support from public funds (including integrated ticketing, 'remote area' petrol concessions, extra aids towards island air and ferry fares and a reshaping of concession fares covering more groups with uniform standards across Scotland)

- establishing new minimum standards for access to facilities for those without easy access to cars

- measures to ensure an integrated approach to transport franchising and contracting

- strengthened guidance and related monitoring on links between transport, city region and community planning – including identification of a reduced range of major infrastructure projects considered to be of national significance (with some aimed to aid shifts away from Edinburgh).

With respect to c), the framework could embrace revised arrangements under the national guidance outlined above for decision taking and monitoring at regional and local level, preferably linked with the introduction of more direct sources of income and, more controversially, transparency between transport income (including congestion charging) and transport spending. Local government has expressed concern that new arrangements for transport could reduce its freedom to use block grant income to achieve the best community results under Community Planning but, without some earmarking or ringfencing of transport related income, there are fears that spending on transport and access could be excessively constrained in favour of other and apparently unjustified local government priorities.

At the organisational level, this framework could be supported by the outcome of the consultation on *Scotland's Transport* (Scottish Executive, 2003d). Rather than a large department covering Enterprise, Transport and Lifelong Learning, there could be reform restricting the Transport function of the Enterprise Department to issues related to external links while restoring the former departmental link between internal transport and planning (now extended to include 'community' and funding issues). This would reflect the evidence that disparities in incomes and access to facilities within Scotland – though never likely to disappear – can be narrowed through policies focused on levels of service to individuals and communities rather than on large scale infrastructure projects. Further research and procedural change is needed to ascertain the extent of convergence or conflict in economic and social objectives and to make clear where social, health, habitat and sustainable growth considerations take precedence over shorter term business aspirations.

Difficulties in creating effective inter-departmental links, the legacy of existing institutional practices and spending programmes and the quirkiness of partnership funding can lead to despair about the ability to establish a new Scottish approach which can deliver progress in reducing economic disparities while also strengthening the total economy. Against this, the limitations of traditional public funding and the dynamics of a new Parliament do open up opportunities for debate and action to secure both economic growth and social gains. Newly released official data has claimed that the Scottish economy, despite restricted public funding for transport investment, has performed above previous estimates and, indeed, ahead of the UK (*The Herald*, 12 February 2004). The Scottish problem is of population decline rather than an economic performance well below the UK average. Restructuring of existing funding, extra income from road pricing and a shift of spending away from major road schemes offer the best prospects for continued economic improvement and measures narrowing income and access disparities. This chapter ends with some conclusions and speculations on transport's role in new frameworks for tackling disparities and achieving sustainable growth.

9.7   Conclusions and Speculations

*   Transport now has a lesser and more responsive role in economic development. The transport intensity of advanced economies (movement relative to income per head) is likely to decline for car movement but with some rise for public transport.

*   As a country peripheral to major markets (and sources of incoming tourists), the external transport intensity, notably in relation to air and rail, of the Scottish economy will continue to rise – though at a lower rate than previous forecasts – but internal transport intensity is expected to stabilise or fall.

*   Measures to improve the quality and range of external transport services will be important for the Scottish economy with particular reference to air, shipping and rail.

*   Given the existence of a good internal road network with little congestion, investment in extra road capacity does not merit priority. Policy should encourage shifts to improved maintenance, demand management (including congestion charging), selective road schemes and upgrading of the rail and bus networks (including tram schemes and direct rail access to Edinburgh and Glasgow Airports).

*   With stability or a slight fall likely in Scotland's overall population, there is little scope for major policy shifts to influence the inter-regional distribution of population and incomes. However, policy should encourage through rail services from the south and west to east and north of Glasgow and shorter trip times to Aberdeen and Inverness.

*   Some specific inter-regional projects should be evaluated to assess their impact on the Scottish economy and the incidence of spatial 'winners' and 'losers'.

There is scope for using transport and funding policies to reduce overheating around Edinburgh and encourage a shift in the balance of economic activity towards the West of Scotland, the Borders, Upper Forth, Fife, Dundee and Aberdeen.

• The principal scope for action to reduce disparities in access to facilities is within Scotland's regions and travel-to-work-areas. Action should include closer links between transport and land use planning and programmes to encourage modal shift from cars and to narrow the access gap between those with and without access to cars.

• 'Deep rural' areas merit action to reduce disparities by car licence rebates and by easing levels of road fuel taxation (or providing rebates), improving rural public transport, encouraging the retention of shops and filling stations and continuing with significant programmes for sensitive enhancement of the road network, new ferry and bus links, fare reductions and selective aid towards air travel and airport costs.

• Policy frameworks and funding should be modified to encourage joined up thinking and more effective use of existing funding within disciplined partnerships and packages aiming to reduce disparities while promoting sustainable overall growth.

• Across the Central Belt, existing councils are too small to deliver effective and integrated planning for travel to work and shopping catchment areas. Consideration should be given to:

a) a more specified Scottish Executive vision for the Central Belt as a whole;
b) strengthening of City Region Plans to include statutory responsibilities for transport, access and area development with earmarked sources of funding – including early introduction of ringfenced finance and road user charging;
c) an enlarged role for local councils, businesses and residents in preparing and delivering Community Plans.

• Since most internal movement is within sub-regions of Scotland, effective delivery of economic and social goals is likely to be helped by a significant transfer of trunk roads (and certain railways) to Regional Transport Bodies acting in a framework set by the Scottish Executive.

References

Christaller, W. (1933) *Die Zentralen Orte in Suddeutschland.*
Department for Transport (2003) *The Future of Air Transport*, White Paper, December.
Dupuit, J. (1844) 'On the measurement of the utility of public works', reproduced in Munby, D. (ed) (1968) *Transport: Selected Readings.*

Hart, T. (1994) 'Transport choices and sustainability: a review of changing trends and policies', *Urban Studies*, 31(4/5), pp.705-727.

Hart, T. and Doar, N. (eds) (1999) *Transport Policy Options for a Sustainable Scotland, 2000-2020: An Assessment of Three Scenarios*, Scottish Forum for Transport and the Environment, February.

Joint Steering Committee (1974) *West Central Scotland Plan*.

Leitch Report (1978) *Report of the Advisory Committee on Trunk Road Assessment*, HMSO.

McKinnon, A.C. (1999/2000a) 'Freight expectations, 2000-2020', *Scottish Transport Review*, 8, p.10.

McKinnon, A.C. (1999/2000b) 'Food distribution and energy efficiency', *Scottish Transport Review*, 8, p.14.

Royal Commission on Environmental Pollution (RCEP) (1994) *Eighteenth Report: Transport and the Environment*, Cm2674, HMSO.

SACTRA (Standing Advisory Committee on Trunk Road Assessment) (1998) *Interim Report on Transport and the Economy*, DETR.

SACTRA (Standing Advisory Committee on Trunk Road Assessment) (1999) *Final Report on Transport and the Economy*, DETR.

Scottish Executive (2000) *The Way Forward: Framework for Economic Development in Scotland*, June.

Scottish Executive (2001) *Scottish Transport Appraisal Guidance (STAG) – Consultation Draft*, July.

Scottish Executive (2002a) *Scotland's Transport: Delivering Improvements*, March.

Scottish Executive (2002b) *Analysis of Cities Review*, especially Chapter 6 on 'Connecting cities'.

Scottish Executive (2003a) *Guide to Transport Assessment in Scotland*, Consultation, January.

Scottish Executive (2003b) *Decisions on Central Scotland Transport Corridor Studies*, January.

Scottish Executive (2003c) *Scottish Transport Appraisal Guidance* (STAG), September.

Scottish Executive (2003d) *Scotland's Transport: Proposals for a New Approach – Consultation*, September.

Scottish Executive (2004) *Planning for Transport Consultation*, Scottish Planning Policy (SPP) 17, January.

Scottish Office (1963) *Central Scotland: A Programme for Development and Growth*.

Scottish Office (1998) *Travel Choices for Scotland: Scottish Integrated Transport*, White Paper, Cm4010.

Scottish Office (1999) *Transport and Planning*, National Planning Policy Guideline 17.

Simmonds, D. (2003) *M74 Completion: Report on Economic and Locational Impact Appraisal*, presented to M74 Public Inquiry, December.

Von Thunen, J.H. (1826 and 1850) *Die Isolierte Staat*, Parts 1 and 2.

Chapter 10

Urban Regeneration in Scotland: Context, Contributions and Choices for the Future

Peter Roberts

10.1 Introduction

Urban regeneration is an important aspect of selective spatial intervention policy in Scotland. It has developed as a discrete activity from the 1960s onwards and it now exhibits a range of modes of operation that vary from small scale prospects of limited duration, to large scale multi-annual programmes which incorporate many aspects of area regeneration. Whilst much of the practice of urban regeneration in Scotland conforms to the general model that is encountered elsewhere in the United Kingdom and the European Union, it is also possible to distinguish a number of distinctive Scottish approaches and contributions; this point is developed later.

In any discussion of urban regeneration it is essential to recognise that whilst practitioners and commentators may refer to a particular set of actions as 'regeneration', it is likely that the component parts of an individual regeneration package will be drawn from a variety of sources. This suggests that urban regeneration, in common with other complex packages of spatial intervention policy, has close links with a wide range of associated policy fields from which it selects elements that are blended together to reflect individual local circumstances and challenges. Equally, the central elements of urban regeneration policy and practice provide a store of approaches and modes of practice that can be, and are, applied in other policy fields. This interchangeability between urban regeneration and associated policy fields is an important feature of the Scottish approach.

Two other points of introduction must be made here. First, urban regeneration has been described as a 'widely experienced but little understood phenomenon' (Roberts and Sykes, 2000a, p.3). This is an indication that, whilst what we describe as an example of urban regeneration may not appear to conform to a single ideal model, this, in itself, need not be considered to represent a barrier to good practice. This characteristic also reflects a somewhat more serious issue: that is, the dangers that are inherent in selecting an approach to regeneration that is drawn from experience elsewhere, without ensuring that an assessment has been conducted of the extent to which the approach is appropriate to another locality (Rifkind, 1999). Second, it is also essential to establish the wider spatial and policy context for an individual regeneration programme or project. Any failure to comply with this basic requirement runs the risk of establishing a 'cathedral in the desert', that is, a regeneration project that exhibits little or no linkage with its host locality or resident community.

The remainder of this chapter concentrates on three topics. First, it presents a discussion of the general characteristics and key features of urban regeneration and discusses the evolution of this area of activity from the 1960s to the present day. Second, it examines a number of the theoretical and practice based foundations for, and forms of, urban regeneration policy in Scotland. Third, it identifies some of the features of best practice evident in Scotland and, learning from this experience outlines an approach to meeting the challenges that urban regeneration will face in the future. The majority of illustrations presented in the chapter are drawn from the experience of urban regeneration in Scotland. However, because the dissemination of best practice is a two way affair, the chapter also draws upon material that reflects experience elsewhere in the European Union and North America.

10.2   Urban Regeneration: Origins, Characteristics and Features

10.2.1 Origins

Urban regeneration policy, as we understand it today, first emerged in the 1960s as a means of exercising positive discrimination on an area basis (McCarthy 1999a). However, in a wider sense, urban regeneration policy has existed since the second half of the nineteenth century. This earlier point of origin for urban regeneration policy can be identified by reference to the great civic schemes for urban improvement that focussed attention on the improvement of sanitary conditions and the provision of fit housing, on the one hand, and on the building of the great Victorian towns and cities, on the other hand. Scottish towns and cities followed this general pathway of housing and health improvement and also developed or redeveloped their core areas, often superimposing a 'new' urban system on an existing pattern of settlement (Hall, 1988).

The intentions behind many of these nineteenth century schemes of urban regeneration were directly associated with the need to respond to the consequences of rapid industrialisation. Chief among these responses was the requirement to provide sufficient housing to accommodate the new concentrations of industrial and domestic workers that were attracted into the towns and cities. In addition, the urban system itself frequently had to be remodelled in order to accommodate new economic activities and infrastructure requirements. However, although in some cases this pattern of adjustment and change was achieved at the lowest possible cost and with the minimum of urban improvement, in many towns and cities the opportunity was taken to provide a grand civic statement of pride and prosperity. Furthermore, in addition to the regeneration and expansion of existing towns and cities, enlightened experiments in 'model village' development offered an alternative to the traditional urban system. New Lanark is the best known of these experiments in Scotland.

The general pattern of civic improvement and expansion continued into the twentieth century, often accompanied by rapid urban growth following the building of commuter railways and the later introduction of the bus and car. Whilst this escape to the suburbs provided a relief valve for the more affluent and mobile, it did little to reduce the problems increasingly encountered in the inner urban areas. In addition, many Scottish towns and cities, especially those located in areas dependent on basic industries and heavy manufacturing, experienced new problems of social, economic and physical decline associated with the recession of the late 1920s and early 1930s.

Following the Second World War, in many Scottish towns and cities considerable emphasis was placed on physical reconstruction and, as a consequence of the need to accommodate a growing population with enhanced aspirations as regards housing, the provision of improved and new housing both in-situ and at the periphery of existing urban areas. The latter point should be noted, because it is this rapid postwar peripheral expansion of urban areas that later spawned a range of new urban problems, many of which have been addressed in recent years.

From the 1950s onwards, urban regeneration followed a pattern of evolution that tracked and reflected a number of dominant trends in associated areas of public and private policy. Although the details of each of these strands of policy will be considered in the following section, the overall pattern of evolution represented a shift away from the domination of policy by the central state and the adoption of an approach that was, and still is, based on multi-level partnership. In parallel with this shift in the method of approach, the focus of urban regeneration has changed, with less emphasis now given to physical and economic factors and greater attention paid to the design and delivery of policies that allow for the achievement of sustainable development.

By the 1960s, the overall pattern of evolution of urban regeneration, as we understand the term today, had generally been set. Subsequent events have seen the rise and fall of different methods of approach, with, not surprisingly, a certain circularity emerging as the various scales and structures of urban regeneration activity emerge or decline. Emphasis has shifted from the immediate neighbourhood to the regional level, and back again. Equally, the emphasis placed in the 1960s on education as the 'key' to 'unlock' the 'urban problem' has re-emerged in the late 1990s and early twenty first century in the guise of education and training for individual and community empowerment.

10.2.2 Changing Characteristics

As has already been noted, a clearly discernible pattern of evolution can be identified which helps to explain the changing nature and characteristics of urban regeneration. In part, this pattern of evolution reflects the general adjustments that can be observed in the philosophy and content of urban and regional policy (Roberts and Lloyd, 1999; Capellin, 1997), but it also represents the introduction of new drivers that are the outcome of the development and adoption of innovative institutional and financial arrangements. Some of these new arrangements have been introduced as a consequence of a genuine desire on the part of central government to encourage a higher level of local content in urban regeneration but it is also evident that other new institutional structures have emerged as a response to a reduction or withdrawal of public sector funding. Irrespective of the initial stimulus, most manifestations of the new institutional arrangements for urban regeneration are based on some form of partnership.

A second new driver of policy evolution emerged in the late 1980s and early 1990s. This was the realisation that many forms of spatial intervention policy, irrespective of their particular design or application, are potentially important vehicles for the delivery of sustainable development. This realisation has subsequently been reflected in a series of changes to both the content and the methodology of urban regeneration. In more specific terms, the requirements of sustainable development caused academics and policy makers to search for new approaches to regeneration that enable seemingly conflicting objectives to be reconciled. This has seen the moderation of early approaches which had emphasised the physical and economic elements of urban regeneration (Turok, 1987) and the encouragement of approaches which have facilitated greater policy co-ordination (Hayton, 1996).

A third driver of change has emerged more recently. This is the search for methods of organisation that allow for different areas of policy and institutional responsibility to be brought together in a single territorial programme. The Scottish manifestation of this approach can be seen with the introduction of community planning (Illsley and McCarthy, 1998), whilst other initiatives that contribute to the achievement of the objective of greater territorial coherence can be seen at a more local level, including the introduction of Social Inclusion Partnerships (SIPs). This search for greater territorial integration in policy is driven by the desire to achieve a higher level of output for a given level of input. Particular emphasis in such an approach is placed upon the minimisation of any duplication in the operation of the processes of administration and the maximisation of 'products'. This search for minimum 'process' and maximum 'product' solutions can be seen at urban and regional levels (Roberts, 2000a).

The influence of these three drivers of change can be traced through the evolution of the various strands of urban regeneration. Table 10.1 illustrates this process.

Table 10.1 demonstrates the ways in which the roles that are performed by the various actors have changed from the 1950s to the present day. It is also possible to trace the influences exerted by other drivers: sustainable development can be seen as a growing force that has guided the more inclusive approach that is now adopted with regard to environmental and social matters, while the search for greater territorial coherence in the design and delivery of a range of policies has led to the reintroduction of a strategic approach to regeneration.

This general pattern of evolution of urban regeneration has also acquired a more explicit Scottish dimension in recent years. A number of authors have outlined and analysed the characteristics of this Scottish dimension. Turok and Hopkins (1998) point to the influence of the decentralising approach that was adopted when the Urban Programme was reshaped in the mid 1990s. This major

Table 10.1   The evolution of urban regeneration

Policy type	1950s	1960s	1970s	1980s	1990s
	Reconstruction	Revitalisation	Renewal	Redevelopment	Regeneration
Major strategy and orientation	Reconstruction and extension of older town and city areas, often based on a 'masterplan'; suburban growth	Continuation of 1950s theme; suburban and peripheral growth; some early attempts at rehabilitation	Focus on in-situ renewal and neighbourhood schemes; still development at periphery	Many major schemes of development and redevelopment; flagship projects	Move towards a more comprehensive form of policy and practice; more emphasis on integrated treatments
Key actors and stakeholders	National and local government; private sector developers and contractors	Move towards a greater balance between public and private sectors	Growing role of private sector and decentralisation in local government	Emphasis on private sector and special agencies; growth of partnerships	Partnership the dominant approach
Spatial level of activity	Emphasis on local and site levels	Regional level of activity emerged	Regional and local levels initially; later more local emphasis	In early 1980s focus on site; later emphasis on local level	Reintroduction of strategic perspective; growth of regional activity
Economic focus	Public sector investment with some private sector involvement	Continuing from 1950s with growing influence of private investment	Resource constraints in public sector and growth of private investment	Private sector dominant with selective public funds	Greater balance between public, private and voluntary funding
Social content	Improvement of housing and living standards	Social and welfare improvement	Community based action and greater empowerment	Community self-help with very selective state support	Emphasis on the role of the community
Physical emphasis	Replacement of inner areas and peripheral development	Some continuation from 1950s with parallel rehabilitation of existing areas	More extensive renewal of urban areas	Major schemes of replacement and redevelopment; 'flagship schemes'	More modest than 1980s; heritage and retention
Environmental approach	Landscaping and some greening	Selective improvements	Environmental improvement with some innovations	Growth of concern for wider approach to environment	Introduction of broader idea of environmental sustainability

Source: Roberts, 2000b.

change in the way in which regeneration policy was to be designed and delivered, focused on the provision of a block allocation of funding to a smaller number of areas. The aim of this new approach was to promote more strategic and integrated urban regeneration. Despite criticism of the procedures which were used to select these new Priority Partnership Areas (PPAs), the emphasis on policy integration and co-ordination has continued. Indeed, this emphasis on the promotion of integration can be seen to have been one of the factors that influenced the introduction of the successors to PPAs, the Social Inclusion Partnerships (SIPs).

Other explicitly Scottish themes that are evident in the recent evolution of urban regeneration policy include the characteristics that have been identified by McCarthy (1999a) and Hayton (1999):

- the lead role that is performed by local government;
- the large degree of consensus on matters of policy and implementation between national and local government;
- the emphasis placed upon strategy, although this is not always evident in practice;
- an increasing attempt to address local needs and involve local communities; and
- the recent downgrading of the role performed by the private sector.

In addition to these overall themes, there are, as always, particular characteristics that are evident at local or regional level and which represent the institutional inheritance that is evident in an individual area.

10.2.3 Key Features

The final part of this section of the chapter examines the key features of urban regeneration that are evident both in Scotland and elsewhere (Roberts, 2000b). Whilst it is unlikely that an individual programme of regeneration will conform to an ideal model, it is reasonable to expect the majority of programmes to reflect most of the features. Reflecting the evolution and characteristics described in the previous parts of this chapter, urban regeneration should:

- be based on a detailed analysis of the condition of an individual urban area;
- be aimed at the simultaneous adaptation of the physical fabric, social structure, economic situation and environmental condition of an urban area;
- attempt to achieve this task of simultaneous adaptation through the generation and implementation of a comprehensive and integrated strategy that deals with the resolution of problems in a balanced, ordered and positive manner;
- ensure that a strategy and the resulting programme of implementation are developed in accord with the aims of sustainable development;
- set clear operational objectives which should, wherever possible, be quantified;
- make the best possible use of natural, human, economic and other resources, including land and existing features of the built environment;
- seek to ensure consensus through the fullest possible participation and co-operation of all stakeholders with a legitimate interest in the regeneration of an

urban area; this may be achieved through partnership or other modes of working;

- recognise the importance of measuring the progress of strategy towards the achievement of specified objectives and of monitoring the changing nature and influence of the internal and external forces which act upon an urban area;
- accept the likelihood that an initial programme of implementation will need to be revised in line with such changes as occur;
- recognise the reality that the various elements of a strategy are likely to make progress at different speeds; this may require the redirection of resources or the provision of additional resources in order to maintain a broad balance between the aims encompassed in a scheme of urban regeneration and to allow for the achievement of all of the strategic objectives.

What is suggested by these features, is that urban regeneration as a discrete area of theory and practice can be distinguished by the combination of activities that is represented in a typical programme and by the attempt which is made to provide a cross sector, co-ordinated and integrated solution. Other authors have recognised this characteristic: Pacione (1997) argues that urban regeneration is the management of urban change across sectors whilst McCarthy (1999b) notes the shift that has occurred in recent years towards the adoption of a more strategic and inclusive approach to regeneration. Despite the fact that some authors claim that much of urban regeneration policy and practice in Scotland has been, and still is, somewhat unbalanced with a 'wholly insufficient emphasis on promoting jobs that are accessible to the unemployed' (Webster, 2000, p.28), this criticism does not detract from the general performance of urban regeneration.

It is important to acknowledge that urban regeneration is both a process and a set of policies. The policy function is widely recognised and accepted, whilst the process aspect is less well researched or understood. Lichfield (2000) has provided a comprehensive assessment of urban regeneration as a managed process of change. Many of the general elements of process arrangement explored by Lichfield are reflected in the experience of constructing and implementing urban regeneration partnerships in Scotland (Chapman, 1998). However, in the final analysis, the distinguishing feature of successful urban regeneration is the bringing together of policy, process and product in order to achieve a desired outcome.

10.3   Urban Regeneration Policy in Scotland: Approaches and Achievements

10.3.1 Approaches

Traditional approaches to urban regeneration in Scotland under the Urban Programme tended to emphasise small scale projects that encompassed a range of elements of local and community development. Following this experience, a key defining event in the evolution of Scottish urban regeneration policy was the establishment of the Glasgow Eastern Area Renewal (GEAR) programme. This programme was the first major regeneration task undertaken by the Scottish Development Agency (SDA) and it introduced a wider, more programmatic approach to regeneration across a large part of inner Glasgow. Even though some commentators have suggested that the SDA displaced local government in terms of the role that it performed in the design and operation of GEAR (Atkinson and Moon, 1994; McCarthy, 1999b); the importance of this scheme should not be underestimated. However, despite having broken with tradition in establishing GEAR, the SDA's approach to regeneration evolved considerably in the late 1970s and early 1980s. In the late 1970s the SDA began to focus on economic aspects of regeneration in areas that had experienced major industrial restructuring, while in the 1980s emphasis was increasingly placed on, first, small area projects and, second, the encouragement of a greater level of participation by the private sector in regeneration schemes.

Alongside the transformation of the role performed by the SDA, the mainstream Urban Programme itself evolved during the 1980s. New Life for Urban Scotland (Scottish Office, 1988) placed emphasis on the need for the greater co-ordination of public sector activities and, in a marked change in policy, shifted attention from the regeneration of the inner urban areas to the problems experienced in peripheral or outer housing estates (Hayton, 1993). This change of direction in urban policy saw the establishment of four major Urban Partnerships: in Dundee (Whitfield), Edinburgh (Wester Hailes), Glasgow (Castlemilk), and Paisley (Ferguslie Park). These new ten year partnership arrangements involved the Scottish Office in working with local authorities, the (then) SDA, Scottish Homes, Health Boards, Manpower Services Commission, and local community and voluntary groups. Emphasis was placed on a strategic, partnership based approach. Underpinning the operation of the partnerships were three principles (Hayton, 1993):

- partnership between the public and private sectors and the local community;
- a central role defined for the private sector;
- the active involvement of the local community.

Furthermore, these principles were to be realised by the adoption of an integrated and strategic approach that would emphasise the development and implementation of a balanced portfolio of economic, social, environmental and physical actions, although it was recognised that the key problem facing the estates was one of economic disadvantage and decline. Even though the Urban Partnerships were successful in bringing about improvements in the physical condition of the estates and in the provision of community facilities, other aspects of the four programmes have been criticised for failing sufficiently to progress economic development (Hayton, 1993; Turok and Hopkins, 1998) or to stimulate certain aspects of environmental and social regeneration. In an independent evaluation of the New Life for Urban Scotland initiative, Tarling et al (1999) concluded that the initiative had been successful in furthering policy development in a more informed and focused way; that it demonstrated the merits of a comprehensive, strategic approach to regeneration; and, in comparison with other large scale regeneration schemes, that it provided value for money. As will be elaborated later, it is evident that some of the initiatives promoted by the Urban Partnerships were considered innovative at the time that they were developed.

Drawing upon the experience of the Urban Partnerships, and attempting also to incorporate the experience of effective regeneration from elsewhere, the review of the Urban Programme conducted in 1991/92 supported the more widespread application of the strategic partnership approach. Turok and Hopkins (1998, p.2026) also point to the desire expressed at this time and subsequently reflected in policy, that 'local communities should play a bigger role in such coalitions'. The consultation paper on the future of the Urban Programme also addressed some of the failings and weaknesses that had become evident in previous rounds of policy, including a recognition that 'increased employment and income levels are the key to the sustainability of other physical and social improvements' (Scottish Office, 1993, p.1). The outcome of the process of review and consultation was the introduction of the Programme for Partnership initiative and the designation in 1996 of Priority Partnership Areas (PPAs) in a number of Scottish towns and cities. These PPAs were to be local or council wide programmes and involved relatively small amounts of funding. Twelve PPAs were designated, each to operate for ten years, covering populations of varying size (see Table 10.2).

Table 10.2   Priority Partnership Areas

Area/PPP name	Population of PPA	UP funding for 3 years (£m)
Aberdeen	5,300	1.55
Dundee	14,700	3.30
Edinburgh - Craigmillar	11,500	3.07
- North	15,400	3.90
Glasgow - East End	29,900	4.14
- Easterhouse	37,500	5.34
- North	29,800	4.58
Inverclyde	29,800	3.87
North Lanarkshire	17,300	2.49
Renfrewshire	28,800	3.88
South Ayrshire	8,300	2.75
West Dunbartonshire	28,200	3.40

The PPAs were selected on a competitive basis, which in the view of Turok and Hopkins (1998) did not fully reflect the adopted criteria and procedures due to the intrusion of additional considerations. Social need, bid quality and the coherence of the proposed programme were supposed to have been the chief factors used to determine the selection of PPAs. However, in practice there 'appears to have been an inclination to spread the winners among different local authorities' and, as a consequence, resources were not always allocated in the expected manner, thereby resulting in Glasgow securing 'far less of the new resources than it probably deserved to' (Turok and Hopkins, 1998, p.2049). For those authorities not designated as having a PPA, a smaller amount of funding – about a third of the total budget – was available. These smaller Regeneration Partnerships (RPs) were also based on partnership arrangements.

A further development, and one which sought more directly to address the question of social exclusion, was the Social Inclusion Partnerships (SIPs) initiative launched in 1998 (Scottish Executive, 2002). There are currently 48 SIPs in Scotland. They are multi-agency partnerships charged with the co-ordination of activities to promote social inclusion. They are funded from the SIP Fund which replaced the Urban Programme in 1999. There are two different types of SIPs. The majority are area based, targeting specific geographical areas of deprivation. Some of these evolved from PPAs and RPs. Thematic SIPs target specific groups such as young people or minority ethnic communities. Communities Scotland currently has responsibility for the SIP programme. However, control of SIPs is now being transferred to local Community Planning structures (discussed further in Chapter 11).

Above and beyond these specific urban policy measures, various other policy fields have contributed to urban regeneration in Scotland. In particular, and perhaps most importantly, mainstream local authority and special agency expenditure on housing, social welfare, education, transport, economic development and environmental management has contributed to local initiatives. Furthermore, many urban regeneration initiatives have been the subject of policy support and financial allocations from the European Union's Structural Funds. In addition, and often ignored or underestimated, both the voluntary or community sector and private investors have provided ideas, resources and a determination to succeed; without these contributions many urban regeneration initiatives would have failed to mature. Finally, and most recently, the *Building Better Cities* review of Scotland's cities (Scottish Executive, 2003) has resulted in the creation of a City Growth Fund which will provide £90m to Edinburgh, Glasgow, Aberdeen, Dundee, Inverness and Stirling over a three year period to help fund a variety of physical infrastructure works. These will include a number of regeneration activities with particular attention being paid to addressing the widespread problem of vacant and derelict land.

10.3.2 Achievements

Urban regeneration programmes and initiatives in Scotland have been the subject of a number of research studies that have attempted to identify and evaluate the key achievements of policy. Some of these assessments have been conducted as official reviews or evaluations of public sector policies whilst other contributions have emerged from academic research and the monitoring and assessment activities of private sector organisations and voluntary or community groups. In some of these exercises a particular aspect or field of policy has been the focus of attention whilst other evaluations have placed specific emphasis on spatial matters or to the implications of particular aspects of policy in, or for, an individual area.

Among other achievements, urban regeneration policy in Scotland, when compared with the general pattern of activity elsewhere in the UK, would appear to have established a particular 'blend' or style of operation. McCarthy (1999a), for example, claims that the features of this distinctive Scottish approach include:

- a lead role for local government, illustrated by the fact that urban development corporations were not designated in Scotland;
- a substantial degree of consensus between national and local government regarding the form and content of urban regeneration;
- an emphasis on strategy and integration, albeit that the degree of emphasis has varied over time and, in some cases, is questionable; and
- an attempt to address local needs and to involve local communities.

Hayton (1999) adds to this list the recent downgrading of the role of the private sector; this contrasts, for example, with the 'business led' approach to regional regeneration that has been adopted as one of the distinctive features of the English Regional Development Agencies. Two additional features of Scottish urban regeneration are, first, the emphasis placed on partnership, which in recent years has extended to include, on the one hand, very small neighbourhood groups that have frequently been ignored in previous regeneration programmes, and, on the other hand, the direct participation of senior members of Scottish Office Staff through secondment to work on local partnership projects. A second feature is the wider 'filtering through' of regeneration objectives into associated aspects of public policy. The latter point also reflects the high level of common purpose that can be detected in Scotland, especially when compared with the somewhat more fragmented public policy system that exists in England (Roberts and Lloyd, 1999).

This combination of the features and characteristics of Scottish urban regeneration policy represents a first layer of analysis, other achievements are associated with individual aspects of policy or with particular methods of policy delivery. Three examples that illustrate these features are presented in the remainder of this section of the chapter:

- the establishment and operation of partnership and collaboration arrangements;
- the importance attached to strategy and its use as a guiding framework for urban regeneration initiatives;
- the development of arrangements for integration and co-ordination in the design and delivery of urban regeneration.

Partnership has emerged as a dominant theme in Scottish urban regeneration. Whilst this could also be claimed as an achievement of urban regeneration practice elsewhere in the UK in more recent years, the introduction of the partnership approach in Scotland predates the general adoption of this mode of working. Chapman, (1998, p.20) points, for example, to the commencement in 1981 of the Dundee city wide partnership and the success of the arrangements in enabling 'key partners to work together and form a broad and well-organised partnership for the city'. Even though some authors have voiced reservations about the structure and operation of partnerships, especially the twin requirements that local or neighbourhood partnership should be set within the context of a city wide perspective, and that they should be comprehensive (Turok and Hopkins, 1998), there is widespread support for the use of an inclusive partnership approach, even though Hayton (1999) has made a valid criticism of some of the attempts to create 'instant partnerships' or to represent ill defined umbrella bodies as partnerships.

Drawing upon the assessments of partnerships that have been conducted by Hayton (1993), Chapman (1998), Carley et al (2000) and McCarthy (1999c), some of the key features of partnership working in urban regeneration in Scotland are:

- the importance of securing the voluntary commitment of the partners and of ensuring a high level of inclusiveness, even if this may not at first sight appear to be the most efficient way of working;
- the creation of partnerships that are equal in terms of the access that each partner has to the decision making process of the partnership, even though the need for strong leadership should not be ignored or avoided;
- the recognition at the outset of the need to link together the various aspects and components of regeneration and to establish a vision and strategy that can be used to guide subsequent processes of choice and implementation;
- the translation of vision and strategy into specific programmes of action, the assignment of responsibilities to partners and establishment of locally based teams that are dedicated to the regeneration programme;
- the need to ensure openness, accountability and transparency in decision making and to encourage the development of a culture of trust and mutual support;
- the provision of assistance, encouragement and facilities in order to enable the personal development of all who are involved in partnerships – this will allow participants to develop their skills of partnership working and can result in the emergence of self supporting structures;
- the desirability of genuinely empowering communities and ensuring that the partnership model becomes embedded in a localities;
- the importance of monitoring and evaluating partnerships and their actions, and the need to ensure the effective dissemination of the lessons of best practice and what should be avoided.

Although individual Scottish towns and cities may display only some of the above characteristics of partnership working, or indeed, may demonstrate other unique features that reflect particular local conditions, it is evident that one of the achievements of regeneration in Scotland has been the gradual establishment of a pool of partnership experience. Learning from the lessons of the 1970s and 1980s, the PPAs and SIPs have sought to incorporate many of the factors noted above.

Strategy and the co-ordinated programming and implementation of urban regeneration initiatives represent a second area of achievement. As has already been demonstrated, strategy is an essential foundation for effective partnership working. However, even if partnership is not the preferred mode of organisation, there is still a need for a clear and well informed view of what is to be done and how the process of regeneration should proceed. Urban regeneration in Scotland started with a somewhat higher strategic 'content' than regeneration policy elsewhere in the UK. This can be seen in the approach in the planning and delivery of GEAR and in relation to other major SDA associated initiatives. In part, this strategic emphasis was an essential requirement given the scale and scope of many of these programmes, but it also reflected the multi organisational nature of the approach used and the general adoption by the SDA of a strategy based model of operation.

Over the past quarter century the role of strategy in Scottish urban regeneration has varied in terms of the extent to which it has been used and it has been expressed in a number of different guises. As was seen in the case of partnership, strategy has become a generally accepted element of many of the urban regeneration schemes designed and developed by local authorities and other partners (Gomez, 1998). Strategy has also figured as an important element in the design and delivery of smaller regeneration schemes, such as the Smaller Urban Renewal Initiatives (SURIs) introduced by Scottish Homes in order to support housing and associated investment and regeneration in smaller towns (Scottish Homes, 1998). Despite this general acceptance of the merits of a strategic approach, some authors have suggested that certain of the more recent initiatives, including some of the Urban Partnerships, have lacked sufficient strategic grounding (McCarthy, 1999b). A final point to note in relation to strategy and partnership, is the way in which this mode of operation has spread to other areas of activity in recent years, such as the arrangements for the management of Scottish Structural Funds regional programmes (Roberts and Hart, 1997) and the exchange of views and approaches that have resulted from this associational relationship.

The third area of achievement to be considered relates to the attempt that has been made to develop and apply an integrated and co-ordinated approach to urban regeneration. Once again, this is an approach which is both an input to, and an output from, the use of a strategic partnership model of organisation. In more specific terms, this issue of the promotion of what is currently referred to as 'joined up' thinking and action, has been the subject of a number of assessments. The conclusion reached by Hayton (1999) is that it is possible to identify the emergence of a more balanced approach in recent urban regeneration policy and that this has helped to reduce the emphasis placed on physical solutions. Other commentators argue that the introduction of the SIPs is an attempt to tackle urban problems in 'a more integrated manner' (McCarthy, 1999b, p.562) and that, at a smaller scale, SURIs were designed as a way of linking together policy fields in order to deliver integrated solutions (Scottish Homes, 1998).

It is in relation to this issue of the integration and co-ordination of urban regeneration policy, that the level of achievement is less easy to assess. Indeed, it can be argued that the overall achievement is substantially lower than is evident in the case of partnership and strategy. Turok and Hopkins (1998, p.2027), for example, have observed that while the Urban Partnerships 'were not comprehensive; they typically focused on particular issues and neglected others', many of their policies and projects did not need to be integrated. Other criticisms of this aspect of urban regeneration, include the concern that insufficient attention has been paid to linking physical regeneration to the provision of jobs that are accessible to the unemployed (Webster, 2000), that the SURIs failed to link housing initiatives strategically with local economic development (Scottish Homes, 1998) and that it has proved difficult for effective links to be established between funding for urban regeneration and funding for mainstream services (Chapman, 1998). More seriously, Hayton has pointed to a failure to integrate urban regeneration initiatives spatially with other aspects of policy and has identified 'a tendency to treat the targeted areas as if they were islands in which policy could be implemented in a way that was insulated from the wider urban area' (Hayton, 1999, p.4).

In summary, therefore, in relation to these three areas of achievement, two – partnership and strategy – can be considered to represent aspects of practice that are widespread in application and mature in terms of their stage of development. The record of the third aspect – integration and co-ordination – is more patchy. However, overall, and when compared with the record elsewhere, Scottish urban regeneration has made steady progress and can demonstrate success at a number of levels.

10.4   Best Practice and Future Challenges

10.4.1 Best Practice

As has been demonstrated in the preceding section, whilst there are a number of matters and aspects of urban regeneration policy and practice in Scotland that require remedial attention in order to correct weaknesses in either the design of policy or its execution, there are also many examples of best practice. It is these examples of best practice that deserve specific attention in order that evidence from the leading edge of urban regeneration may be encapsulated in future policy and in practice guidance.

Before examining specific examples, it is important to set the context for the best practice of urban regeneration in Scotland. One manifestation of this context, which allows for comparisons to be made with practice elsewhere in the UK, is provided by the annual Best Practice Awards made by the British Urban Regeneration Association (BURA). Scottish urban regeneration has figured prominently in the BURA Awards. The schemes awarded range from regeneration programmes in historic city centres to community-based actions undertaken in peripheral estates. Five examples of what can be achieved are presented in order to illustrate the overall standard of urban regeneration practice in Scotland.

Examining these examples of best practice, what can be identified are a number of characteristics of best practice (Roberts and Sykes, 2000b), these include:

- the contribution made to the economic regeneration of an area and the importance of ensuring the financial viability of an initiative;

- the extent to which a scheme has acted as a catalyst for further regeneration in an area and/or in adjacent neighbourhoods;
- the contribution made to community spirit and social cohesion;
- the contribution made to building the capacity of local people to the plan and influence the future development of their area;
- the environmental sustainability of a scheme;
- the presence of a firm foundation for sound management and future development;
- the involvement of a wide range of partners;
- the qualities of imagination, inspiration and determination.

Some or all of these characteristics are evident in the following examples drawn from the list of BURA Best Practice Awards; examples are provided here of various types of urban regeneration scheme:

a) Dunbar Initiative – Historic Town Regeneration

This programme of improvement and regeneration concentrated initially on the town centre of Dunbar. From 1995 onwards the emphasis extended to include housing improvements and tourism related activities. The Dunbar programme was based on an original agreement between the (then) district and regional authorities, Edinburgh and Lothian Enterprise, the SDA and Scottish Homes to make staff available to the Initiative, to prioritise spending from existing budgets and to integrate projects. Over £22 million of public money has been spent, together with substantial private and community investments in both cash and kind.

b) The Whitfield Partnership, Dundee – Estate Regeneration

Whitfield is a peripheral housing estate on the north east side of Dundee. Planned in 1965 to have a population of 12,000 people, it had become by the 1980s an area of multiple deprivation. The Whitfield Partnership was established in 1988 and total expenditure on regeneration from all partnership sources during the first six years was in excess of £55 million, with a leverage of approximately 6:1 between public and private funding. A major programme of housing improvement has been accompanied by various economic development initiatives that have reduced unemployment and raised local incomes. Environmental improvements and enhanced community facilities have also been provided.

c) The Italian Centre, Glasgow – Mixed Use Regeneration

This scheme was concerned with the regeneration of a group of derelict warehouses and tenements in Glasgow's Merchant City. High quality classical and contemporary art is incorporated into the scheme, which provides a quality setting for residential and office accommodation alongside shops, cafes, a restaurant and a wine bar. The programme was developed under a public-private partnership and involved investment of over £7 million.

d) New Lanark – Model Settlement Regeneration

New Lanark represented a major step forward in the design and development of industrial settlements when it was established in the late eighteenth century. Robert Owen's self contained cotton spinning community housed 2500 people, provided decent housing and a range of social facilities. Cotton production ended in 1968 and the village population had shrunk to 50 people. By the early 1970s the village was subject to increasing decay. From 1973 there have been many contributions to the regeneration programme, co-ordinated by the New Lanark Conservation Trust. The village now attracts over 400,000 visitors a year, has 150 permanent jobs and provides homes for 200 people.

e) Irvine Harbourside – Regenerating a Declining Port

Irvine, originally one of the main commercial ports on the west coast, had fallen into neglect by the 1960s. The regeneration of the town began in the late 1960s, initially led by the Irvine New Town Development Corporation. The programme of regeneration included a new leisure centre, small business workshops, various tourist attractions, a range of residential developments and a number of social and community facilities.

These five examples are illustrative of the many urban regeneration programmes in Scotland. The examples are not a representative sample, rather they demonstrate the points of good practice that were discussed in the previous section. In particular, the examples demonstrate that urban regeneration is a long term business and that, if it is to be successful, it should involve all aspects of urban activity.

10.4.2 Future Challenges

Drawing on the experience of best practice, and learning from successes and failures of previous rounds of policy, the future of urban regeneration in Scotland is likely to be guided by a number of important considerations. Chief among these are the desire of the Scottish Executive and the vast majority of stakeholders to promote greater integration between the various policies that contribute to urban regeneration; the increased emphasis placed on social factors and environmental aspects of regeneration; and the essential requirement that urban regeneration should be guided by strategy and that it should be set within a wider framework of national and regional policy. These considerations are already influencing practice through, for example, the increased budget allocated for SIPs (SURF, 2000), and in the emphasis now placed on integration and a strategic perspective in community planning and other initiatives (Lloyd and McCarthy, 1999).

Other important themes for the future can be detected in the support given to the further extension of the partnership mode of working in order to include a wider selection of local and community representatives, and in the adoption of procedures aimed at allowing for a high level of transparency and accountability in the design and operation of urban regeneration policy. A new theme that has emerged in the past two years in the SIPs is the shift away from geographically focused policy and an increased emphasis on sectoral measures. Finally, it has been argued by some commentators that insufficient attention has been given in recent years to physical improvement and the provision of quality infrastructure in order to bring derelict sites back into use (Webster, 1999 and 2000); what is less evident in such suggestions is the validity of the mechanism proposed to achieve such a task – the establishment of urban development corporations.

In addition to these direct influences on urban regeneration policy, it is also important to appreciate that, more so than in the past, the influence of associated policy fields is likely to prove decisive in achieving success. Infrastructure policies play an important role in influencing a wide range of regeneration decisions, especially the availability of telecommunications facilities and the provision of fast, efficient public transport. Of equal importance is the influence of the European Structural Funds and the possible difficulties that will be experienced as the provision of European funding is reduced. A third source of influence is the shape and structure of mainstream policies and budgets for education, housing, social welfare, environment and health; these are all essential activities that can help to ensure that urban regeneration initiatives are incorporated into the mainstream of policy rather than allowing 'initiative-itis' to spread (SURF, 1999). Cutting across all of these and other direct sources of influence will be the need for increased attention to be paid to monitoring evaluation and review; preferably as an integral part of an urban regeneration programme.

Scotland has developed a wide range of urban regeneration policies and programmes over the past thirty years. Much of this experience is highly regarded and can provide best practice guidance for use elsewhere. Equally, there are lessons from practice outwith Scotland which can be of value in determining the future content of policy and practice in Scotland.

Establishing and maintaining links with practice elsewhere in Europe is of increasing importance and can help to avoid the waste of scarce resources. Equally, it is essential that policy makers, practitioners and communities continue to experiment and innovate; old solutions may fail to address new problems or to maximise the benefits that can be obtained from developing new opportunities and initiatives.

References

Atkinson, R. and Moon, G. (1994) *Urban Policy in Britain*, Macmillan, London.
Cappellin, R. (1997) 'Federalism and the network paradigm' in Danson, M., Lloyd, M.G. and Hill, S. (eds) *Regional Governance and Economic Development*, Pion, London.

Carley, M., Chapman, M., Hastings, A., Kirk, K. and Young, R. (2000) *Urban Regeneration Through Partnership*, Policy Press, Bristol.

Chapman, M. (1998) *Effective Partnership Working*, Scottish Office, Edinburgh.

Gomez, M. (1998) 'Reflective images: the case of urban regeneration in Glasgow and Bilbao', *International Journal of Urban and Regional Research*, 22, pp.106-121.

Hall, P. (1988) *Cities of Tomorrow*, Basil Blackwell, Oxford.

Hayton, K. (1993) 'Progress in partnership: the future of urban regeneration in Scotland', *Quarterly Economic Commentary*, 19, pp.51-56.

Hayton, K. (1996) 'Planning policy in Scotland' in Tewdwr-Jones, M. (ed) *British Planning Policy in Transition: Planning in the 1990s*, UCL Press, London.

Hayton, K. (1999) *Baseline Paper – Urban Regeneration*, RTPI Scotland, Edinburgh.

Illsley, B. and McCarthy, J. (1998) 'Community-led planning? The case of Dundee', *Scottish Geographical Magazine*, 114, pp.103-108.

Lichfield, D. (2000) 'Organisation and management' in Roberts, P. and Sykes, H. (eds) *Urban Regeneration*, Sage, London.

Lloyd, M.G. and McCarthy, J. (1999) 'Urban regeneration in Scotland – programmes for change', *European Planning Studies*, 7, pp.809-813.

McCarthy, J. (1999a) *Encouraging Sustainable Urban Regeneration in Scotland: Learning from Europe*, paper presented at the 39th Congress of the European Regional Science Association, Dublin, August.

McCarthy, J. (1999b) 'Urban regeneration in Scotland: an agenda for the Scottish Parliament', *Regional Studies*, 36, pp.559-566.

McCarthy, J. (1999c) 'Implications of the Scottish Parliament for urban regeneration', in McCarthy, J. and Newlands, D. (eds) *Governing Scotland: Problems and Prospects*, Ashgate, Aldershot.

Pacione, M. (1997) 'Urban restructuring and the reproduction of inequality in Britain's cities: an overview' in Pacione, M. (ed) *Britain's Cities: Geographies of Division in Urban Britain*, Routledge, London.

Rifkind, M. (1999) *Learning from New Life for Urban Scotland*, Scottish Urban Regeneration Forum, Glasgow.

Roberts, P. (2000a) *The New Territorial Governance*, Town and Country Planning Association, London.

Roberts, P. (2000b) 'The evolution, definition and purposes of urban regeneration' in Roberts, P. and Sykes, H. (eds) *Urban Regeneration*, Sage, London.

Roberts, P. and Hart, T. (1997) 'The design and implementation of European programmes for regional development in the UK: a comparative review' in Bachtler, J. and Turok, I. (eds) *The Coherence of EU Regional Policy*, Jessica Kingsley, London.

Roberts, P. and Lloyd, M.G. (1999) 'Institutional aspects of regional planning, management and development: lessons from the English experience', *Environment and Planning B*, 26, pp.517-531.

Roberts, P. and Sykes, H. (2000a) 'Introduction' in Roberts, P. and Sykes, H. (eds) *Urban Regeneration*, Sage, London.

Roberts, P. and Sykes, H. (2000b) 'Current challenges and future prospects' in Roberts, P. and Sykes, H. (eds) *Urban Regeneration*, Sage, London.

Scottish Executive (2002) *Social Justice Annual Report 2002*, Edinburgh.

Scottish Executive (2003) *Building Better Cities: Delivering Growth and Opportunities*, Edinburgh.

Scottish Homes (1998) *Smaller Urban Renewal Initiatives (SURIs): An Interim Evaluation*, Scottish Homes, Edinburgh.

Scottish Office (1988) *New Life for Urban Scotland*, Scottish Office, Edinburgh.

Scottish Office (1993) *Progress in Partnership: A Consultation Paper on the Future of Urban Regeneration Policy in Scotland*, Scottish Office, Edinburgh.

Scottish Urban Regeneration Forum (1999) *Scottish Regeneration 12*, SURF, Glasgow.

Scottish Urban Regeneration Forum (2000) *Scottish Regeneration 15*, SURF, Glasgow.

Tarling, R., Hirst, A., Rowland, B., Rhodes, J. and Tyler, P. (1999) *An Evaluation of the New Life for Urban Scotland Initiative*, Scottish Executive Central Research Unit, Edinburgh.

Turok, I. (1987) 'Continuity, change and contradiction in urban planning' in Donnison, D. and Middleton, A. (eds) *Regenerating the Inner City*, Routledge, London.

Turok, I. and Hopkins, N. (1998) 'Competition and area selection in Scotland's new urban policy', *Urban Studies*, 35, pp.2021-2061.

Webster, D. (1999) 'Targeted local jobs', *New Economy*, 6, pp.193-199.

Webster, D. (2000) 'Scottish social inclusion policy: a critical assessment', *Scottish Affairs*, 30, pp.28-50.

Chapter 11

Community Planning in Scotland: Prospects and Potential for Local Governance?

M. Greg Lloyd and Barbara Illsley

11.1   Introduction

The Local Government in Scotland Act (2003) provides the statutory basis for community planning, alongside related aspects of local governance, including arrangements for best value and the provision of a power to advance well being in communities. The main aims of community planning are described as 'making sure people and communities are genuinely engaged in the decisions made on public services which affect them; allied to a commitment from organisations to work together, not apart, in providing better public services' (Scottish Executive, 2003a, p.7). Essentially this is the foundation of the modernisation of arrangements for regional and local governance in Scotland. The Partnership Agreement between Labour and the Liberal Democrats, which sets out the programme for the second term of the Scottish Parliament, for example, envisages a Scotland 'where enterprise can flourish, where opportunity does exist for all and our people and our country have confidence to face the challenges of a global society' (Scottish Executive, 2003b, p.3). To this end, the Executive seeks to encourage the delivery of local services of the highest possible quality and to promote the empowerment and inclusion of communities.

Clearly, there are a number of very important questions being raised here about the nature of the processes of modernisation which are taking place, and the changing relations between the new and existing arrangements for local and regional governance. This chapter examines the background to community planning in Scotland, the progress made in putting community planning into effect and discusses the issues arising from this innovation in planning and management for strategic planning, development and service delivery in a modern devolved Scotland.

11.2 A Modernising Agenda for Local Governance

The modernising agenda for local governance draws its intellectual rationale from a synthesis of the political ideas associated with social democratic thinking and that of neoliberalism – known as the Third Way (Giddens, 1998). This has informed the particular features of modernisation with respect to the redefined, reconfigured and reinvigorated relationships between government, business, communities, localities and individuals. This interest is relatively long established. Prior to its election in 1997, for example, the (New) Labour Party had initiated a practical experiment in a new partnership process for local governance (Rogers, 1998). This was articulated through a modest pilot programme of a small number of local authorities in England and Scotland, which set out to consult their communities about the nature and effectiveness of local strategies. This was a relatively focussed attempt to secure greater empowerment and involvement by communities in the affairs of local authorities (Billingham and Kitchen, 1999). It was, however, an explicit attempt to address the issues associated with the highly fragmented arrangements for the delivery of local services. Following its election to office in 1997, the Labour Government published a White Paper which asserted the importance of enhancing the leadership and enabling roles of local government (Department of the Environment, Transport and the Regions, 1998). This brought together ideas of leadership, well being and improved participation from diverse local communities (Kitchen, 1999). In England and Wales, this led to the Local Government Act 2000 which introduced a power of community well being, and the concept of community strategies. In Scotland, the same principles, line of reasoning and concerns about appropriate governance resulted in the legislative provision for community planning.

11.3 A Scottish Context: Devolution and Community Well Being

Against this broad programme of modernisation, change and inclusion, there was a distinctively Scottish dimension to the interest in community leadership, well being and planning. First, the concept of community planning has a particular resonance in the Scottish polity as it draws on and reflects certain distinctive features of established Scottish public administrative practice. The broad meso- corporatist ethos that has characterised the emphasis on partnership working is important, and indeed it has been argued that there is evidence 'to support the view that, although there may have been a rejection of corporatist or consensual politics south of the border, in many respects they have survived in some areas of policy in Scotland' (Brown et al, 1996, p.106). Further, the concept of community planning represents an attempt to reorganise the fragmented institutional relationships and inter-organisational processes that prevailed in Scotland: the inherited effects of the hollowing out of the state associated with the market dominated neoliberal political agenda of the 1980s (Rhodes, 1996). This in itself demands particular attention in attempting to devise cost effective delivery of local services provided by a range of organisations.

Secondly, there is the strong historical link between the idea of community planning and the earlier regional report initiative which had taken place in the

1970s (Sinclair, 1997). The Local Government (Scotland) Act, 1973, had created a
two tier structure of regional councils and district councils with an attendant
division of responsibility between strategic and local functions. The legislation
introduced the idea of the regional report in order to enable the new regional
authorities to establish a strategic framework. The intention was that the regional
reports would contextualise their subsequent agenda setting, preparation of
structure plans, arrangements for resource allocation and decision making. The
reports were to be vehicles for assessing the available resources and competing
priorities of the regional authorities and thereby providing a strategic context to
decision making and investment planning by district councils, private interests and
other public sector bodies. The reports were intended to provide a structure and a
process for strategic planning, to concentrate on policy decisions and to reflect the
corporate approach of the regional council to its economic, social, environmental
and land use issues (Lloyd, 1997). In practice, however, the emphasis of the reports
was on outcome rather than process. Nonetheless, regional reports are an
appropriate historical touchstone for community planning because they facilitated
both a strategic planning process and corporate outcome and represent a historical
link to past practice in Scottish public administration (Sinclair, 1997).

Thirdly, the proposed creation of a Scottish Parliament, led to concerns on the
part of Scottish local authorities that their established community leadership role
might be compromised. It was argued, for example, that the relationship between
the unitary Councils and a new Scottish Parliament needed clarification in order to
avoid any unnecessary conflicts between the levels and processes of government
(Alexander, 1997). The concept of community planning emerged as a possible way
of addressing the uncertainties attendant upon this relationship and the associated
balance of power between the local government and the Parliament. Community
planning was advocated, therefore, as a means of reasserting the role of local
authorities at a time when new relationships, policy agendas and national priorities
were being developed in Scotland (Sinclair, 1997). In other words, community
planning may be seen as representing an attempt to provide a strategic framework
for the activities of the multifarious institutions engaged in local governance,
community capacity building and regeneration.

11.4   First Steps Towards Community Planning in Scotland

In July 1997, the Secretary of State for Scotland and the Convention of Scottish
Local Authorities (COSLA) established a joint working group – the Community
Planning Working Group – comprised of officials from the two organisations. Its
responsibility was to examine the ways in which Scottish local authorities could
engage in viable partnerships with other bodies to provide for and promote the
economic, social and environmental well being of their respective communities. In
particular, the Community Planning Working Group (1998) highlighted the
leadership role of local government in asserting local agendas for the delivery of
services and in providing a managed framework for effective inter-organisational
relations. The importance of the leadership role ascribed to community planning

was also echoed in the deliberations and recommendations of the McIntosh Commission (1999) which considered the emerging relationship between local government and the Scottish Parliament. Community planning was presented as a process through which a Council would come together with other organisations to plan, provide for or promote the well being of communities they serve. This was expected to operate across an entire Council area, and at the level of local communities within a given Council area.

The Community Planning Working Group (1998) described the aims of Community Planning as follows:

- to improve the service provided by Councils and their public sector partners to the public through closer, more co-ordinated working;
- to provide a process through which Councils and their public sector partners, in consultation with the voluntary and private sector, and the community, can agree both a strategic vision for the area and the action which each of the partners will take in pursuit of that vision; and,
- to help Councils and their public sector partners collectively to identify the needs and views of individuals and communities and to assess how they can best be delivered and addressed.

The Working Group conducted a mapping exercise of the myriad of existing planning and resource allocation processes that were in place in Scotland. This confirmed the extent to which local governance was being achieved through a complex of statutory and non statutory plans, partnerships, projects and other initiatives emanating from a wide range of different organisations. These included, inter alia, structure and local planning, local authority decentralisation schemes, and the arrangements which had been put in place for specific functions such as Care in the Community and Children's Services. It was evident that the non statutory provisions were equally as diverse in character as the statutory ones, and covered urban regeneration, physical development, housing, lifelong learning, social inclusion partnerships and community regeneration (Community Planning Working Group, 1998). The complexity of this institutional landscape becomes even more evident when the different internal processes associated with the bodies involved were considered.

The extent to which there was fragmentation in the institutional landscape in Scotland was further demonstrated by the results of a survey of the direct economic development activity undertaken by local government (Ekos, 2000). Direct economic development was defined as including processes related to business competitiveness, physical business infrastructure, training and human resource development, tourism and economic inclusion, and community economic development. Furthermore, there was considerable diversity in the approaches adopted by individual Councils in working with a wide range of public, private and voluntary organisations to deliver economic development services. These characteristics reflected the broader shifts that had taken place in the arrangements for local governance across Europe (Goldsmith, 1993).

The Community Planning Working Group (1998) argued that there was a need to establish a more systematic approach to ensure greater co-ordination between the processes in place for service delivery, and the communities for which they were intended. It concluded 'that there is at present a lack of structured overview across the various agencies about how they collectively could best promote the well being of their communities. The kaleidoscope of local and subject-specific plans and partnerships was not related to a consistent attempt to develop a shared strategic vision for an area and a statement of common purpose in pursuit of that vision. Neither was it always clear who had the lead in developing this shared strategic vision' (Community Planning Working Group, 1998, p.3). Against this fragmented institutional context, the Working Group (1998) argued that the benefits of community planning would include, inter alia:

- an increase in the collective capacity of public sector agencies to tackle problems which require action from more than one agency;
- strategies linked more closely to the needs and wishes of individuals and communities;
- an increase in community involvement and the avoidance of conflicts between programmes.

For an individual Council area, the purpose of the community planning process would be to present an informed view of the challenges and opportunities facing the geographical communities and the different communities of interest. A community plan was envisaged as holding for between five and ten years, and to be subject to annual review with clear statements of progress to the commonly agreed agenda for action. It would involve full consultation with communities, voluntary organisations and the private sector although it would be driven from within the public sector. The community planning process was also envisaged as working at more local community levels of interest. It is clear that the concept of community planning involved an outcome (the Plan) and a process of negotiation whereby the different interests and policy positions of all the bodies concerned with community were drawn together into a common agenda for action. In particular, it was intended that community plans would be prepared by local authorities enabling them to demonstrate greater leadership. This would involve a process that would involve all local agencies to submit their annual plans to the Council. On the basis of this material and consultation the Council would then produce a community plan which 'would incorporate not only the Council's own proposals, including a statement of the standards and quality of service it would provide to the local community, but also the plans of the local appointed bodies and how these plans would contribute to the overall well being of the community rather than, as at present, being developed and published in isolation' (Sinclair, 1997, p.17). The expectations of community planning remain high in this particular approach to achieve improved local governance.

11.5   Learning from Practice: The Pathfinder Community Plans

The Community Planning Working Group, which reported in July 1998, provided Councils and their partners with an initial framework for embarking on the process of community planning. The framework built on and extended the experience of partnership working throughout Scotland (Community Planning Working Group, 1998). It was made clear, however, that individual community plans should be unique in reflecting the prevailing, inherited and anticipated economic, political and social conditions, the different inter organisational relationships involved, and the specific processes of learning to address the needs of individual communities. The Community Planning Working Group recommended that Councils and their partners should aim to produce the first community plans by the end of September 1999.

To facilitate this ambitious time frame, the Working Group suggested that a small number of Pathfinders engage with the process in order to identify emerging experience and good practice as the basis of dissemination across Scotland. Five local authorities – Highland Council, City of Edinburgh Council, Perth and Kinross Council, South Lanarkshire Council and Stirling Council – were invited by the Scottish Office to pilot the initiative and to draw up draft community plans by the end of 1998. These were published in mid 1999.

An evaluation of the five Pathfinder projects was then carried out to identify the lessons from this initial stab at putting community planning into practice. The study was based on a review of the relevant material for each area and interviews with representatives of the partner organisations involved in the community planning process (Rogers et al, 1999). It found that there was general support for the concept of community planning from those organisations involved in the Pathfinders and concluded that the value of the process was beyond doubt. It was asserted that there was a high level of agreement about the fundamental value of community planning within local councils and their partner organisations – in establishing a shared vision for an area, to improve consultation with local people, and to promote partnership working (Rogers et al, 1999). A number of points may be highlighted from the evaluation exercise.

First, the research confirmed the diversity of approach adopted in each of the Pathfinder areas. Highland Council, for example, built on existing joint working arrangements with a range of agencies which had been involved in past initiatives, such as the creation of the University of the Highlands, the Highlands and Islands European Partnership, and the Well being Alliance. This was also the case with Edinburgh, where the community planning process drew on the experience of over seventy existing partnerships operating in the city. In contrast, in South Lanarkshire, despite the short timescale available for the production of the draft community plan, the principal partners attempted to engage the local community through the creation of a citizen's panel, the distribution of leaflets, workshops and a major conference of the partners. In Stirling, however, the Stirling Assembly was central to the its community planning process. This had been set up by Stirling Council in 1997 to bring together a range of community interests, such as community councils, voluntary groups, business people and individuals, to discuss strategic and national issues affecting the area. It now formed the basis of the community planning process.

Second, the diversity in approach was reflected also in the plan outcomes. The Highland community plan, for example, reflected the issues and challenges which were considered unique to the region – a changing population, the impact of its peripheral location, and a range of associated environmental conflicts. The community plan set out a vision of a prosperous and dynamic future for the Highlands 'which has the people, organisations and infrastructure for a growing, inclusive economy; which is healthy, safe and provides high quality services for all of its people; known for its wonderful, productive natural environment and high standards of stewardship; which has a strong sense of identity; where confident, sustainable communities are engaged in the democratic process; and which makes a unique and valuable contribution within Scotland, the UK and Europe' (Highland Council, 1999, p.2). The diversity of themes, set out in the initial pathfinder community plans, is shown in Table 11.1.

Table 11.1   Community plan themes

Edinburgh	Highland	Perth and Kinross	South Lanarkshire	Stirling
Social inclusion		Social inclusion	Successful and inclusive communities	Social inclusion
Community well being	Safe, healthy communities	Health and welfare	Safe and healthy communities	Community safety
				Caring community
Economic growth	Prosperous communities	The economy	Working and learning communities	Prosperity, income, jobs, opportunities
Information and learning	Learning communities			
Environmental sustainability	Sustainable communities			Environmental and sustainable development
	Capable and confident communities			
		Young people		
		Older people		
				Quality services
				Local democracy and accountability
Major development projects				

Source: Rogers et al. (1999).

Third, whilst proselytising the advantages of this approach to local governance, the evaluation study also highlighted a number of tensions that had become evident in the execution of the different community planning processes. In particular, these concerned the execution and implementation of community planning. There was a perceived need to secure robust and effective arrangements for partnership working and community engagement in the process of community planning. There was the related matter of the capacity required to implement community plans. In effect, would the partners be in a position to discharge their stated commitments to the community plan itself? In this respect, concerns were raised about the lack of coterminosity of the geographical boundaries of institutions, their stated responsibilities and available resources in delivering the expectations set out in the individual community plans (Rogers et al, 1999).

Notwithstanding these issues, the community planning idea was taken forward with a vengeance and initial community plans were subsequently prepared by local authorities and their associated partnerships across Scotland. In 2001, the Scottish Executive set up the Community Planning Task Force to facilitate the development of the Community Planning process, by advising central and local government bodies as well as other partners, sharing good practice, and helping develop a coherent relationship between the Community Planning process and other local plans and strategies.

Community Planning into Action?

In 2002, the Scottish Executive published a Green Paper on its legislative proposals for local government. Amongst a raft of proposed measures, the Green Paper asserted the Executive's intention to introduce a power of community initiative and to provide a statutory basis for community planning. A statutory power of community initiative represented a significant change in the powers of local authorities. It would empower local authorities to do anything for the benefit of their communities which is not already reserved, prohibited or provided for under other legislation. The intention was to enable local authorities to become stronger leaders in their communities. In broad terms, a power of community initiative would empower local authorities to do anything that promotes the economic, social and environmental well being of their communities. Community planning was an integral part of this thinking. There was a close correspondence between experiences of local authorities and the political agenda for change and improvement in the delivery of local services.

Subsequently, the Local Government in Scotland Act (2003) provided a statutory framework for community planning. It places community planning within a spectrum of related aspects of local government activity, including Best Value arrangements and Power to Advance Well Being. Under section 16 of the Act, local authorities have been given the duty to initiate and facilitate the Community Planning process, due in part to their democratic credentials and in part to the range of services they provide to the public. However, a number of other bodies, notably NHS Boards, Scottish Enterprise, Highlands and Islands Enterprise, Joint

Police Boards and Chief Constables, Joint Fire Boards and the Strathclyde Passenger Transport Authority, have also been given a statutory duty to participate in the community planning process. Furthermore, the legislation requires local authorities to consult and co-operate with community bodies.

Guidance has been drawn up in conjunction with the Community Planning Task Group and it is intended to provide a national framework for all those engaged in community planning. The guidance 'seeks to strike a balance between providing clarity in what is expected from the community planning process and the need for local discretion in tailoring the process to the needs and opportunities of local communities' (Scottish Executive, 2003a, p.4).

11.7   Community Planning and Collaboration?

What is the significance of community planning in Scotland? A number of points may be made. First, there is a resonance between the assumptions underpinning community planning and the ideas associated with collaborative planning theory. Collaborative planning is described as a process of planning that reflects the dynamics of contemporary social and economic change, together with the inclusion of local needs and expectations (Innes, 1995). This approach is clearly compatible with the ideas associated with the Third Way political agenda. As a contemporary expression of planning practice it seeks to secure a modern approach to the management of change through devising and executing appropriate institutional responses to that change (Healey, 1998). It is essentially a call for action in an uncertain world which 'sets a new challenge for the design of institutional mechanisms through which political communities can address their common problems about the management of environmental change in localities, that is, the design of planning systems and planning practices' (Healey, 1997, p.5). More specifically, collaborative planning is seen as involving 'defining and developing policy agendas and strategic approaches about shared spaces among the members of political communities [which] serve to build up social, intellectual and political capital which becomes a new institutional resource' (Healey, 1997, p.311). It provides a means by which integration of forward planning and service delivery can be facilitated in the context of highly fragmented institutional settings. Clearly, these ideas may be identified in the community planning concept.

Over the past five years, there is little doubt that community planning has resulted in the creation of new institutional mechanisms, in the form of Community Planning Partnerships, which bring together public sector agencies, private sector interests and community bodies. Different structures have developed, in some places emerging from existing partnerships, in others being created for the first time. Four broad approaches have been found to exist across Scotland: 'new build' infrastructure, developed around the themes of the community plan; 'incremental gap filling' where structures are focused on issues with no existing mechanism; 'restructuring' of existing arrangements to match community planning priorities; and 'organic networking' which relies on informal collaboration between agencies (RDS Consultancy Services, 2002). The way in which the community is integrated into these arrangements is equally important. Most partnerships have created opportunities for communities to be represented on the main strategic body and various strategies have been developed to secure input from the wider public.

Community planning is predicated on the notion of consensus building within communities, between communities and service providers, and between providers to deliver to the agreed community plan. The key test, therefore, is the extent to which the new institutional arrangements result in the provision of a more holistic and responsive approach to the delivery of local services. Is information and knowledge being shared amongst partners, including the community? Are working practices and expectations changing as a result of co-operation? Are new and better solutions being found to complex problems? Are the agendas of local communities and interest groups being valued in formal planning processes and in the administration of established institutional arrangements?

Community planning in Scotland is still in its infancy and it is too early to judge the success of the formal, statutory process. However, positive and encouraging evidence is emerging from a number of partnership initiatives across Scotland which have embraced community planning principles. Aberdeenshire Towns Partnership (ATP) provides one such example. ATP is a partnership between three public sector bodies, Aberdeenshire Council, Scottish Enterprise Grampian and Communities Scotland that was set up in 1998 in order to enhance the social, economic, cultural and environmental vitality of Aberdeenshire's five main towns. Working closely with local stakeholders in each town, town strategies and action programmes have been prepared and implemented. Community engagement has been given a high priority in this process, with a range of initiatives such as community training using Planning Aid for Scotland; focus groups, workshops and Planning for Real exercises to develop strategies; and Town Partnership meetings to review progress. A total of £12.9 million was spent on projects between 1999 and 2002 with a further £10 million committed for the 2003 to 2006 period. Work has included environmental enhancement schemes, business promotion, social housing provision, health and arts initiatives. A holistic approach to the management of change has been developed with the main partners successfully integrating key aspects of policy development and decision making. ATP was created before the emergence of community planning but it demonstrates many of the benefits of the collaborative planning approach. Not surprisingly, the Partnership was relaunched in 2003, placing it squarely in the context of delivering community planning.

Despite apparent successes in practice, it is important to acknowledge that there are a number of fundamental criticisms of the collaborative planning approach which relate to the underlying assumptions and the practicalities of consensus building between diverse interests (Hooper, 1992; Ball, 1998). Yet, community planning would appear to satisfy many aspects of broader collaborative planning thinking and certainly draws down on the contemporary promotion of ideas associated with institutional capacity, social inclusion and environmental sustainability.

Second, community planning involves an active or assertive role for local government in providing leadership to the devising of common agendas for inter-organisational action. Clarke and Stewart (1998), for example, have set out a number of defined principles of leadership for local authorities:

- that the concern of a local authority should extend beyond the services provided to the overall welfare of the area;
- that the local authority's role of community leadership is only justified if it is close to and empowers the communities within and the citizens who constitute them;
- that the local authority must recognise the contribution of other organisations and enable that contribution;
- that the local authority should ensure that the whole range of resources are used to the full for the good area;
- that in order to make the best use of resources, the local authority will need to review rigorously with other agencies how needs are best met and to be prepared to act in many different ways to meet them;
- that in showing leadership the local authority must seek to reconcile, to balance and in the final resort, to judge the diversity of views and interests; and,
- that in all of this the local authority must work with other organisations and with the communities and actors that constitute the community of its area.

Certainly, community planning in Scotland would appear to address those aspects necessary for local authority action and leadership in enabling diversity and innovation at the local community level. The intention is that a local authority, in putting the process of community planning into effect, will consider the overall range of services provided for the welfare of the area. This is where the community planning process draws down on all the key players concerned and, in order to fulfil that role, the local authority must recognise the contribution of other organisations in the overall delivery of services to the common good. In practice, there is general acceptance of the leadership role of councils within community planning partnerships (RDS Consultancy Services, 2002), partly because of the major role played in service delivery and partly in recognition of their democratic nature. The evaluation of the pathfinder community plans suggested, however, that the local authorities involved met some but not all of the features of community leadership (Rogers et al, 1999).

In particular, the role of community leadership in community planning 'requires a capacity for innovation because the system of community governance has to be capable of responding to local problems and issues and also to local aspirations. It should be the special contribution of local authorities to enhance that capacity for innovation and hence of diversity' (Kitchen, 1999). In this context, the local authority becomes the focal point for effective action. Leadership requires assertive action by the local authority and this role has a strong parallel with the associational economy. This is concerned with innovation and development in which the contemporary role of the state is re-energised to become that of an animateur, essentially what is described as a driver for innovation (Cooke and Morgan, 1998). In discharging this role, the partnership approach is stressed as an appropriate way forward. Community leadership involves also certain soft or invisible factors in the management of change and inter-organisational relations, such as trust, voice and loyalty, which are linked to the creation of social capital and community capacity in specific localities (Cooke and Morgan, 1998). Community planning provides a vehicle which would involve these attributes and this would suggest it is very much to the fore with respect to contemporary thinking in local governance.

Third, combining the characteristics of community planning and the parallel powers to promote community well being, may herald the beginnings of a period of assertive local authority activism in Scotland. The bringing together of diverse bodies, policies and expenditure plans to focus on an integrated cost effective service delivery portfolio may provide local government with a new role. But can local government deliver this new agenda for action? Can it sustain it in a highly competitive institutional context? Do local authorities have the skills and resources to discharge the expected leadership role? Are local authorities capable of the reticulism required to overcome jurisdictional boundaries which impede an effective response by an organisation to a problem?

A reticulist approach provides an inter-organisational communications link between policy systems (Fischer, 1981). To achieve this outcome involves a number of pre-requisites, including, inter alia, the exploration of the issues of joint concern to the bodies involved to establish a common agenda for action; an ability to conduct an assessment of the policy arenas involved in the process; establishing a link between both the external and internal policy environments; and mediating between the key players involved in any conflict. Essentially, local authorities have to become a bargaining agent between the different interests involved and be capable of addressing the substantive issues as well as the tactical, localised decisions (Fischer, 1981). To do this requires adequate skills, energy and resources on the part of local authorities, otherwise community planning may simply prove to be a further burden on individual councils (Lloyd and Illsley, 1999). In parallel to this potentially assertive role for local government there is a real interest in mediation in resolving land use planning outcomes (Watchman, 2002; Lloyd and Peel, 2003a).

11.8 Wherefore Community Planning?

A major challenge for community planning will be its relationship to new and existing initiatives. In England, for example, there is concern about the relationship between community strategies and the ongoing reform of the statutory land use planning system (ODPM, 2003). In Scotland, there remains a considerable strategic vacuum in terms of managing the subnational economy (Lloyd, 1999). There is a lack of a regional framework for assertive strategic priorities for the highly fragmented institutional activity which is taking place across Scotland. For example, the Enterprise and Lifelong Learning Committee (2000-01) cited evidence of congested institutional arrangements, with confusion, overlap, duplication and inter-organisational competition for available resources (discussed further in Chapter 7). It advocated an economic development strategy for Scotland, based on growth through competitiveness and sustainability, but at the same time taking into account regional development and social integration. Such a national perspective would include an implicit spatial dimension. There are positive moves in this direction. The economic development framework for Scotland, for example, asserts the need to 'consider the basic organisation of economic activity and the degree to which it promotes entrepreneurial dynamism. The environment must facilitate a range of activities including the establishment of new enterprises, the establishment of productive bases in Scotland by overseas enterprises, the expansion of small enterprises, collaboration and joint ventures between productive enterprises and centres of knowledge and research, and the development of the formal and informal networks that help to lower the costs of economic transactions' (Scottish Executive, 2000, para.4.1). At a subnational level, Local Economic Forums have been established and these include a responsibility to provide an economic input to their respective community plans. Questions arise as to the mediation of the different perspectives and priorities being articulated here and the ability of the community planning process to reconcile them.

The preparation of a national planning framework for Scotland, as currently proposed by the Scottish Executive, will be of particular importance in providing the spatial context to community planning. A national planning framework will allow the assertion of Scotland's distinctive spatial identity, within a broader (and regionalised) European agenda, and the better management of its internal space. The Convention of Scottish Local Authorities, for example, has suggested that such a national 'overview should express social, economic and environmental policy and provide a spatial framework for the sustainable development of Scotland' (Geoff Peart Consulting, 2002). COSLA has further asserted that the 'purpose, content and process for preparation of this national framework would provide the necessary national counterpart to the local partnership working on strategic visions for social, economic and environmental well being which is being developed through community planning' (Geoff Peart Consulting, 2002). Community planning could form an integral part of this strategic framework. The national planning framework is intended to be a non statutory planning policy document which will inform strategic investment decisions and development planning. It will, however, serve as a material consideration in future decision making. The framework will consider Scotland from a spatial perspective, and set out a vision to 2025, with the purpose of ensuring different areas can fully realise their potential in the national interest. The emerging agenda for action includes issues associated with economic development, transport, energy and water and telecommunications development. The overarching theme is that of connectivity, both internally and externally, so as to create greater certainty for planning and development into the future (Lloyd and Peel, 2003a and 2003b). It is here that community planning will contribute to promoting the interests of local communities within a national spatial context.

11.9 Conclusion

As the process of community planning matures it needs to assert greater leadership in the governance of local communities. It must remain as inclusive as possible to bring legitimacy to this specific intervention in the face of expectations, fragmented institutional capacities and rapidly changing social and economic milieux. Community planning now has to deliver within the emerging national economic development agenda and the national planning framework. Thus, community planning has a role at different levels of governance, and it must guard against creating an additional and unnecessary layer of public administration. Community planning is about liberating agencies to act in partnership at a strategic level of interaction, to combine resources where appropriate and make the links between national and local clearer for all concerned. It must allow for a regional consensus as well as local ones. It has to address the trade-off between economy, society and environment throughout Scotland. These are big questions that have not yet been adequately framed let alone debated.

References

Alexander, A. (1997) 'Scotland's Parliament and Scottish local government: conditions for a stable relationship', *Scottish Affairs*, 19, pp.22-28.

Ball, M. (1998) 'Institutions in British property research: a review', *Urban Studies*, 35(9), pp.1501-1517.

Billingham, Z. and Kitchen, H. (1999) 'Diversity and innovation: an analysis of the Government's proposals' in Local Government Information Unit (ed) *Turning Community Leadership into Reality*, London, LGIU, pp.90-103.

Brown, A., McCrone, D. and Paterson, L. (1996) *Politics and Society in Scotland*, London, Macmillan.

Clarke, M. and Stewart, J. (1998) *Community Governance, Community Leadership and the New Local Government*, London, LGIU.

Community Planning Working Group (1998) *Report of the Community Planning Group*, Edinburgh, Scottish Office, July.

Cooke, P. and Morgan, K. (1998) *The Associational Economy: Firms, Regions and Innovation*, Oxford, Oxford University Press.

Department of the Environment, Transport and the Regions (1998) *Modern Local Government: In Touch with the People*, London, HMSO.

Ekos (2000) *Survey of Economic Development Activity of Scottish Councils*, Edinburgh, COSLA.

Enterprise and Lifelong Learning Committee (2000-01) *Report*, Inquiry into the Delivery of Economic Development, Edinburgh, Scottish Parliament.

Fischer, D.W. (1981) *North Sea Oil: An Environment Interface*, Norway, Universitetsforlaget.

Geoff Peart Consulting (2002) *Review of Strategic Planning: Digest of Responses to Consultation*, Edinburgh, Scottish Executive Central Research Unit.

Giddens, A. (1998) *The Third Way. The Renewal of Social Democracy*, Cambridge, Polity Press.

Goldsmith, M. (1993) 'The Europeanisation of local government', *Urban Studies*, 30, pp.683-700.

Healey, P. (1997) *Collaborative Planning. Shaping Places in Fragmented Societies*, London, Macmillan.

Healey, P. (1998) 'Collaborative planning in a stakeholder society', *Town Planning Review*, 69(1), pp.1-21.

Highland Council (1999) *Draft Community Plan*, Inverness.

Hooper, A. (1992) 'The construction of theory: a comment', *Journal of Property Research*, 9, pp.45-48.

Innes, J. (1995) 'Planning theory's emerging paradigm: communicative action and interactive practice', *Journal of Planning Education and Research*, 14(3), pp.183-191.

Kitchen, H. (1999) 'Turning community leadership in reality: a programme for new powers' in Local Government Information Unit (ed) *Turning Community Leadership into Reality*, London, LGIU, pp.7-27.

Lloyd, M.G. (1997) 'Regional reports and strategic planning innovation: lessons from Scotland', *European Planning Studies*, 5(6), pp.731-739.

Lloyd, M.G. (1999) 'The Scottish Parliament and the planning system: addressing the strategic deficit through spatial planning' in McCarthy, J. and Newlands, D. (eds*)* *Governing Scotland: Problems and Prospects*, Aldershot, Ashgate, pp.121-134.

Lloyd, M.G. and Illsley, B. (1999) 'An idea for its time? Community Planning and reticulism in Scotland', *Regional Studies*, 33(2), pp.181-184.

Lloyd, M.G. and Peel, D. (2003a) 'Mediating mediation in land use planning', *Scottish Planning and Environment Law*, 99, pp.102-103.

Lloyd, M.G. and Peel, D. (2003b) 'Planning for a better Scotland – Carpe Diem'. *Town and Country Planning*, 72(6), p.196.

Local Government Association (2003) *Powering-up: Making the Most of the Power of Well-being*, London, LGA.

McIntosh Commission (1999) *Local Government and the Scottish Parliament*, Edinburgh.

Office of the Deputy Prime Minister (2003) *The Relationships between Community Strategies and Local Development Frameworks*, London, ODPM.

RDS Consultancy Services (2002) *Getting "Under the Skin" of Community Planning*, Local Government Research Programme, Edinburgh, Scottish Executive.

Rhodes, R. (1996) 'The new governance: governing without government'. *Political Studies*, XLIV, pp.652-667.

Rogers, S. (1998) *Community Planning and Engagement*, Birmingham, Inlogov.

Rogers, S., Smith, M., Sullivan, H. and Clarke, M. (1999) *Community Planning in Scotland: An Evaluation of the Pathfinder Projects*, Edinburgh, COSLA/Scottish Executive.

Scottish Executive (2000) *The Way Forward: Framework for Economic Development in Scotland*, Edinburgh, Scottish Executive.

Scottish Executive (2003a) *Local Government in Scotland Act Community Planning Statutory Guidance*, Edinburgh, Scottish Executive.

Scottish Executive (2003b) *A Partnership for a Better Scotland*, Edinburgh, Scottish Executive.

Sinclair, D. (1997) 'Local government and a Scottish Parliament', *Scottish Affairs*, 19, pp.14-21.

Watchman, P. (2002) 'Mediation in the planning system', *Scottish Planning and Environmental Law*, 89, pp.9-12.

Chapter 12

Policy Implications

Mike Danson and John McCarthy

12.1 Introduction

The substantive chapters of this book have considered a range of aspects of the disparities within Scotland, and many have clearly implied the need for policy interventions of various kinds and at various levels. This chapter aims to carry forward and consolidate the arguments for such policy interventions. The chapter is structured as follows. In sections 12.2-12.6, the broad policy implications arising for each of the substantive cross-cutting policy areas – economic development, education and training, transport and communications, urban regeneration, and community planning – will be considered, taking account of the evidence from the substantive chapters, as well as the area case studies. Links will be drawn out between separate policy themes, and areas of consensus highlighted. Finally, in section 12.7, conclusions in terms of policy priorities will be proposed.

With regard to the thickness and capacity of institutions to address the need for these strategic interventions, Scotland appears to have adequate coverage (Macleod, 1996). However, paradoxically in many instances there is concern about duplication and overlap with a lack of an holistic approach to joining up governance structures (ELLC, 2000). Community planning and local economic fora are beginning to confront some of these difficulties, potentially releasing resources for more effective and efficient policy interventions. Whether these will be sufficient both to raise the competitiveness of Scotland as a whole and to achieve a degree of equity between regions and localities will depend on how appropriate are the detailed proposals below, and whether they are implemented.

12.2 Economic Development

There is a need to build a stable environment to promote confidence, to establish linkages and to create support mechanisms to deepen and embed economic activities with Scotland. In this context, as with most other policy areas, there are tensions between different jurisdictional levels over the delivery of sustainable economic development. On the one hand, there are advantages in promoting consistency and in controlling inefficient competition between regions by having top down national strategies, policies and programmes. However, delivery is often most effectively undertaken by local or regional partnerships addressing priorities determined at these levels, with discretion over policy mix and balance.

Good practice in terms of planning to ameliorate the effects of economic withdrawal of enterprises is available in both North America and Europe. There would seem to be a need to encourage such planning here – in partnership with the relevant enterprises and employers themselves, and underpinned by good intelligence. This would be applied for instance in relation to both the likelihood of withdrawal and the potential impact of withdrawal. Moreover, there is a need for encouragement for innovation and development in the tourism sector, and for area tourist boards to be incorporated more directly into economic development strategies and fora. In addition, there is a need to consider the linkages between elements within economic development strategies more holistically. It is significant in this respect that one of the Scottish Executive's regional objectives is balanced development. This of course has implications for all aspects of policy. Specifically, the worst effects of disparities – on the traditional industrial areas of the west of Scotland and the peripheral regions to the north and south – are to be addressed through mainstream top down, supply side polices. However, it is questionable whether these are adequate, since the evidence suggests that market failure will continue, and that disadvantaged communities and regions will not benefit from the 'trickle down' of benefits arising from general economic growth. Consequently, explicit intervention in the economy is required to bring about sustainable growth in such areas.

Furthermore, regarding the role of agencies and institutions within Scotland, there is a clear danger of lack of progress and inattention to opportunities if the same standard of packages is imposed throughout Scotland. As Mike Danson argues in Chapter 7, this 'nationalised' regional framework risks preventing the emergence of innovative, 'bottom up' approaches. Instead, it seems that a context-specific set of programmes is required. Recent moves to provide nationwide support products for enterprises through Business Gateway, and for internationalising businesses through Business Gateway International Trade, confirm the arguments for more discretion at the regional level to meet regional priorities (Danson et. al., 2004). Cluster strategies, similarly, have to recognise the significance of distance and the higher costs of involvement for those in the periphery removed from the core of economy, and not least in food and drink sectors.

Overall, however, there seems to be a case for a credible national economic development strategy which could in turn inform an effective regional development policy, as in the case made by Douglas Scott in Chapter 6, relating to the South of Scotland. Scott emphases that such a strategy would have the potential to address the historically unrecognised problems of the South of Scotland, as well as areas such as the Highlands and Islands. In fact, until 2000 there had been no national economic development strategy for Scotland since the White Paper on the Scottish Economy in 1965. However, national economic development strategies have proved effective in small countries such as Finland and Ireland in providing a clear focus for regional development. Clearly, such a national strategy could go further than merely combining the economic strategies of Scottish Enterprise and

Highland and Islands Enterprise, as in *Smart, Successful Scotland* (Scottish Executive, 2001). All relevant stakeholders at national level could, and should, be involved in the formulation of such a strategy. While the Executive's *Framework for Economic Development* (Scottish Executive, 2000) provides an important step in this direction, there seems to be a need for a strategy with less reliance on mainstream top down, supply side policies and trickle down or trickle across growth. Instead, explicit intervention to ensure sustainable economic growth would seem to be a pre-requisite for such a strategy, if it is to address the core needs of de-industrialised communities.

The case of the Highlands and Islands, as set out in Chapter 5 by Stuart Black, provides an example of how some of these points can be applied. For instance, given the problems faced in the agricultural sector, which has faced some of the poorest years for several decades recently, there is a need to focus efforts on the production of better quality agricultural products such as the 'Orkney Gold' premium beef brand. Moreover, given the downturn in tourism demand, and the greater dependence of the region on tourism than other parts of Scotland, there is also a need to improve the quality of the tourism experience. This could be done by encouraging the upgrading of facilities and attractions, thus building on work that has been carried out using European funding. There is also a need to encourage the development of e-commerce within the tourism industry in the Highlands and Islands, as well as to focus attention on marketing initiatives to encourage tourism.

In addition, initiatives to encourage knowledge driven industries are a potential means of addressing the income differential between the Highlands and Islands and other parts of Scotland. Particular possibilities include encouraging new opportunities in new media such as software production and broadcasting, particularly related to Gaelic. Specifically, there are opportunities to develop broader expertise in nuclear decommissioning, which has a global market, and in making use of the North Sea for the removal and disposal of offshore structures. In terms of education, encouragement of the University of the Highlands and Islands and the associated prospects for enhancing the capacity for economic development is very important. Research institutes such as Dunstaffnage marine laboratory present important means of creating new employment in marine biotechnology through the UHI. Perhaps most important, however, the information economy is key to the future of the Highlands and Islands, and indeed it seems that this issue needs to be considered for rural Scotland as a whole since otherwise there is a danger of further divisions being created between urban and rural areas of Scotland in terms of a so-called 'digital divide'.

The case of Edinburgh, as set out by Ron McQuaid in Chapter 3, also illustrates many policy needs in relation to economic development. McQuaid makes clear that there is a declared intention by the Scottish Executive to, where possible, disperse its functions to areas outwith Edinburgh. Indeed, the Executive has stated that it will keep the policy under review with a view to extending it. Dispersal is clearly of potential benefit to areas of Scotland facing decline and its extension should be supported, particularly where this is seen to benefit those areas that demonstrate high levels of disadvantage, and which have not yet benefited from the policy. While there will be costs associated with such dispersal, the benefits to the recipient communities, and indirectly for the country as a whole, are likely to outweigh such costs. However, it is important that location criteria and information are transparent, given the possible dominance of political considerations that may not conform with the reduction of disparities within Scotland. Moreover, there is a need to ensure that social criteria are adequately considered otherwise it does not seem likely that rural areas will be able to benefit from the dispersal policy, given their disadvantages in terms of physical communications for instance.

12.3   Vocational Education and Training (VET)

Given the need for a more coherent national policy context, the Scottish Executive's (2003) strategy seems to provide a framework to allow a more distinctively Scottish approach to lifelong learning. However, as John Fairley makes clear in Chapter 8, VET in Scotland remains fragmented, based upon voluntarism and largely driven by UK priorities. This is clearly inappropriate in the context of distinct and local circumstances in Scotland in terms of education and training. Furthermore, part of the problem in this field is lack of data to justify policy. There is a need for more emphasis on the collection of data on education and training needs in Scotland. The establishment of new local delivery facilities has been successful in Argyll and Ayrshire in broadening access to VET, suggesting more investment in further education in rural and deprived communities should be encouraged.

More generally, as tertiary education continues to face uncertainty over funding, student numbers and support, planning for both individuals and institutions is problematic. The Scottish Executive, SHEFC (Scottish Higher Education Funding Council), and colleges and universities need to address this if lifelong learning is to be realised across the country. Debates about the relative private and social costs and benefits of such investment in human capital must also include consideration of the development of vocational and non degree based occupations in Scotland. Domination of the labour market by qualifications is helping to create skill and labour shortages which impact on certain areas more than others.

12.4   Transport and Communications

There is a need for a shift in funding priorities away from roads to non roads transport projects. This is because road schemes give rise to small time savings that have no discernible effect on business competitiveness, as demonstrated by Tom Hart in Chapter 9. For instance, funding presently applied to trunk road investment could be reallocated to projects to improve maintenance, traffic calming and traffic management. All these measures would help to reduce congestion, as opposed to trunk road investment which generates greater road use, leading to further congestion and the need for further road investment. There should be a coherent national approach to road pricing, so as to help to reduce congestion. This would also allow selective transport projects to be implemented supported by lorry operators for instance – if funds were hypothecated. Clearly, this must be done at the national level otherwise there would be the danger of reduced competitiveness if one area were to introduce such projects before another. There is also a need to address the specific needs of rural areas. In particular, economic disparities in 'deep rural' areas could be reduced by lowering levels of road fuel taxation, introducing car licence rebates, improving public transport, and encouraging retention of shops and filling stations. It is necessary to upgrade the quality of interregional rail services, including improved freight facilities, and proposals for direct rail access to Glasgow and Edinburgh airports should be accelerated. Moreover, investment in schemes such as airports could be closely linked with broader aims to reduce interregional disparities. This could be done for instance by increasing the share of investment in Glasgow airport at the expense of Edinburgh airport, which could reduce the economic overheating of the Edinburgh region and shift the balance of economic activity within Scotland towards less pressured areas.

Overall, there is a need for a more coherent framework for funding of transport in Scotland. This would of course contribute to the achievement of policy integration, an important aim of the UK government and the Scottish Parliament. In particular, there is a need to integrate transport related elements as key elements of regeneration and spatial planning, depending on local circumstances. For instance, modification of public transport services could facilitate commuting. Similarly, amendment of land use strategies could encourage settlement patterns that favour public transport use (particularly if such strategies were supported by appropriate ancillary regulatory and pricing measures), require lower levels of parking and lower levels of access by single occupant cars. Moreover, public transport provision could be integrated with plans for new employment uses for instance in relation to business and industrial sites.

However, these suggestions raise important issues of administrative capacity and governance. Specifically, it would seem that existing council areas in Central Scotland are too small to deliver an effective and integrated transport policy for travel-to-work and shopping catchment areas. Consequently, it may be appropriate for the Scottish Executive to focus on transport policy in terms of a strategy for the Central Belt as a whole. This could be combined with the strengthening of City Region Plans so as to allow them to assume responsibility for transport, access and area development with earmarked sources of funding (including early introduction of ringfenced finance and road user charging). There should also be a significant transfer of trunk roads (and certain railways) to Regional Transport Bodies acting in a framework set by the Scottish Executive.

Using the Highlands and Islands as an example, it may be argued that transport policy is having a detrimental effect on the region, particularly in terms of higher fuel prices. Hypothecation of fuel tax revenue could benefit the region, as could development of infrastructure for information and communications technology (ICT) (thereby avoiding a 'digital divide'), and the encouragement of affordable housing for local people. Douglas Scott argues in Chapter 6 that there is also a need for a credible rural transport strategy to benefit the South of Scotland.

12.5   Urban Regeneration

First, there is a need for the Scottish Executive to promote greater integration between policies that contribute to urban regeneration. Second, there is a need to emphasise the social and environmental aspects of regeneration. Third, there is a need for urban regeneration activity to be guided by strategic considerations – namely within a wider framework, as suggested above in the context of transport. While all these factors are currently influencing practice, as Peter Roberts illustrates in Chapter 10, there is a need to maintain their impetus. There is also, however, a need to widen community involvement in partnership, increase transparency and accountability, and also perhaps to re-emphasise the need for adequate physical infrastructure, without reverting to the simplistic property led approaches of the 1980s. In addition, wider policy fields are also important to achieving aims for urban regeneration, for instance in terms of infrastructure, European Structural Funds, and mainstream budgets in relation to education and social services. Hence there is an urgent need to ensure regeneration activity is incorporated into the mainstream of policy. Moreover, it is essential that monitoring and review be accorded a higher priority so as to ensure that the lessons from policy initiatives – particularly those explicitly considered as experimental – should be learned effectively.

The case of Edinburgh, as set out in Chapter 5 by Ron McQuaid, illustrates some important policy implications in the context of urban regeneration. This arises in part from the need for dispersal of employment away from the 'overheated' economy in Edinburgh, to other areas such as the cities of Dundee and Glasgow which face problems of high unemployment. In addition, there are implications for Edinburgh itself, which faces significant disparities within the city. In particular, policy could seek to address the needs of the long term unemployed within Edinburgh, by encouraging employers to recruit such people. The possibilities for this – normally an extremely difficult task – are enhanced by the 'tight' labour market. Arguably, given the high demand for labour within Edinburgh, action to address 'supply side' barriers (based, for instance, in education, personal adaptability, transport provision, childcare, employer prejudice), which may prevent long term unemployed people from gaining access to employment opportunities, are even more important than in other areas where this is less of a realistic option. However, such initiatives should be tailored more closely to the need of individuals, given the failure of 'volume' initiatives to achieve their objectives.

Moreover, given the falling number of unemployed in many of the disadvantaged areas of Edinburgh, there would seem to be a need to provide services related to job search and training at the city rather than neighbourhood level, in order to capture economies of scale. However it may be argued, of course, that addressing the needs of unemployed people in Edinburgh is of less concern than shifting resources to areas of Scotland with greater overall need. The implication of this is that action within Edinburgh should demonstrate the additional advantage of expanding the economy as a whole.

The case of the Glasgow region, as indicated by Ivan Turok and Nick Bailey in Chapter 4, is also of relevance here. Indeed, as Turok and Bailey show, there is a particularly striking contrast between the slow, steady growth experienced in Edinburgh in recent decades (as well as the more recent 'overheating' of the local economy) and the accumulation of problems experienced in Glasgow, for which the biggest problems are in relation to employment and derelict land. As in the case of Edinburgh, however, there are also significant disparities within Glasgow, and declining sectors and localities exist in conjunction with areas where new investment has been made and which are physically regenerating. This polarisation is a particularly important issue for Glasgow in view of the absolute levels of disadvantage faced in the city. In terms of policy, the priority is to accelerate the rate of growth and to consider enhancing the traditional role of the public sector in employment creation (Marshall et al, 2002). It is also important to target the core urban areas for support measures in order to meet local needs most directly.

In terms of institutional co-operation, since Glasgow is an extremely large and fragmented city, it is crucial to prioritise closer institutional co-operation at the level of the city-region in order to avoid duplication and to ensure that initiatives are integrated and strategic in orientation. The Scottish Parliament clearly has a role to play in this respect by establishing an appropriate strategic perspective to encouraging economic opportunities in order to meet social needs, a point made also by Tom Hart and Douglas Scott. But there is also a need to make concrete the commitments that have been made to furthering social inclusion, economic development and urban regeneration, and to broaden the composition and location of economic growth to ensure that benefits are distributed more widely. Green (2003) has discussed how balancing such objectives in different ways leads to varying alternative scenarios with differing spatial implications. In turn, these would seem to require both appropriate policy development and sustained investment in physical infrastructure in full recognition of the locational impacts.

12.6 Community Planning

As argued by Greg Lloyd and Barbara Illsley in Chapter 11, the community planning function involves a potentially heightened role for local authorities in terms of reticulism and leadership. This implies the need for a wider review of local government and associated institutional structures in order to facilitate the execution of community planning. Otherwise, community planning may prove to be little more than an additional burden on individual councils, and there may be the added damage of raised but unrealised expectations of what community planning can deliver, on the part of local communities. Nevertheless, it is clear that community planning indeed has the potential (as yet unrealised) to bring together diverse bodies, policies and expenditure plans to focus on an integrated, cost effective service delivery portfolio. It could act as a valuable counter balance to the fragmentation of inter-organisational relations in contemporary local governance. However, even with community planning providing such a function there remains a strategic vacuum in terms of managing the sub-national economy, as indicated above in the contexts of transport and urban regeneration. Hence community plans could form the basis for regional strategic guidance within Scotland, which could truly achieve a strategic context for the provision of services and infrastructure.

Furthermore, Douglas Scott argues in Chapter 6 for the need for a more effective rural policy context in Scotland. This, he argues, is not yet evident, as illustrated by the need for consolidation of local development activities, which are extremely fragmented at present, with an increasingly wide range of bodies involved. This suggests that too much attention has to be given to co-ordination as opposed to implementation. Scott also argues that there is a lack of government policy explicitly addressing rural aspects of social disadvantage, a lack of a policy focus on smaller towns, relatively low financial allocations to rural authorities, and the threat of closure of a range of rural services. This links with the need for a national strategy for transport highlighted by Tom Hart in Chapter 9.

12.7   Conclusion

The substantive chapters of this book show, as indicated above, that there is a degree of consensus on the most urgent priorities for Scotland in terms of policy implications for reducing social, economic disparities without compromising economic development and competitiveness. These priorities may be summarised as follows:

Spatial and Transport Issues

- develop a national, integrated indicative plan for transport and development
- initiate regional and sub-regional plans as appropriate
- incorporate funding elements into national/sub-regional transport strategies
- shift spending priorities from road to non road transport modes
- increase investment in rail
- ensure more explicit links between urban regeneration policy and mainstream funding and service delivery
- develop an integrated strategy for urban regeneration, with sustained investment in physical infrastructure
- introduce a strategic governance dimension to facilitate urban regeneration
- ensure benefits of economic growth are shared more equally within Edinburgh
- address specific issues affecting rural areas in terms of transport (e.g. with respect to costs)
- review the community planning function.

Economic and Social Issues

- support the development of niche markets in agriculture
- develop a national economic development strategy
- develop withdrawal strategies where appropriate

- encourage innovation in the tourism sector
- encourage innovation and development of knowledge based industries
- disperse employment away from Edinburgh to areas of need (using transparent criteria for locational decisions)
- develop policy for vocational training and education which meets specifically Scottish needs in terms of national coherence and public sector orientation.

Clearly, these are only a fraction of the policy implications thrown up by the substantive chapters of this book. Nevertheless, they serve as a possible starting point from which policy makers in Scotland can begin to formulate a strategy to achieve the key aim of social justice, which, after all, involves 'reducing inequalities between communities' (Scottish Executive, 1999, p.16).

References

Danson, M., Helinska-Hughes, E., Hughes, M. and Whittam, G. (2004) 'National and local agency assistance for Scottish SMEs: lessons for small transition economies from supporting internationalisation activities', *Europe at the Margins: EU Regional Policy, Peripherality and Rurality*, Regional Studies Association International Conference, Angers.

Enterprise and Lifelong Learning Committee (2000) *Inquiry into the Delivery of Local Economic Development Services in Scotland*, ELCC, Scottish Parliament, Edinburgh.

Green, A. (2001) *The Scottish Labour Market – Future Scenarios*, Issue Paper Number 3, Futureskills Scotland, Scottish Enterprise, Glasgow.

Macleod, G. (1996) 'The cult of enterprise in a networked, learning region? Governing business and skills in Lowland Scotland', *Regional Studies*, 30(8), pp.749-756.

Marshall, R., Boyes, L. and McCormick, J. (2002) *The Full Employment City*, Scottish Council Foundation, Edinburgh.

Scottish Executive (1999) *Social Justice ... A Scotland Where Everyone Matters*, Scottish Executive, Edinburgh.

Scottish Executive (2000) *The Way Forward: Framework for Economic Development in Scotland*, Scottish Executive, Edinburgh.

Scottish Executive (2001) *A Smart, Successful Scotland: Ambitions for the Enterprise Networks*, Scottish Executive, Edinburgh.

Scottish Executive (2003) *Life Through Learning, Learning Through Life: the Lifelong Learning Strategy for Scotland*, Scottish Executive, Edinburgh.

Index

Divided Scotland?